Women, crime and the courts
in early modern England

Women, crime and the courts in early modern England

edited by

Jennifer Kermode
University of Liverpool

&

Garthine Walker
University of Warwick

The University of North Carolina Press
Chapel Hill & London

© Jenny Kermode, Garthine Walker and contributors 1994

First published in the United States in 1994 by
The University of North Carolina Press

Library of Congress Cataloging-in-Publication Data are available

ISBN 0-8078-2192-6 (cloth)
ISBN 0-8078-4500-0 (paper)

First published in Great Britain in 1994 by UCL Press

UCL Press Limited
University College London
Gower Street
London WC1E 6BT

Typeset in Bembo.
Printed and bound by
Biddles Ltd, England.

Contents

Notes on contributors

Malcolm Gaskill is completing a doctoral dissertation for the University of Cambridge, on attitudes to crime in early modern England. He is currently lecturing in history at Keele University.

Laura Gowing is a British Academy Postdoctoral Fellow at Royal Holloway and Bedford New College, University of London. She is writing a book on women, sex and honour in early modern London.

Geoffrey L. Hudson is completing a doctoral dissertation for the University of Oxford. His research interests include gender relations, war and society, and the social history of medicine.

Martin Ingram is a Fellow of Brasenose College, Oxford and lectures in history at the University of Oxford. He has published extensively on early modern social history and is author of *Church courts, sex and marriage in England, 1570–1640* (1987).

Jenny Kermode is Senior Lecturer in Local History and Director of the MA in Women's History at the University of Liverpool.

Jim Sharpe is Senior Lecturer in History at the University of York. He has published extensively on the history of crime and is author of *Early modern England: a social history 1550–1760* (1987). He is currently writing a major study of witchcraft in early modern England.

Tim Stretton studied history and law at the University of Adelaide before working for his PhD at the University of Cambridge. After teaching for a year at the University of Durham he is researching a book on women and litigation in Elizabethan England.

Garthine Walker studied history at the University of Liverpool where she is completing a doctoral dissertation on crime, gender and social order in early modern Cheshire. She was a Research Fellow at the Institute of Historical Research, University of London and is currently lecturing in history at the University of Warwick.

Acknowledgements

The editors are grateful for the helpful advice and support received from Bernard Capp, Chris Lewis, Michael Power, Brian Quintrell and Andy Wood. Malcolm Gaskill and Martin Ingram are especially thanked for searching out appropriate illustrations.

Introduction

Garthine Walker & Jenny Kermode

Until the mid-1970s the historiography of early modern society was structured around the notion of crisis. Since that time historians have increasingly concentrated upon the themes of continuity and stability in the period between roughly 1550 and 1750.[1] That later interpretation is now experiencing its own crisis. The historiographical emphasis on continuity and a latent anti-Marxism formed two of the central organizing themes of the "new" social history of early modern England. The central assumptions of that recent emphasis are now being fast eroded in the face of the apparent collapse of both conventional modernist historical periodization and of Marxist meta-narratives. There is now a need not only to dismantle old and perhaps inaccurate interpretations, but to rebuild historical explanation in the period.[2]

The past 20 years has, however, also been a period of major historiographical accomplishment. Nowhere, perhaps, is this more clearly demonstrated than in the ascendency of social history. Social historians have brought to the discipline a rigorous reappraisal of manifold aspects of historical enquiry and interpretation.[3] New perspectives and methodologies have been applied to old and new sources with profound consequences. The standard nostrum that "it is the essence of the poor that they do not appear in history" can no longer apply.[4] "Political" history can no longer be confined to the actions of an elite minority.[5] And women have been rescued from the periphery of historical enquiry to a position of central concern.[6] Indeed, the study of gender has been recognized not only as a crucial component of social relations, but as an integral element in the formation and operation of the legal, political and economic frameworks of society.[7] The challenge that now faces social historians is to integrate the most positive aspects of the recent historical literature into a coherent whole rather than a series of scattered, if occasionally brilliant, interventions into the realm of the "proper" history of kings, bishops and battles.

In order to create an integrated social history of the period that extends the parameters of the subject while remaining true to its essentially interpretive traditions, new and more positive themes and problems need to be developed. A series of possibilities present themselves: language, locality, identity, power, diversity, collectivity and class. But surely one of the most essential requirements to a reconstitution of early modern social history is a greater understanding of the rôle of gender in the construction of ideas and the structures of life. The investigation of the cultural implications of women's position before the law raises provocative questions. It is the purpose of this volume to address some of these questions and to pave the way for new ones to be posed.

Much of the agenda for both women's history and the social history of crime has been set within the shifting parameters of "continuity and change". There is now, for example, an extensive literature regarding women and work which largely focuses on the nature and timing of women's economic marginalization. This is located within "far-reaching changes in the economy and of society", and definitions of what construed "women's work" across the centuries.[8] The history of the family, and of women's position within it, has been concerned with the changes and continuities of affective relationships.[9] Studies of the relationship between gender and social order have adhered to models of transformation or crisis, and have sought to connect the changing position of women to that of the economic superstructure and the regionally specific infrastructure of early modern society.[10] Similarly, the upheavals of the English civil wars have been considered in the light of short- and long-term effects on women's social rôle and position, especially regarding women's self-perception and self-confidence.[11] Whilst such work is invaluable, a fundamental problem of conceptualization remains. By considering the ramifications for women (or indeed, for the concept of gender) of societal changes, there has been a tendency to employ "women" as a static historical category against which the effects of transformation and immutability can be measured. This remains so even where particular groups of women are isolated for scrutiny.[12]

The same is largely true of studies of crime and criminality in early modern England. In recent years, historians have sought to identify changing patterns of prosecution and punishment, which they have then attempted to explain in terms of economic, religious and political phenomena. Connections have been made between processes of fundamental religious and economic readjustment and an increase in intrusive regulation and legislation. The obvious conclusion that legislation led to increased litigation itself suggests that a society becoming accustomed to institutional intrusion would increasingly turn to litigation to settle festering personal disputes, to establish social boundaries, and to make individual statements.[13]

Thus historical analysis of the records of secular and ecclesiastical courts has provided vital evidence for our understanding of a variety of social and political relationships. Local and regional studies have illuminated aspects of the dynamics of interpersonal disputes and have stressed the participatory nature of the legal process, locating it within community norms. The business of courts of church, state and manor has been seen as the product of a consensus for orderly life and the maintaining of preferred behavioural standards. While prosecution has correctly been seen to reflect wider social issues, albeit in a form manipulated and defined according to law and legal procedure, crime itself has been recognized as the outcome of constantly shifting definitions of acceptable behaviour. The fact that much litigation was between people of similar social status, and that ordinary people were involved to varying degrees both in litigating and in administering the legal system, means that the entire notion of consensus, even that which is perceived to vary over time and place and according to different social groups, must be qualified. Despite the recent emphasis on the broad participatory base of the legal system, any real consideration of what this meant for women has been conspicuously absent.[14]

It is accepted that many court actions were not strictly confined to the cases as stated but were the culmination of, or one stage in, often lengthy disputes. The law itself did not clearly establish immutable principle and considerable discretion existed in categorizing behaviour within the legal process. People might have used a common language of legality and order, in much the same way that they might have used the language of deference: as a common language deployed in the context of legal procedure. This language was informed by the prevailing conceptual framework of social order and might mask a multiplicity of meaning which is not readily explained by essentialist or functionalist readings.[15] The essays in this book demonstrate how fluid and negotiable relations in early modern England were, both before and during the formal legal process. The conventional language of social description, predicated upon patriarchal and hierarchical norms, cannot be taken at face value.[16]

The development of a rich and thriving social history has depended heavily upon court records of various kinds for the reconstruction of the lives of ordinary people in the early modern period. Court records are, after all, among the most illuminating of all early modern sources for social history. Yet the experience of ordinary women who came before the courts as defendants, plaintiffs and witnesses has remained largely obscure. Within studies of litigation, gender has rarely been dealt with *per se*.[17] Assumptions about women have been made with little regard to gendered meanings and representations, save only for the most obvious which imbue our own culture, and which may or may not have had similar resonances in the early modern period.[18] In this respect, Malcom Gaskill's plea for a "more self-consciously 'past-centred' approach which seeks to insert the speech and action contained in recorded accusations back into the fluid structure of mentalities which shaped them" is surely not confined to studies of witchcraft.

Much has been made of the fact that studies of criminality in all periods from the fourteenth century to the twentieth show women to have been a minority of those officially prosecuted. An emphasis upon the quantification of source material, despite being fruitful in many ways, has consequently resulted in women being duly counted and then discounted. Aggregation inevitably raises interpretative difficulties which are illuminated by (although not restricted to) the study of women's crime. Broad theories based largely upon a quantitative methodology applied to the formal records of the courts by definition neglect the dynamics of human interaction and deny agency to historical actors. Arguably, in searching for statistical patterns, historians have often categorized and compartmentalized criminal activity, whilst glossing over crucial elements in understanding it. As women do not appear in the records in comparable numbers to men, they simply cannot be compared in a like manner. Female activity is marginalized if it is measured only against male criminality; only by considering women's actions in context does their significant rôle in the legal process become evident. Thus, prevalent methodologies of historians of crime have restricted rather than facilitated our understanding of the nature of female criminality in the past.

Moreover, the conventional sources chosen for quantification are often inappropriate for the study of women's rôle within the legal process. Recent research has highlighted the extent to which women used forms of prosecution other than the indictments upon which so many studies have been based. Prosecuting by recognizance, for instance, was an alternative way in which women entered the legal process as plaintiffs at quarter sessions and assizes, although the popularity of this practice may have varied regionally. Not only was it a cheaper method of litigation than indictment, but even married women could and did request on their own behalf that their adversaries were bound over to keep the peace or to be of good behaviour towards them. As recognizances were not subject to the degree of legal categorization and form which applied to indictments, they often provide a more discursive and detailed account of allegedly unacceptable behaviour. Studies of this type of prosecution suggest that women took recourse to the courts over a wide range of issues, and not only those which have been hitherto allotted to the female domain, whatever that is supposed to be.[19]

It is becoming increasingly apparent that qualitative material can tell us far more about the activities and attitudes of ordinary people than can aggregates of litigation alone.[20] This is true for both men and women, but it is particularly pertinent to any study of women's relationship to the courts and the law, for women tend to get lost in the broad overview. By closely examining the context of cases the dynamics of interpersonal disputes can be revealed; the reconstruction of recorded words and actions is an important preliminary to deciphering the encoded social, cultural and individual meanings which informed court actions. Even so, we are left with the perennial problem confronting all social historians as to exactly what we have measured and how typical it is. One way of negotiating this is to stop holding up typicality as a yardstick of historical worth. Women's crime is, after all, atypical if we compare the sheer number of prosecutions of men and women, but it is surely as valid an indicator of human experience as any other. Moreover, it is often within the abnormal that the construction of norms themselves can be understood.

There are conceptual problems too. Behaviour for which women were more commonly prosecuted has often been labelled "female" crime, witchcraft, infanticide and scolding being cases in point. In fact, verbal violence in general has been characterized as the feminine equivalent to the supposedly masculine recourse to physical blows. But there has been little attempt to conceptualize the gendered differences in either the behaviour itself or the meanings of such behaviour. The net result is that these "female" crimes have been inadvertently sensationalized, and those activities for which the label "male" has been applied tend to be those which are thought to involve a certain degree of courage, initiative and physical strength. Thus, highway robbery is a "male" crime, not only because virtually all persons prosecuted for the offence were men, but because our image of the successful highway robber encompasses positive and exciting male attributes. Conversely, such characterizations tend to curtail useful discussion of those women who committed crimes other than the "female" ones. A recent account of crime in the eighteenth century, for instance, refers to "demons in female form", "psychopathic brutality" and so on, when describing female violence, yet emotive and judgemental language does not set the tone of the corresponding chapter on male violence.[21] The noted aversion to both theory and conceptualization[22] of many of those working within the field, along with a failure to acknowledge the gendered construction of many formal sources, has contributed to the unimaginative (or perhaps too imaginative) treatment of women who came before the courts, and a less than rigorous degree of contextualization.

The equivocal legal position of women has also been partly responsible for this state of affairs. As women had little agency according to common law, secular litigation in particular has not, perhaps, been seen as the richest of sources for historians of women's history. Much of the published work on female crime has tended to emphasize women's dependent social position in early modern society. Dependency on husbands, fathers and the community has been used not only to explain the low rate of female prosecution, but also as evidence of the minor types of offences which they committed.[23] Women's status in legal, institutional and conventional terms was indeed derivative, defined in terms of their subordinate relationship to men and the status and occupation of their menfolk. Their social identity was also bound up with the life cycle. Women were described in formal discourses as daughter, wife or widow of "X". Although they could claim an independent identity as spinster, spinsterhood rarely offered opportunities in which women would be offically recognized in formal documentation. Once married, as *femes covert*, they lost much of their legal capacity for independent action under common law with regard to property, including their own clothes as well as real estate; they were unable to sue, be sued or contract on their own behalf; and they were disadvantaged in disputes over custody and access to their children. Widows were entitled to only one third of their husbands' real property by common law, which was often not enough to maintain their self-sufficiency. While they constituted a great number of those receiving poor relief, they are less often found as independent traders in urban records, and despite the stereotype of the merry widow, the majority of widows of middling status remarried. Since women were excluded from most skilled work it was not usual for them to claim an occupational ascription of their own, and because their wages were usually significantly lower than those of men doing similar work, much work done by women was automatically of lower status and was labelled unskilled by default, no matter what degree of skill was actually involved. Less visible, but perhaps even more powerful, were attitudes towards women's daily conduct derived from gendered constructions of what constituted appropriate and acceptable behaviour.

Crucially, though, this is not to say that women have been thought to have had no economic or legal significance in early modern England. The well known figure of the wealthy heiress was a key figure within the family: occasionally such women were given free agency, but they were more often manoeuvred as pawns in strategies for accumulating land and wealth.[24] Amy Erickson's pioneering work on women and property shows that generalizations based on the common law are misleading. Daughters in ordinary families were not universally disadvantaged by inheritance compared with sons, although they were more likely to receive bequests of personal property than land, and, despite legal coverture, wives maintained substantial property interests of their own. Widows, too, appear to have been far better off than is suggested by their legal rights to marital estate alone, although too much optimism about their material wellbeing would be misplaced.[25] The reality of family life and the immediate value of domestic management in lesser households has also been confronted. Even after domestic chores ceased to include the manufacture of saleable goods, women continued to provide essential services and research confirms the sizeable economic contribution that women made to the family. By re-defining work to include non-waged employment, it becomes clear that women occupied a central position in managing the family's survival.[26] Historians of later periods are becoming increasingly aware of the enormous importance of women's labour in the process of industrialization.[27] However, explicit acknowledgement of women's real economic contribution has been difficult to find and, within both the rhetoric of social order and the practicalities of male organizational institutions, women were nevertheless seen as subordinate and peripheral.

Given the ways in which women's lives were circumscribed and constrained, the ways in which women used the courts to bring their own concerns into an officially sanctioned arena is telling. Within this male world of legality women claimed an authority derived from their own intimate knowledge. As these essays demonstrate, women were far from being passive victims or bystanders, and it is no longer adequate to discuss their experiences within the simple paradigm of active/passive or public/ private. We find women moving easily from one to the other, indeed exploiting the paradoxes between the two as they constructed stories which utilized or manipulated convention for their own ends. By exploring the dynamics of female behaviour, we dramatically expand our perception of the legal process, of women's engagement with it, and of the gendered attitudes of early modern England. Each of the chapters in this book serves to qualify a model of oppressive patriarchy with women as passive victims. A crucial challenge for historians is to understand the way in which the whole of society, including women, constructed gender and allocated and imagined rôles for either sex. By closely examining behaviour when individuals exhausted social tolerance or broke fundamental taboos we gain insights difficult to achieve by other means.

Laura Gowing's chapter provides a useful conceptual framework for the study of women in early modern England, by addressing both the tensions between the prescriptive evidence of the law within a system where women's agency was severely circumscribed, and the words and actions of women themselves. Gowing explores the opportunities and limitations which defamation offered women through the dual procedures of speaking sexual insult and the pursuit of legal redress. Focusing on prosecutions at the London consistory court where sexual slander between women dominated the proceedings, she reconstructs the contexts and words of defamation. She demonstrates the ways in which women shaped both language and legal process to their own ends and negotiated their tenuous position before a tribunal in which stories told by men were accorded greater belief and credit. In doing so, she explains the very particular opportunity which defamation offered women, and suggests some different ways of interpreting the meaning of such litigation in the context of early modern ideas about gender and honour.

An often associated aspect of female activity is discussed by Martin Ingram: scolding. In this period "scold" was a highly potent, negatively charged term, second only to "whore" as a pejorative female label. Scolding was, however, also a criminal offence, and women found guilty could be judicially ducked, fined, bound over by recognizance, or subject to numerous informal sanctions. By carefully analyzing court records of several regions, Ingram shows that legal action against scolds was fairly rare in most communities, and offers a persuasive critique of David Underdown's recent argument that contemporaries were obsessed with scolding and that any assertive woman was liable to prosecution. Ingram demonstrates that both official and non-official plaintiffs drew on a distinct and well developed notion of what kind of woman a scold was, and explores the possibility that some women did display such characteristics. In doing so, he offers an alternative explanation of how and why a small minority of women were subject to the humiliation of the cucking-stool at the hands of their neighbours.

Garthine Walker's essay considers women's involvement in property offences. Focusing on the rôle that women played in theft and related activities such as receiving stolen goods, she argues that if women's involvement is to be understood, historians must expand the conceptual and methodological parameters of their inquiry to take account of the spheres of women's knowledge and influence in their communities. By analyzing the records of the Cheshire criminal courts, she shows that women and men had different patterns of criminal activity, both in the types of goods they stole and in their choice of partners in crime. Qualitative sources provide evidence that as victims, defendants, witnesses, informers and neighbours, women were active within female networks of social transmission, thus offering a new perspective on their participation as both breakers of the law and as the informal agents of its enforcement. Women appear to have had a developed and distinct investment in certain types of moveable property which was different from men's and which bears little correlation to legal categories of ownership. Walker shows that the significance of female criminality is seen, not in crude relation to male criminality, but in the context of women's wider economic and social rôle.

Jim Sharpe investigates the rôle of women in the legal process through the medium of witchcraft accusations and trials, and shows that, here too, women's rôle in the community as the holders of certain forms of knowledge allowed them to participate in a particular way. Witchcraft has frequently been portrayed as a gender related offence, and many commentators have asserted that witchcraft trials show women to be the victims of a patriarchal and misogynistic early modern society. While not losing sight of this issue, Sharpe focuses on a number of aspects of the trial procedure in which women played an ambiguous part. The rôle of women in searching for the witch's mark, the involvement of women as witnesses against other women and the conduct of accused women in the courtroom and convicted women on the gallows, all demonstrate the much broader issues at play. Using evidence from various regions and diverse legal tribunals, Sharpe shows that the nature and extent of active female participation in the legal process was both more tangible and more tenuous than traditional interpretations of witchcraft prosecution have allowed.

Malcolm Gaskill combines an interpretation of witchcraft as a fantasy of power with a specific case study from seventeenth-century Ely, in which Margaret Moore allegedly exchanged her soul in compact with the devil to save her last living child and proceeded to cause maleficent harm to others using the familiars that came to serve her. Gaskill argues that central to the popular perception of witchcraft was the exercise, or imagined exercise, of power by persons who were otherwise relatively powerless in terms of wealth and social status. The part played by madness, delusion and fantasy, and the forms in which mental states were expressed, are discussed in the context of valid contemporary belief and popular culture. By employing this model of interpretation, yet locating the incident within the topography of the Isle of Ely and prevalent contemporary tensions, he shows how Moore's sacrifice represents an imaginary power extension, where her intangible soul is reified in an imaginary sphere as something with which she is able to bargain. Through this case, Gaskill illustrates how conflicts and the struggle for survival in early modern England could be played out on an elevated mental plain, and ultimately be resolved in the material world of criminal legal process where such supernatural evidence was deemed to be viable proof.

Moving away from the more familiar aspects of women's involvement in the courts, Geoffrey L. Hudson and Tim Stretton both explore ways in which women actively negotiated with the courts in order to claim what they perceived to be rightfully theirs. Hudson examines the provision of state pensions for war widows in the mid-seventeenth century – a phenomenon which did not recur in England for over 300 years. He shows that, for the first time, women joined maimed soldiers in a previously male category of the impoverished where relief was merited for their contribution to the state, only to be excluded after the Restoration when the attitudes of the Stuart administration brought dramatic and detrimental change for women. Examining the records of quarter sessions of several counties, he argues that both the provision for war widows and the women's response to it represent a practical shift in gender based discrimination with regard to the poor. By looking at the law, its results and the tactics of the widows themselves to secure pensions, Hudson not only gives us a new perspective on the relationship between women and the courts, but also raises important questions regarding women's own attitudes to entitlement. Far from being passive recipients of relief, war widows in the mid-seventeenth century actively sought their pensions, and were as successful in their endeavours as the maimed soldiers with whom they were in competition.

Tim Stretton focuses upon customary litigation in Elizabethan Somerset that was sued at the Court of Requests. Despite an increasing interest in custom generally, the relationship between custom and women has been under investigated. Stretton's essay demonstrates that customary disputes are a rich source not only of women's perceptions of their rights generally, but specifically with regard to women's rights to property and inheritance. He shows that whilst custom was itself mutable, in the later sixteenth century there was a gradual shift in equity courts away from oral, plebeian evidence towards a formal system of written evidence, and he questions the consequences of this for women. In the developing conflict between common land and customary law, the equity courts are shown to have had a mediating rôle. He argues that due to the nature of early modern English land law, shifting definitions of women's property rights were often more to do with local customs regulating the transfer and inheritance of copyhold rights. Women's, and especially widows', property rights were coming to be defined on a local level in the course of a more general redefinition of property.

A number of themes have emerged independently from these essays, all offering insights into behaviour and attitudes that go far beyond a single social group or any one region. Foremost is the continual interplay between women's active participation and strategies *vis-à-vis* the contextual constraints placed upon them, including the construction of gendered meanings. Other themes raise issues of approach, particularly the use of quantification, the acceptance of stereotypes, both by contemporaries and historians, and the dominance of modern rationalism in historical explanation.

As we have seen, women's lives in early modern England were more circumscribed than men's in a number of ways, but as the essays in this volume suggest, we can no longer regard women as passive players. Gowing and Hudson show how women could manipulate both the system and the expected rôle of the defenceless, dependent female. War widows pursuing government pensions and the women involved in defamation suits at the London consistory court were evidently knowledgeable of legal procedures, and could manipulate versions of stereotyped femininity accordingly. Women could and did claim a knowledge of matters which have been identified as male concerns. Women did engage with the court system, and to an extent made it work for them as plaintiffs. It is becoming increasingly clear that studies of crime which focus primarily upon felonies prosecuted at the courts of assize and quarter sessions under-represent the degree and nature of women's involvement in litigation. Not only do the strictures of the common law often preclude official prosecution by women, but legal categories are not always coterminous with common practice and perceptions.

Other jurisdictions, such as those of church and manor, could provide arenas in which women could play out their disputes.[28] Certain offences likewise offered opportunites for women to bring private concerns into public, and to gain official sanction. Gowing suggests that the language of slander was used by women to perform functions for which men could far more easily turn to official, institutional and legal spheres. Thus, women brought suits at the London consistory that were ostensibly about sexual insult, but might be rooted in personal and community disputes over a range of issues. Similarly, Sharpe indicates that witchcraft accusations provided a forum in which a variety of disputes between women could be played out. Stretton's study of customary law also shows how women might draw on other forms of authority than the common law in order to establish their claims to property. The mutability of customary law, largely unwritten and potentially open to reinvention, allowed women to partake in creating the evolving customs of their communities. Although the greater credence given to male witnesses in other jurisdictions appears to have existed in the Court of Requests, further research into the archives of local customary courts may well illuminate gendered aspects of local knowledge. In customary disputes brought to the Westminster equity courts, for instance, male deponents from northwest Derbyshire cited their grandfathers' times and opinions whilst the few old women who gave evidence tended to draw upon the recalled experience of their female ancestors.[29] Moreover, the institutional exclusion of women from various legal processes did not necessarily prohibit a detailed and extensive knowledge of the law itself. The war widows of whom Hudson writes took every opportunity to exercise their new rights. They did so not as the passive recipients of male patronage, but on their own merits and through their own agency. Although, as Hudson suggests, these widows may have learnt how to work the system once they had access to it, the extent of their knowledge need not have itself been newly acquired. Women's silence was a consequence of institutional exclusion – it might not denote an ignorance of the process.

One of the most striking aspects of several of the papers in this volume is the location of female power and knowledge. At first sight this appears to be in domestic and economic areas which have traditionally been categorized as "private". Yet women's concerns can be seen to have existed within much wider parameters than this would suggest, with implications which sometimes greatly expand the perceived social rôle of women. As Gowing shows, it was through women that sexual honour was mediated, thereby creating a female responsibility for the sexual honour of whole communities as well as of individual households. Feminine honesty in all respects was imagined almost entirely through the language of sexual honesty. It is not surprising, therefore, that Walker's paper suggests that women were similarly concerned with the honesty of other women who stole or received stolen goods. In female networks of communal interaction, women assumed responsibility for regulating other types of feminine dishonesty. In both cases, this was extraneous to the formal institutional processes of the common law, and has therefore received little attention. Walker's discussion of women's involvement in the secondhand trade raises further issues about the gendered honesty of the marketplace. It has been noted that, although trust and community values were the nexus upon which the market operated, a social history of the market which focuses on the language of credit and honesty has not yet been written.[30] Such a study, if undertaken, should include a consideration of the ways in which credit and honesty interrelated conceptually with gender if the "community values" on which the market is based is not to be an anachronistic term.

Women's relationship to property, both moveable goods and land, is far more complex than historians have traditionally assumed. As Stretton points out, widows universally claimed their widow's estate, and must have usually been successful as only a minority of claims were legally contested. Moreover, most deponents gave examples to the court of widows in the past whose rights had been recognized. Contrary to the standard view that women had few legal rights, the women who were defendants and plaintiffs at the Court of Requests evidently believed otherwise. Likewise, it is clear from Walker's paper that women considered certain goods to be theirs, notwithstanding the legal ownership of those goods according to common law.[31] The notion of women's rights and their perception of entitlement goes beyond property, of course, and is crucial to furthering our understanding of the position of women in early modern society. Even women accused of witchcraft could both display knowledge of the legal process and demand justice for themselves, as Sharpe shows.

The stake which women held in their households and communities was more than a defensive one. By appropriating certain concerns as their own, even those which might easily be used against them, as in the case of sexual reputation, women could and did wield a considerable amount of power. In much the same way, women could use their sex and knowledge of female physiology to claim authoritative expertise in important public matters. As juries of matrons especially empanelled to deduce whether convicted women were pregnant, and in cases of rape and incest, and as those who searched women for evidence of witches' marks, women made the crucial decisions that could determine whether the accused would live or die. It is an acknowledgement of the same areas of specialist knowledge that led women to claim that they could tell whether or not another woman was pregnant, or a virgin, even in the absence of any physical examination. In the context of defamation cases, publicly airing one's views about the chastity of other women might have been based upon supposedly specialist skills, yet imparting such information might well have resulted in the speaker being prosecuted.

The very act of repeating incontinent language in court placed women in an ambiguous position, and there was a fine line between upholding the moral order of the neighbourhood and participating in its destruction, as Gowing demonstrates. This was not a boundary maintained by men alone. The collusive nature of women's part in perpetuating and defending social norms is clearly visible in the use London women made of the consistory court. The language and process of slander litigation allowed women to bring personal grievances into a wider sphere, as in cases where women sought redress against adulterous husbands by defaming their mistresses. But in doing so, women were complicit in supporting a dual standard that placed responsibility and culpability for sexual misdemeanor not with the adulterous husband, but with his mistress. The expertise of midwives was similarly double edged: knowledge of pregnancy and childbirth was also potentially that of abortion and infanticide; midwives might withhold practical aid to the woman in labour who refused to name the father of her bastard infant about to be born, but they were also in a position to withhold that same information from justices of the peace. Therefore, the midwives and other women who were allocated the task of searching for witch's marks were chosen not for their technical expertise alone, as Sharpe points out, but for their honesty and credit in the community. The same applies to juries of matrons in criminal cases.

Yet the ambiguities and tensions in attributing "honesty" to women who were experts in the very sphere in which women's dishonesty was imagined, that of sex and its repercussion, pregnancy, are crudely evident in the by then obsolete practice of "honest" women being appointed to sexually arouse allegedly impotent men. But it may also underlie the ambivalence with which women often described personal knowledge of their own bodies. Women appear to have explained away alleged witches' marks by drawing on positive feminine rôles: they claimed the marks were caused by childbearing, or carrying thorns, for instance, or were other physical manifestations of the labours of their dutiful occasions; or, they claimed to have no knowledge of the physical fact of the alleged marks. The women in Sharpe's paper who protested ignorance of marks beneath their clothes might or might not have been telling the truth, but their professed bodily ignorance might itself have been part of a strategy to portray themselves as good, "honest" women. In a different type of case in 1667, a Halton woman, Elizabeth Heath, used precisely this means to claim innocence for herself when she charged two men with abusing her. Employing the common disclaimer of passivity in unconsciousness, Heath reinforced her inculpability by claiming that she was oblivious to the marks left upon her body by the alleged abuse until she heard rumours which brought them to her attention.

> she . . . heard it openly reported by her neighbours that [the two men] had abused [her] body . . . whilst she was senseless by cutting or pulling of her hair from her secrett partes and by other abuses of her body which [she] after perceived to be true for that she found her hair to be wanting, and for that her theighes and secrett partes were black and sore.[32]

In cases of demonic possession, too, we find a paradoxical connection between female power and non-engagement. Here, as in Elizabeth Heath's testimony, trance is a powerful means of removing the female self from culpability. Non-action for women is important in establishing that they are not themselves responsible.[33] For women like Heath, senselessness laid the blame firmly at the feet of their male adversaries. For the possessed girls whom Sharpe describes, the trance is doubly significant as the fact of suspected possession implies not only that they themselves are not guilty per se but that their waking selves are, by contrast, innocent. Thus, out of fits, Margaret Muschamp is merely an "innocent, bashfull girle".

The realm of childbirth with its related knowledge of the female body provides another link between the various forms of social, economic and biological reproduction and transmission in which women were engaged. Whilst Michael MacDonald stresses the importance that contemporaries generally attached to this aspect of the female world, it is not surprising that his evidence suggests that it had a very different significance for women and men.[34] The rituals of childbirth could breed dissension between women as well as being an area of female strength, both practically and symbolically. Whilst the women's world of childbirth might have displayed female solidarity, the pivotal place of the female body served to undermine female authority at the same time as elevating it, perhaps *because* it did so. Ideas about female physicality and sexuality were inextricably linked, as Gowing makes clear in her discussion of the ways in which sexual insult between women focused on the physical manifestations of whoredom. And as Gaskill demonstrates, Margaret Moore's confession relocates her positive femininity as nurturing mother at the centre of her diabolical pact. Even Sharpe's possessed girls draw our attention to the tensions and fears of female power manifest in the female form. The harrowing details of the denial of corporality through burning a young woman's skin till it blistered, at the same time point towards a belief in the power of female physicality. Women's bodies, open as they supposedly were to manipulation, defiance and deceit, could swell into a "monstrous and vast bigness", or become heavy enough for three strong men to find carrying a young woman burdensome.

The question of labelling is also broached in this volume. In modern western criminology, there has been a tendency for men who commit crimes to be termed "criminal", whereas women who do so have been labelled "mentally ill". The motivation attributed to men and women is in a similar vein: men's criminality is normal, explicable and rational; women's is irrational, if not pathological.[35] The inverse of this is that "what we consider madness whether in women or in men . . . is either the acting out of the devalued female role or the total/partial rejection of one's sex-role stereotype".[36] The vituperative, violent woman is a common representation of insanity: a woman out of her own control, and that of others. Ingram is surely right to present the possibility of a link, in some cases, between the alleged characteristics of scolding and those of emotional instability, despite the problematic nature of the association. We may, of course, never know if some women who were mentally unstable were prosecuted as scolds because of their instability. Gaskill, too, suggests the manner in which emotional factors might rest at the core of witchcraft accusations in considering the state of mind of the accused witch who believes in her own supernatural powers.

Ingram's paper on scolds also raises a series of other issues about labelling by historians and contemporaries. His consideration of the offence and the behaviour of the women who were so prosecuted is a welcome departure from the accepted and unsubstantiated interpretation of scolding as an unproblematic gendered category.[37] He notes that the legal meaning of the term "scold" encompassed far more than "mere female loquacity or assertiveness", and that the type of behaviour for which women were so labelled was not itself peculiarly feminine. Aware that the distinctions between scolding and other types of unacceptable behaviour, notably barratry, were blurred, Ingram has focused his inquiry upon scolds alone in order to avoid confusion, and has not included accusations that arise from specific acts of defamation. Future research might build on this through a more detailed consideration of the relationship between scolding and related offences, which would take account of variations in practice in different localities and jurisdictions, and which might thereby shed further light on the contexts in which the label of "scold" was applied.

Overlapping definitions and the interplay between the procedural and personal context of specific cases are recurring themes in this collection of essays. By focusing discussion on a particular event – scolding – issues of gender and legal process may be explored further. In Cheshire, for instance, scolding and barratry as prosecuted at common law were often compounded; barratry was rarely used exclusively to denote a malicious or repeated litigation. The wording of indictments for each event was almost identical, the only difference on the indictment usually being in the choice of *barractator* or *objurgator*.[38] As with all indictments, there is the endemic problem of how one interprets a formulaic document. Yet in the vernacular and often detailed presentments by local officials, and in witnesses' examinations and neighbours' petitions, the two offences are often indistinguishable. Contemporaries appear to have compounded the legal categories as well as the reported behaviour. Alice Meyre, for instance, was indicted as a scold in 1620, but when her neighbours petitioned against her at the same sessions, they referred to her prosecution as that of barratry. Similarly, a note on Elizabeth Adams' indictment for barratry states that the prosecution rests upon information given by one John Burges that she is a common scold; a petition against her also terms her a scold, among other things.[39]

Many defendants who were dealt with by recognizance allegedly displayed behaviour which neatly fits the description of barratry or scolding, despite neither offence being mentioned. Sometimes husbands and wives were prosecuted as barrators and scolds for their respective parts in the same incident. In disputes over diverse issues, petitioners to the bench commonly denounced opponents of both sexes as scolds and barrators as a form of discrediting them, without officially prosecuting them as such, and their opponents often responded in kind with counter-claims that the original complainants were themselves scolds or barrators. Labelling one's adversary as a disruptive antisocial person gave credence to the accuser's story. Women were painted as harassers and haranguers by drawing on a powerful convention of "the scold", and we must be aware that the misbehaviour ascribed to such women may be evidence as much of that convention as it is of perceived or actual behaviour exhibited by the women concerned. In this sense, accusations of scolding often followed similar patterns to those which Gowing has found in defamation cases.

The problem remains to ascertain the criteria upon which complainants labelled defendants as scolds (and barrators). The key may lie in the nature of the legal offence itself. As Ingram makes clear, the legal definition of scolding was both precise and flexible. Scolding must not, therefore, be understood as a catch-all for diverse behaviour. Legal definitions could, in practice, encompass a wide variety of alleged activity and a considerable degree of flexibility in interpretation which could easily be manipulated by complainants. Ingram's observation that most accused scolds appear to have been in contention with their immediate neighbours may be crucial. Just as Gowing shows for sexual slander, prosecutions for scolding might be understood in the context of the tense relationships between individuals.

The contexts of specific cases can therefore be extremely illuminating. At the Easter quarter sessions held in Cheshire in 1626, Thomas Cole and his wife Mary were indicted and found guilty of barratry and scolding respectively. The Coles were in the midst of a dispute with one George Poole; the quarrel took the form of accusation and counter accusation over several months. Poole also prosecuted Mary Cole for assaults on himself and his friend William Morris, and Thomas Cole for causing a nuisance by leaving his hedges open. At the following sessions in July, Thomas Cole responded by prosecuting Poole for barratry and for trespass and damage. He also filed indictments against Poole's daughter Jane for scolding, William Morris and a kinsman for assault, and two other men together for trespass. Poole then attempted to indict the constable who let the Coles go free before they had found sureties to keep the peace towards him. Thomas and Mary Cole and George and Jane Poole were all bound over to be of their good behaviour; the Coles towards the Pooles and *vice versa*.[40]

It is not possible to consider scolding and barratry in isolation in this type of compound case. The evidence may suggest that the Coles were litigious and quarrelsome, and that therefore the labels are appropriate and unproblematic, but the Coles were prosecuted for scolding and barratry *before* they entered into litigation at common law, not because of it. Unfortunately, there is no extant examination or petition stating Poole's position, but Thomas and Mary Cole's petition has survived. Two-thirds of their petition is aimed at discrediting Poole. The Coles inform the bench that he is an active recusant, keeping recusant tenants, and persuading others to convert to Catholicism. They charge him with harbouring recusant women, "suffering them to be brought to bed in his house and so to returne backe the Child being neither christened nor they Churched, unless by some popish priest". As regards barratry, they briefly mention that he is a common sower of sedition amongst his neighbours,[41] but they do not privilege this charge above his alleged taking of partridge eggs and "setting them under his owne hens to be hatched". Perhaps most telling are the charges of his abuse of the Coles themselves. George and Jane Poole have "with most uncivil and opprobrious speeches called [Cole] theefe and Cuckold, his wyfe a whore and a murderer, and their children foxes with many more slanderous and undecent termes . . .".[42]

Prosecutions for barratry and scolding at the secular courts were one way of dealing with defamatory words, especially when those words were spoken within the context of a wider dispute.[43] That wider context might also encompass religious tensions within a neighbourhood, as this case suggests, either as the sources of tension or to cloak other matters.

Rather than scolding and barratry always alluding to distinct activities then, a distinction may perhaps be drawn between *a priori* prosecutions for particular kinds of verbal disruption, which is the emphasis of Ingram's essay, and those that exploit the category as part of a quarrel about an entirely separate issue in much the same way that indictments for trespass were often intrinsically about disputed property rights. Women and men who were accused of scolding or barratry were portrayed as quarrelsome, verbally abusive persons. To understand more fully the dynamics and implications of prosecutions for scolding and related offences, substantial research must be undertaken in all jurisdictions where the offence was prosecuted. It must be stressed that quarter sessions, the court from which the above evidence is drawn, was not the main forum for scolding prosecutions. Such litigation involving scolds reflects the ways in which ordinary people used the legal process for their own ends as much as it reflects assumptions about the offence itself. A more detailed and local cross-court survey may illuminate diverse applications of the term. The terms "scold" and "barrator" as used in official prosecutions could sometimes be those of convenience. "Scold", in particular, was a potent and inclusive term, which, like "barrator", could be used to the advantage of complainants with relative ease. After all, a heated quarrel is by definition likely to produce behaviour "typical" of scolds and barrators.

We must also consider the conceptual implications of contemporary labelling. A distinction must be made not merely between rhetoric and actuality, but between prescriptive, expected and apparent behaviour, with all their anomalies and complexities. The fragility of the verbal and legal authority attributed to women which Gowing has identified in London defamation cases can likewise be found in the prosecution of scolds. As Gowing shows, defamation litigation was often the result of complex interpersonal disputes, in which the term "whore" could be made a symbol for every kind of female misbehaviour. The term "scold" was similarly both vague and precise. Although its meaning was less overtly linked to sexual reputation, it encompassed an alternative stereotype of negative femininity: that of the vituperative woman.

All of the chapters offer explicit challenges to previous historical writing. Some stress the diversity of female experience across time and locality. Others are concerned with conceptual frameworks within which women have been considered. Studying women's experiences offers us a particular challenge. We are familiar with the pitfalls inherent in documents which are filtered through the agency of male-oriented institutions, and are learning to deploy a multistranded approach to our subject. It is, of course, axiomatic for all historians that they must unravel their own cultural and individual preconceptions before they can address the past on its own terms. Political and religious ideology can stimulate debate because the bias is readily visible.[44] The manner and extent to which ideologies of gender are woven into our presumptions are far harder to uncover and disentangle. To understand gender in its historical context, it is crucial for the functional to be distinguished from the constructed, and for the constructed in turn to be contextualized.

The conceptual category of gender limits the extent to which "women's" history can be considered in isolation from women's relation to men. Gender as an historical category discourages the treatment of women as an homogenous group with a common interest, viewpoint and experience. But it also challenges the supposed unity of the household and forces the historian's attention to focus more critically upon the relative power of women and men. We have chosen, however, to deploy "women" rather than "gender" as the signifier in the title of this book for the following reasons.

First, "women" is a useful category of analysis for it describes the general concerns of all the contributors in a way that "gender" does not. To have used "gender" in the title may have indicated a political and theoretical agenda common to all the contributors which would have been misleading. This being the first collection of its kind, the theoretical frameworks of the authors are distinct and various. The emphasis is on diversity, with alternative methodologies and differing degrees of theoretical and conceptual rigour according to the types of sources, topics and intellectual interests of the authors. Whereas a simple binary model of comparison of men and women is entirely inadequate, and women's experience – psychically, socially and physically – cannot be held to be universal or constant, there are, nevertheless, constraints and processes that may be common to women in a way that is incommensurable to men. That is not to say that these are experienced similarly by individual women. In this volume "women" is employed as a general category of analysis: we are not claiming that the women's experiences here were universal. In all of the essays, women have emerged as far more feisty, individual and complex than simply grouping them as a single gender would allow.

Secondly, given that the institutional subordination of women is a commonplace, the language of gender might more properly signify the importance of structures rather than agents. Yet, more than anything else, perhaps, this volume is characterized by its emphasis upon female agency in the face of a legal system institutionally biased towards men. There is, after all, no such concept as men's legal position. Rather than offering essentialist explanations of the differential power of men and women, the overall theme of this book encompasses female power, female knowledge and female experience. Although all chapters broach the relative power of men and women to some extent, this is often tacit. Amy Erickson, the author of the most recent study of women's property rights in early modern England, has remarked on the relativity of the study of women, mediated as it is through male channels. Her study "aims to make it an occasion for professional comment and self-doubt for any historian to summarize English women's legal and economic position in the early modern period without asking the women themselves".[45] In a different way, using different sources and methodologies, *Women, crime and the courts in early modern England* shares that aim.

Notes

1. For example: G. R. Elton, *The Tudor revolution in government* (Cambridge, 1953), cf. D. R. Starkey *The reign of Henry VIII; personalities and politics* (London, 1985); C. Hill, *The world turned upside down: radical ideas during the English revolution* (London, 1972) & *idem, The English revolution, 1640: an essay* (London, 1955), cf. Conrad Russell, *The causes of the English civil war* (Oxford, 1990); C. Hill, A one class society?, in *Change and continuity in seventeenth-century England*, ed. C. Hill (London, 1974), pp. 205–18 & E. P. Thompson, Patrician society and plebeian culture, *Journal of Social History*, **7**, 1974, pp. 382–405, cf. J. D. C. Clark, *English society, 1688–1832, ideology, social structure and political practice during the ancien regime* (Cambridge, 1985); R. H. Tawney *The agrarian problems in the sixteenth century* (London, 1912), cf. E. Kerridge, *The agrarian problems in the sixteenth century and after* (London, 1969) & see T. H. Ashton & C. H. E. Philpin (eds), *The Brenner debate: agrarian class structure and economic development in pre-industrial Europe*, (Cambridge, 1985); K. Thomas, *Religion and the decline of magic: studies in popular beliefs in sixteenth and seventeenth century England* (London, 1971), cf. M. Ingram, The reform of popular culture? Sex and marriage in early modern England, in *Popular culture in seventeenth-century England*, ed. B. Reay (London, 1985), pp. 129–65.
2. K. Wrightson, The enclosure of social history, *Rural History*, **1**, 1990, pp. 73–81.
3. Several aspects of this are discussed in *New perspectives on historical writing,* ed. Peter Burke (Oxford, 1991).
4. G. R. Elton, *England under the Tudors* (London, 1955; 1991 edn), p. 259.
5. J. Walter, A "rising of the people"? The Oxfordshire rising of 1596, *Past & Present,* **107** (1985), pp. 90–143.
6. S. D. Amussen, *An ordered society: gender and class in early modern England* (Oxford, 1988).
7. L. Davidoff & C. Hall, *Family fortunes. Men and women of the English middle class, 1780–1850* (London, 1987).
8. J. Thirsk, Introduction, *Women in English society,* ed. M. Prior (London, 1985), p.1; *Women and work in pre-industrial England,* eds L. Charles & L. Duffin (Beckenham, 1985). See also, A. Vickery, Golden age to separate spheres? A review of the categories and chronology of English women's history, *The Historical Journal*, **36** (1993), pp. 383–414.
9. L. Stone, *The family, sex and marriage in England 1500–1800* (London, 1977); R. Houlbrooke, *The English family 1450–1700* (London, 1984).
10. Amussen, *Ordered society*; D. Underdown, The taming of the scold: the

enforcement of patriarchal authority in early modern England, in *Order and disorder in early modern England,* eds A. Fletcher & J. Stevenson (Cambridge, 1985), pp.196–218.

11. P. Crawford, Public duty, conscience and women in early modern England, in *Public duty and private conscience in seventeenth-century England. Essays presented to G. E. Aylmer,* eds J. Morrill *et al.* (Oxford, 1993), pp. 57–76; P. Mack, The prophet and her audience: gender and knowledge in the world turned upside down, in *Reviving the English revolution,* eds G. Eley & W. Hunt (London, 1988), pp. 139–52.

12. J. Butler, *Gender trouble* (London, 1990), pp. 1, 3; J. Scott, Women's history, see Burke (1991), pp. 42–66.

13. D. Hay *et al.* (eds), *Albion's fatal tree* (London, 1977); K. Wrightson & D. Levine, *Poverty and piety in an English village: Terling 1525–1700* (New York, 1979).

14. Introduction, Fletcher & Stevenson (1985), pp. 1–40; C. B. Herrup, *The common peace: participation and the criminal law in seventeenth-century England* (Cambridge, 1987); M. Ingram, *Church courts, sex and marriage in England, 1570–1640* (Cambridge, 1987); J. Sharpe, The people and the law, see Reay (1985), pp. 244–70; K. Wrightson, Two concepts of order, in *An ungovernable people: the English and their law in the seventeenth and eighteenth centuries,* eds J. Brewer & J. Styles (London, 1980), pp. 21–46.

15. Wrightson, Two concepts of order; K. D. M. Snell, Deferential bitterness: the social outlook of the rural proletariat in eighteenth- and nineteenth-century England and Wales, in *Social orders and social classes in Europe since 1500,* ed. M. L. Bush (London, 1992), pp. 158–84.

16. K. Wrightson, The social order of early modern England: three approaches, in *The world we have gained: histories of population and social structure,* eds L. Bonfield *et al.* (Oxford, 1986), pp. 177–202; P. Burke, The language of orders in early modern Europe, see Bush (1992), pp. 1–14.

17. Important exceptions include J. H. Beattie, The criminality of women in eighteenth-century England, *Journal of Social History,* **8**, 1975, pp. 80–116; B. Hanawalt, The female felon, *Viator,* **5**, 1974, pp. 253–68; R. B. Shoemaker, *Prosecution and punishment. Petty crime and the law in London and rural Middlesex, c. 1660–1725* (Cambridge, 1992), pp. 207–216.

18. See for example, C. Z. Wiener, Sex-roles and crime in late Elizabethan Hertfordshire, *Journal of Social History,* **8**, 1974–5, pp. 174–5; F. McLynn, *Crime in eighteenth-century England,* (Oxford, 1991).

19. Shoemaker, *Prosecution and punishment,* pp. 207–216 ; G. Walker, Crime, gender and social order in early modern Cheshire, PhD thesis, Department of History, University of Liverpool.

20. N. Z. Davis, *Fiction in the archives: pardon tales and their tellers in sixteenth-century France* (Oxford, 1987); G. Levi, On microhistory, see Burke (1991), pp. 93–113.

21. McLynn, *Crime in eighteenth-century England*.
22. J. M. McMullen, Crime, law and order in early modern England, *British Journal of Criminology*, **27**, 1987, p. 264; J. A. Sharpe, The history of crime in England, *c.*1300–1914: an overview of recent publications, *British Journal of Criminology*, **28**, 1988, pp. 124–37.
23. For example, see J. A. Sharpe, *Crime in seventeenth-century England. A county study* (Cambridge, 1983), p. 101 and Wiener, Sex-roles and crime.
24. P. Hogrefe, Legal rights of Tudor women and the circumvention by men and women, *Sixteenth Century Journal*, **3**, 1972, pp. 97–105.
25. A. L. Erickson, *Women and property in early modern England* (London, 1993), pp. 19, 61–2, 157, 224–6, 202–203, 221–2, 199, and *passim*.
26. Charles & Duffin (eds) *Women and work*; M. Prior, Women and the urban economy: Oxford 1500–1800, in *Women in English society*, see Prior (1985); M. Roberts, Women and work in sixteenth-century English towns, in *Work in Towns 850–1850* eds P. J. Corfield & D. Keene (London, 1990), pp. 86–102.
27. P. Hudson & M. Berg, Rehabilitating the industrial revolution, *The Economic History Review*, second series, **XLV**, 1992, pp. 35–8; M. Berg, What difference did women's work make to the industrial revolution?, *History Workshop Journal*, **35**, Spring 1993, pp. 22–44.
28. W. R. Prest, Law and women's rights in early modern England, *The Seventeenth Century*, **6**, 1991, pp. 169–187.
29. A. Wood, Industrial development, social change, and popular politics in the mining area of north west Derbyshire, *c.*1600–1700, PhD thesis, University of Cambridge, 1993, ch. 3.
30. C. Muldrew, Interpreting the market: the ethics of credit and community relations in early modern England, *Journal of Social History*, **18**, 1993, pp. 163–83.
31. See also Erickson, *Women and property, passim*.
32. Public Record Office [PRO], CHES 24/135–6, [unfoliated] Examination of Elizabeth Heath, wife of Thomas Heath of Halton.
33. For a discussion of gendered responses to violence, see Walker, Crime, gender and social order, forthcoming, especially ch. 2.
34. M. MacDonald, *Mystical bedlam: madness, anxiety and healing in seventeenth-century England* (Cambridge, 1981), pp. 108–9.
35. A. Morris, *Women, crime and criminal justice* (Oxford, 1987), pp. 52, 55.
36. P. Chesler, *Women and madness* (New York, 1972), p. 56.
37. Underdown, The taming of the scold; Amussen, *Ordered society*, pp. 103, 122–3, 132.
38. For "barrator" and "scold" respectively.
39. Chesh RO QJF 49/1, ff.15, 141; QJF 49/3, ff.13, 81.
40. Chesh RO, QJF 55/1 ff.24, 25, 26, 27, 29; QJF 55/1 f.65; QJF 55/2 ff.8, 18, 23, 151, 159, 161; QJF 55/2 ff.83, 84, 95.
41. This is done in the manner of the majority of petitions involving cases within the category of those against the peace or of non-lethal violence.

42. Chesh RO QJF 55/2 f.118, Petition of Thomas and Mary Cole. George Poole took the oath of allegiance at the Michelmas Sessions: Chesh RO QJB 1/5 f.166r.
43. See also the ongoing feud between Robert Steele and Richard Jolly and his wife Joan: Chesh RO QJF 53/3 f.84; QJF 53/4 ff.49, 102; QJF 55/2 ff.112, 120; QJF 55/4 ff.89, 90; QJB 2/5 f.130v.
44. See for instance, M. Spufford, Puritanism and social control?, in Fletcher & Stevenson (1985) pp. 41–57.
45. Erickson, *Women and property*, pp. 18–19.

Chapter Two

Language, power and the law: women's slander litigation in early modern London

Laura Gowing

"A married woman perhaps may doubt whether shee bee either none or no more than half a person", wrote the anonymous author of the first exposition of women's equivocal legal position, *The lawes resolution of womens rights*, in 1632. Legally, women's agency was vested in their husbands: "Women have no voyse in Parliament, they make no lawes, they consent to none, they abrogate none. All of them are understood either married or to be married and their desires are subject to their husband, I know no remedy, though some women can shift it well enough".[1]

For much of the legal practice of early modern England this outline was an accurate one. In particular, while contemporaries observed increased levels of litigation, women's access to this kind of participation in the law was restricted. Technically, married women could not sue cases at the common law: their desires, and their legal authority, were "subject to their husband". But among those who could "shift it well enough" must surely have been the women who fought cases at the church courts. There, married, single and widowed women sued cases in their own names over disputed wills, tithes, and, most often, sex and marriage. In the most popular type of litigation, suits alleging sexual slander, they brought cases up to five times more often than men did. A typical case in London in 1628 involved Magdalen Lewis and Mary Record, neighbours from near Bridewell. The two had fallen out after Magdalen's husband persuaded Mary's lodgers not to go to her wedding feast. Mary interpreted this as a slur on her pre-marital conduct and, in return, launched an attack on Magdalen's honesty, calling her "a pore sorry thinge a common thinge and one that was familiar with every hattmakers boy", adding "that she had had a bastard by a hattmakers boy before she was married". The slander stuck. Six months later a witness testified that as Magdalen went about her business "people thereabouts do mocke at her and say that she must goe into poules to try her honesty". Magdalen followed their advice to "goe into poules", bringing a suit against Mary at London's principal church court, the consistory court held in St Pauls.[2]

Such legal recourse was expensive and time consuming, yet Magdalen and Mary were only two of around 230 women suing and defending defamation cases every year in the early seventeenth-century consistory court. The ecclesiastical courts dealt with sexual slander because it imputed spiritual, rather than temporal, sin. Sexual slander had always been sued predominantly by women, and in the early seventeenth century suits for slander were increasing in all courts.[3] But after 1600, the volume of both defamation cases and women litigants increased to such an extent in London that sexual slander accounted for the largest part of the consistory court's business. By 1633, as many as 70 per cent of cases at the court concerned defamation, and 85 per cent of those were sued by women.[4] In a legal system where women's testimonies were rarely accorded the same measure of credit as men's, defamation cases also involved higher numbers of female witnesses than other suits.[5] This chapter examines the contexts and meanings of the slander litigation that women fought at the London church courts in the late sixteenth and early seventeenth centuries.[6] Looking first at the language of slander, and then at women's litigation, it examines the ways gender determined ideas of sexual honour, uses of slander, and the effects of insult; how women used the courts, and what kinds of opportunities litigation offered women; and how the particular circumstances and definitions of women that obtained in early modern society both circumscribed women's actions, and provided a base from which they could claim verbal, local, and legal authority.

Ostensibly, defamation was concerned with morality and reputation. Slanderous words attacked immoral behaviour; lawsuits in response to them fought to restore a person's damaged reputation. To historians, the increase in slander litigation has suggested the possibility of tracing a growing popular intolerance of illicit sexuality through the currency of insult; but the evidence of dispute has also shown the extent to which defamation disputes arose from complex local and personal conflicts.[7] For early modern commentators, rising levels of litigation were evidence most of all of the pollution of ideals of neighbourliness by malicious dispute.[8] Slander litigation was far more than a response to dishonour. The battles that were fought out in the words of slander and at the court were complex and heterogenous, and their context was far wider than the incidents retailed to the court. Defamation was also an imaginative enterprise. The words of slander did not echo the view of sexual responsibility that contemporary moralists were endeavouring to enforce. While the homilies, sermons and law of the church stress the culpability of both men and women for illicit sex, the idiom of slander holds women entirely responsible for it, contains no words to condemn male sexual misconduct, and judges men and women by two sets of incommensurable values. Women and men used that idiom to produce personal, creative complaints that used, rather than absorbed, contemporary visions of morality.

The motives and functions behind sexual slander, predominantly targeted at and fought at law by women, cannot be understood without taking gender into account. Women's use of both language and lawsuits was determined by their specific places in the economies of language, law, sex, household and community. In a culture where a host of prescriptions limited women's words, and where women's participation in the law was explicitly restricted, sexual insult and legal action represented particular opportunities. Women in London used those opportunities, in conjunction with a set of established customary and practical powers, to claim a verbal and legal authority that was at once powerful and fragile.

London women's involvement in slander was shaped by their particular situation. The women who fought defamation were mostly married or widowed. Gentlewomen did not bring defamation suits, nor did the poorest women. Most litigants were the wives, daughters and widows of middle-status tradesmen and craftsmen, working in shops or markets, nursing, washing, or in service. Their litigation made London's principal ecclesiastical jurisdiction look like a women's court.[9] Here, the metropolitan experience seems to have been unique: although sexual defamation cases regularly attracted large numbers of women plaintiffs, it was only in London that women's business came to take up so large a part of the court's time.

This might be traced in part to London's demographic situation. With a constantly increasing population, sustained by immigration, the city was characterized by a changing topography and a high degree of mobility.[10] A sample of inhabitants between 1572 and 1640 shows that only one in ten Londoners were living in the parish in which they were born, and three-quarters came from outside London and Middlesex.[11] The daily experience of urban life, with its crowded conditions and fragile boundaries, must have exerted considerable strain, particularly on those women and men new to it, and conflicts over property boundaries and shared resources were frequently at the root of defamation. More generally, most people were living in a community where they had a short personal history, and no family past. Public discussions of past sexual behaviour might provide one forum for the exploration of those gaps and the voicing of anxieties about geographic and economic mobility. The specific conditions of urban gender relations were also likely to influence these women's contact with the courts. Many women were working in shops in the fronts of their houses, in their own alehouses, or selling goods at markets; in the eastern parishes, women married to sailors spent much of their time living and working in a predominantly female world. All these circumstances both increased their public profile and made them more likely to be involved in social dispute.

Slander in London was determined by particular urban circumstances, but it was expressed in a language of insult whose themes are recorded in defamation cases across the country.[12] Central to this language was the word "whore", the focus for a dialogue about the honesty of women. Insults like "base whore", "common whore" or "pocky whore" were used not to denote the actual financial and sexual relations of prostitution, but as a shorthand for a fuller exposition of sexual misconduct. The language of defamation construed the whore as the exact opposite of the honest woman. Defamers accused whores of looking "brazen-faced" and dressing luxuriously. Other slanderers complained of women "nightwalking and daywalking", spending their time on the street instead of in the house, and being proud, insubordinate and immodest. All these proofs of dishonesty were familiar from the literature, sermons and biblical texts that advised women on their rôle and behaviour.[13] But defamers also used rumour, elaboration, and invention to construct their own condemnations, transforming the stock cultural images of whoredom into personal insults. Their language established a set of associations through which the word "whore" could be made a symbol for every kind of female misbehaviour.

As the primary targets of insult, women occupied a very particular place in the negotiation of sexual guilt and honour. Insults of women played on a culpability for illicit sex that was unique to them. The personal, verbal, social and institutional sanctions against "whores" and "bawds" had no counterpart for men. Men were less likely than women to be presented for illicit sex. Men's adultery was never an accepted ground for marital separation, as women's was. And the word "whore" had no male equivalent. Instead, men fought cases over insults like "whoremonger", "pander", or "cuckold", concerning not their own sexuality but that of women for whom they were in some sense responsible. In these insults male sexual behaviour was perceived not through its promiscuity, but through the measure of men's control over women's sexuality. Through the power, simultaneously vague and immense, of the word "whore", sexual honour was imagined entirely through women, and in the language of abuse women's dishonesty was interpreted through its direct and material effects on the whole household. The reputation of the house itself rested on women. In 1613 Anne Gibbons complained of a series of sexual insults directed at her husband but focusing on her: "cuckold", "wittall" and "everyone that passeth by thy house and seeth thy wife saieth there is a whore and there is a bawdye house".[14] Women were at the pivotal centre of the circulation of blame and dishonour for sex: responsibility was channelled entirely through them.

That responsibility made women the natural targets for sexual insult, but it also gave some women an investment in the regulation of sexuality inside and outside their households. Sexual honour was overwhelmingly a female concern, and as much as women were the targets of the regulation of honesty, they made themselves the agents of its definition. Women used the broad and powerful possibilities of the word "whore" in every sort of local and personal conflict. They called other women whores loosely, with little or no further details, as one weapon in disputes about money, goods or territory; and they told circumstantial stories of actual, rumoured or imagined sexual transgressions. It seems that women were using the language of slander to perform a function for which men were more likely to look to official, institutional and legal spheres.

The publicity of defamation was central to its power for women. Insulting other women in the street, they made themselves responsible for the honesty of the whole neighbourhood. Defamations regularly began "Goe you whore" or "away you whore", and defamers referred particularly to the localities notorious for prostitution and bawdy houses, Clerkenwell and Turnmill Street.[15] The spirit behind regulations that confined prostitutes to a particular area outside the city walls acted equally effectively for women insulting each other.[16] Ellen Tilbury's abuse of her neighbour in "angrie and malicious manner" in 1625 was typical: "hang thee whore thou keepest a bawdy house" and "Turnbull Street is a more fitt place for thee than to laie here amongst thy neighbours".[17] In insults like these women assumed a particular responsibility for local honesty, claiming the right to define and enforce the moral character of their neighbourhood.

Within the neighbourhood, women drew on a set of other powers from the realms of custom, tradition and law. Some conventionally female areas of power gave women's words a forceful backing. One of these was pregnancy. As midwives, women's sphere of action in the realm of childbirth extended from practical knowledge about pregnancy, abortion and miscarriage and supervision at the time of labour, to the quasi-legal task of questioning illegitimately pregnant women for the names of their partners at the times when labour pains were supposed to make them most truthful. As neighbours, women assisted in the rituals of childbed and the time of seclusion that followed the birth and ended with the re-entry into a mixed world at the moment of churching.[18] So both professionally and socially they were invested with an access to the truth of the physical experience of pregnancy. In the words and actions of slander women exploited this access to expand upon the results of whoredom. In 1624 Anne Pomeroy claimed to be able to detect loss of virginity at sight. In a kitchen of the Inns of Court, she heard someone call Elizabeth Maskall "maid". She intervened "I warrant she is no mayd, for she hath had a child", and told the others there "doe you all thincke that I have some skill, I cann tell upon the sight of one whether she be a mayd or no".[19]

More often women proclaimed their skills at noticing the specific signs of pregnancy, defined exactly by one woman's observation of the changes in her neighbour: "her great belly milking of her brests her lookes and shortnes of her coates".[20] Others claimed medical or visionary skills, like Susan Chaddocke of Wapping, who told a neighbour in 1613 that "she had found in the house of Elizabeth Barwicke an urinall And yt she . . . did looke upon the water which was in the same urinall and saied that whose water soever that was they were with child". At this Elizabeth "did take the same urinall and did throw the water which was in it into her parlour chimney saieing unto . . . Susan Chaddocke that she had as much skill as the dog". Susan had recently herself been presented by Elizabeth's father for bastardy, and she took her assertions to Elizabeth's parents and told her father "nowe it was quid pro quo or it was come home by his . . . dore".[21]

More invasive tests of pregnancy included the squeezing of other women's breasts to check for milk.[22] And once children were born it was women who had the first and fullest chances to examine their features for the evidence of dubious paternity. Ellen Fanch, visiting a neighbour in childbed in 1631, was asked about her sister-in-law's young daughter. She replied "she cared not how they did and further . . . that Richard Wood didst beget her husbands brothers wife", and "I will take mine oath that he didst beget [it] and it is like his Children . . . and I . . . cannot love it".[23]

All the knowledge of female bodies with which women were credited and their authority in the area of childbirth established a source of power that was immensely productive in the shaping of abuse.

Pregnancy was perceived as the natural punishment of whoredom: one frequent insult was "if she is not with child, she has deserved to be so". But women also interested themselves in particular physical, ritual and communal punishments, both informally and through the law. Community custom included an established set of symbolic rituals to punish infringements of sexual rules, and in those rituals women were prominent. In London there is little evidence of the skimmingtons or ridings with which disturbers of the sexual order were received in rural areas.[24] Instead, defamers and their witnesses refer to public rituals that were in many cases specific to women. Broken windows were supposed to mark a bawdy house, and some women had their windows broken to show their whoredom. In 1628 Catherine Ripon was accused of calling Sibill Brosse whore and breaking both her head and her windows, in an action that combined the symbolizing of whoredom with physical violence against the whore.[25] Like the rituals of rough music recorded in other areas, the banging of basins and pans at women was used to accuse them of whoredom or scolding, and this too found its way into the vernacular of defamation. Alice Fullham and Ellen Alsop called each other "quean" and "bitch" in the street in 1611, and Alice said to Ellen "a cart and a basen tyng tyng, a cart and a basen tyng tyng, a cart and a basen if thou wilt not be quiet".[26] Here, as so often, verbal and sexual incontinence were conflated.

A more personal punishment involved an actual mutilation of the whore, to make her as visible as she was meant to be. In Stepney in 1618 Alice Squire scratched Katherine Berry's face and said she had given her a "whores marke". This mark was a slit nose, traditionally conceived as the injured wife's revenge on her husband's mistress.[27] Other women threatened the same penalty. In 1619 Joan Hickman accused her neighbour Joan Bird of "keeping her husband" and threatened to "slitt her nose and marke her for a whore". Witnesses described this as having "used her pleasure of Joane Bird in speeches", echoing the familiar phraseology of sexual pleasure in the shape of the pleasurable verbal revenge for it.[28] Given the way that noses, in early modern culture, could stand in for phalluses, it is a revenge that looks like castration.[29] Symbolic actions and threats like these sustained the tradition of this corpus of women's sanctions, encompassing sexual sin in contexts as broad as the neighbourhood and as narrow as the household.

Women's power to punish whoredom was not confined to the communal, informal sphere. Whereas men decided and enforced the temporal and spiritual law's penalties for illicit sex, many women made explicit reference to those punishments and proclaimed their own power to invoke them. Women found guilty of whoredom or bawdry at the sessions were regularly sentenced to be carried in a cart through specified neighbourhoods, and carting proved an institutional punishment that satisfied with its ritual humiliation and local visibility. The church courts had an equally powerful ritual, the penance that adulterers and fornicators were ordered to do in a white sheet, sometimes with a paper proclaiming their sins at their heads, and this furnished an equally fruitful source of insult.

Many defamers linked the two kinds of punishment so their insults called down a whole range of sanctions against the whore. Margery Hixwell and Phoebe Cartwright fell into an argument in Margery's shop in Fleet Street in 1613, and a woman in the shop next door heard Margery say to Alice "Thou art a quean and a wrymouth quean and I will make thee do penaunce in a white sheet And I will have thee carted out of the street".[30] Anne Johnson was sitting in her shop selling fruit with Marie Buckle's child in her arms, when Elizabeth Lee came past and

> tooke the child and kissed yt sayeing Thow art a pretty child and Marie Buckle did not stand in a white sheete for nothinge, and . . . further that Alice Clerke . . . was a Bawde and she would cause her to be carted for a bawd, which words she . . . spake verie loude.[31]

Such institutional punishments had a clear neighbourhood character. The church courts' penance was staged in the parish church of the offender, and included asking forgiveness of the congregation. Carting brought the offender through selected neighbourhoods connected with her crime. It was these local contexts that gave such punishments their effect and, as in women's use of the idea of neighbourhood honesty to insult "whores", it was the local and communal context that enabled women to claim their part in the male judicial system. Punishments like carting or ordering the penance of a white sheet were the public manifestations of a formal, male legal institution; but in form they were closely related to community rituals in which women could claim more agency.[32] And whereas male constables, churchwardens, and local officials presented women for sexual misconduct to the secular and spiritual courts, the procedures of informal complaint and formal presentment by which discipline was invoked were also open to women. In the words of defamation, some women made an explicit and public claim to the power of local punishment.

This claim found its fullest expression when women were concerned with sexual misconduct not in the neighbourhood, but in the household. While many of the insults exchanged between neighbours or acquaint-ances used sexual words as a useful weapon rather than an accurate descrip-tion of misconduct, and many others produced sexual stories from vague rumours, insult also provided a means of complaining publicly about more concrete situations. In one household situation, that of a husband's adul-tery, slander was particularly useful for women. In the idiom of sexual insult there was one phrase that had meaning only between women and it was used again and again: "thou art my husband's whore". Men were most unlikely to refer to even the potential of sexual relations between their wives and other men. But women complained of their husbands' adultery in long and specific detail, explaining its damages in sexual, emotional and financial terms, and directing the blame always onto other women. Joan Marwent said that Prudence Hosegood was "a base quean and that she kept company with her [Joan's] husband and what he got he spent upon her and when he came from her he alwaies beat her".[33] In 1632 three men and women testified how, in midsummer of that year, Mary Sadd had come to Horne Alley to find the woman she called her husband's whore. Sara Saunderson, hearing "a greate noise" in the alley, went down "and finding a woeman standing at her husbands house door railing with a great company of people about her she . . . demanded of the woeman what she meant to kepe such a railing at her doore". Mary pointed at the house where Margaret Eddis lodged and replied "I would have the whore out of that house . . . for she is a base whore and a hospitall whore" and said that "her [Mary's] husband pawned her goades and . . . her childrens clothes to maintaine her [Margaret], and that she had rousted her out of one place already, and yf she staied but til tomorrow she would roust her out of this".[34]

Incidents like this reveal the prime concerns of women who suspected their husbands of adultery. Sexual, financial and physical injuries are evalu-ated with care to explain the disruption of marriage through the conse-quent disorganization of household consumption. If these women were making allegations they believed to be true, they were engaged in an endeavour with particular significance for women. Although both sexes could, in theory, sue their spouses for adultery at these same courts, women hardly ever did so. In legal practice, it was women's and not men's adultery that was culpable, and this was underlined in 1650 when women's adultery was made a capital offence. Through defamation, women were able to invoke a public humiliation in response to adultery, and, following the legal system, they directed the blame not toward their husbands but toward other women. Mary Sadd's threats reveal a repertory of specific actions with which this blame could be pursued by women against the women they called their husbands' whores: going to confront them, defaming them in front of landladies, workmates or neighbours, "rousting" them out of lodgings and forcing them to move.

Less specific insults served as fuel for disputes that turn out to have had little to do with sex, where "whore" became a shorthand for much wider grievances. Because the sexual honesty of women had implications for so many other spheres, from their speech to their financial honesty, it easily became the focus for disputes about a whole range of familial and community issues. Most often these disputes were concerned very closely with the organization of neighbourhood relations, between houses or within streets. Women's conflicts over children or servants, about shared fences or walls, or neighbourhood resources like water, shifted through defamation into sexual dispute. A typical exchange in 1629 reveals the steps through which this translation of dispute into the realm of the sexual was effected. Elizabeth White heard Rachel Townsend persuading her husband not to pay the debts he owed Elizabeth's husband, and to make Elizabeth instead "take her course by law". Confronting Rachel, she told her "she was a scurvy woman in soe doing"; Rachel responded "I am not so scurvy a woman as you for I never sould my daughters maydenhead for money", and she accused Elizabeth of taking £5 for her daughter's virginity.[35] Rachel transposed the financial issue into another accusation of economic misdealing; in this way, disputes that were fought out between women became focused on the sexual.

The slanderous words that women exchanged in cases like these functioned both as complaint about sexual misconduct and, much more broadly, as one step in wider neighbourhood conflicts. Slander has often been conflated with gossip, understood as a way of regulating behaviour and social relations through the emphasis of group values, consonant with a larger moral system represented in various forms of contemporary culture, custom and law.[36] But the categorizations and condemnations through which slander was effected constituted a project more creative and more disruptive than this interpretation allows. The voicing of sexual slander was far more than a perpetuation of predefined condemnations of women's sexual sin. The word "whore" was used with no reference to the real financial–sexual exchanges of prostitution, and the stories that were woven around it referred to incidents from the concrete to the imaginary. It was used with imagination and elaboration: the words of slander defined with care the exact lines that delineated honesty. Clearly, in many cases, slander worked as a way of calling men or women to account for sexual grievances, and as such it was particularly important for women who had few other avenues of effective response. But slander worked very often against, not in concord with, prescribed moral values; more than normative regulation, it represented a creative offensive. Ostensibly concerned with the detailed mechanics of heterosexuality, slander was also about another kind of relationship, the social ties between women.[37] At this level, the established language of insult operated as a sign for other grievances or disputes, and when women spoke sexual insult they adopted a discourse whose idiom and meaning were already set up to focus on women's sexual faults, and used it towards their own ends. The exchanges of slander represent not normative regulation of heterosexuality, but disruptive interpersonal abuse in a larger social context.

More than sex, slander was about gender. Women who used the language of insult claimed for themselves responsibility for the definition of honest femininity. And, as women's unchastity had implications for their whole character, so defining sexual honesty meant defining womanhood. The constant repetition of the word whore, and its associated terms "jade", "bawd" and "quean", presented femininity through the terms of honesty, distributing blame so as to differentiate men from women and honest women from whores. If, as Judith Butler has argued, we understand gender not as a static division but a definition in progress, mobilized through the repetition of particular acts, sexual slander might productively be read as a set of representations and performances in which women defined honesty and femininity.[38]

★ ★ ★

In many ways, then, the language of slander offered particular linguistic powers to women, through which they asserted their verbal, physical and legal agency to judge and condemn other women. But such sexually explicit speech had its risks for women. Using sexual insult to prove other women dishonest left slanderers themselves open to charges of impropriety. Incontinence of speech and sexuality were directly linked in contemporary sources. In New England, although not in England, women found guilty of defamation could be punished by ducking in the same way as scolds:

women's sexual slander was a crime against verbal and social norms.[39]

The dangers of women's speech about sex were particularly apparent when women alleged seduction, assault or rape. Men regularly sued women for their attempts to fix sexual responsibility on them. Even the most conventional forms of such attempts were liable to interpretation as defamation. In 1613 Martha Day was sued by John Cowell for confessing to her midwife that he was the father of her illegitimate child, and for saying as he passed her that "I was his whore". More assertive claims and complaints against men's sexual misconduct were even more liable to prosecution as slander. Many involved complaints against masters, employers and landlords. In 1624 Susan Turton, a servant, protested to a local gentleman about her master's treatment of herself and her fellow servant: "I could not be in quiet for him for he would fynde me out in anie room of the house"; "he would be tousing and mousing[40] of them and urging them to follie and did take upp their clothes and would have had the carnal knowledge of their bodies"; "she was sometymes out of breath to resiste him and [he] did throwe her upon a bed and strived with her by pulling up of her Cloathes".[41] When her master heard of her complaints he sued her for defamation. Dorcas Newton accused her landlord William Garrad of "lying with her against her will in ye malt room at her dwelling house" and of making her pregnant. Her servant testified to hearing her cry out, and her husband brought a suit at common law against Garrad, yet Garrad was able to sue both Dorcas Newton and her servant for slander.[42] The early modern legal system offered most women little recourse against rape, particularly when men's stories were given more credit by economic and social advantage.[43]

The stories that men told about sex automatically received more credit than those of women. Accusations like these by women were pitted against this credit and against all the legal, literary and customary practices of penalizing sexual sin, where only women could be characterized as "whores", where only women were sued for adultery, and where men's honour never involved their sexual behaviour. Some men even defamed women for being "whores" with them, as one man did in 1587: "Thow . . . art an arrant whore, aye and I have lyen with thee and my friende too have lyen with the".[44] Men spoke with a self confidence about their own sexual behaviour that was entirely absent from women's speech. Women talked of their own sexual behaviour from a very different angle. Their references to men's misconduct were not so much insults as complaints that attempted to fix blame upon the men who had dishonoured them. With neither the rhetoric of insult nor the framework of sexual honour on which sexual insults of "whores" depended, women who accused men of sexual sin were redefining the very grounds of slander to insist upon a male culpability that was not enforceable in practice.[45]

★ ★ ★

From women's disputes in the street, I want to turn now to their confrontations in the courts. Like the language of defamation itself, the litigation by which victims complained of slander was a complicated transaction, involving a set of particular and gendered purposes, meanings and results, and functioning in a much broader context of personal and neighbourhood relations and disruptions. When women uttered slanderous words they set in motion a train of consequences that had a place in larger conflicts. After slanderous words were spoken their victims might complain of their abusers to other neighbours, to local gentry or to the clergy. Attempts might be made at informal and formal mediation to resolve the dispute; at the same time the dispute might spread as family, neighbours and friends took sides or repeated the slander. If every other attempt at settlement failed, the case might end up in the church courts.

The pursuit of words like these at law assumed that their effects were so damaging as to require public retraction and apology. The law of defamation posited a direct link between the words of temporal and spiritual slanders and their material effects. What were those effects, supposedly so powerful? Treatises on defamation discuss the various effects of slander on men but say little about its results for women. For men, slander posed a material threat to profession, inheritance, advancement or livelihood, and hence a man's good name was, as John Godolphin wrote, "Equilibrious with his Life".[46] The same kind of effects were understood to apply to women, but women's livelihood and "advancement" were conceived in a much narrower sphere than men's. In these texts women's material livelihood is affected not through their own earnings, but through their marriage prospects: marriage is women's only opportunity for the kind of advancement that makes up men's careers.[47]

At the church courts, witnesses for single women sometimes spoke of "discredit" to "a mayden . . . in the waie of preferment in marriage",[48] but in most cases, the victims were married and the conflation of "chastity" and "virginity" that was assumed by writers on honour could not apply. Instead, plaintiffs and litigants described how husbands might treat suspicion of their wives' infidelity as a threat to their marriage. When Margaret

Smith was accused of saying to Anne Fanne "thou art a whore thou hast dishonested my house for I did see Hopkins and thee togither he with his breeches downe", one witness testified that Anne's husband had been so offended he would not let her lie with him and Anne had gone to her mother in the country.[49]

Other people spoke of the broader ways slander might damage women. As sexual behaviour had implications for women's whole characters, so, in theory, sexual insult could affect their whole lives. Witnesses for slandered women assessed the damage in phrases like "[she is] discredited in her reputation and calling to be so evil spoken of"; "upon the speaking of the said words [she] imagined very ill of the producent and she yet doth till she hath cleared herself"; "notwithstanding that [he] was great friends with the producent he did tell his . . . wife that he was persuaded that the words about the falling out . . . was a bad matter and very suspicious and as yet [he] cannot think well of the producent until she hath cleared herself".[50] The key words are "imagined", "persuaded" and "suspicious", suggesting the way reputation developed: influences and suspicions might be effective through their very imprecision.

In another case one witness attempted, in contrast, a material assessment of damage. In 1590 in Woodford, Essex, Elizabeth Dymsdale was reported to have called Susan More "an arrant whore . . . that laye first with the master and then with the man in Mill Lane", and said "there were two dozen men witness to it". A witness to the words estimated the effects on Susan's reputation:

> Susan Mores name is by reason of the saide scandalls uttered by Elizabeth Dymsdall as aforesaid spreaded about all the country there-abouts and she is talked about commonly amongst the neighbours, to the great discredit of the producent, And he verily thinketh the producent to have rather given twenty pounds than to have had such a speche goe upon her, as that the said speaches is gonne and doth yet goe and is talked of, for he saieth the producent hath byen taken by the neighbours hereabouts as a very honest woman.[51]

This is an unusually lengthy account of how defamatory speeches were perceived as circulating, damaging as they went. It would have been in the interests of plaintiffs to produce witnesses who could elaborate on the exact damage done by slander, but few did so. The effects of insult, and its relationship to the actual operation of honour, remain elusive; the most substantive result of slander seems to be talk. Anne Pridgen, who sued

Christopher Thompson in 1588 for calling her whore "in fleering manner", brought a witness to testify: "foreasmuch as people are commonly given to speake the worste of a woman whome they heere to be evell spoken of she thinckelth the good name of Anne Pridgen to be impayred and hurte by the said Thompson".[52] Evil words lead to more evil words, nothing more substantial.

This consistent failure to mark out the exact effects of defamation suggests that more was at stake in litigation than the urge to defend a materially damaged reputation. Historians have tended to stress, through the evidence of slander, an idea of popular honour as both consonant with the standards of ecclesiastical and secular morality, and homogenous across differences of age, geography and class.[53] But the enterprise of defamation was as much about defining honesty as repeating predefined prescriptions: in practice, both women and men worked out codes of sexual honour that served certain purposes.[54] The ideas of honesty and morality that church law, household advice, sermons, or popular literature suggested did not dictate popular morality. They provided, rather, a set of ideals that could be invoked, adapted or transformed in daily life. The imprecisions of the effects of slander suggest the potential for accommodation, negotiation and reproduction of ideas about sex and honourable behaviour. Given this flexibility, the functions and meanings of litigation require a more fluid and complex analysis.

Litigation was in itself a potentially ambiguous response to slander. Some people insisted that it was dishonouring to let an insult go unchallenged. Elizabeth Aldeworth took Christopher Mortimer to court in 1572 for impugning her honesty by saying that she had been "called whore, and prevye whore to yor teth, and ye were gladd to take it quyetlye and putt it upp". Elizabeth responded in defence of her record of litigation, saying she had sued a previous detractor to protect her name, and another neighbour intervened to support her.[55] But taking sexual insult to court was hardly consistent with the ideas of women's honour that provided the basis for defining honesty and dishonesty. Perfectly chaste and honourable women should not, technically, have discussed their sexual reputation in court; self-defence against accusations of whoredom could be seen as contributing to dishonour, in perpetuating the discourse about sex. While some women were accused of dishonesty for not pursuing defamation in the courts, others were attacked for being too litigious. One woman defended herself against such suggestions in 1610: "Had I had any more lawe than an honest woman should have?"[56] Clearly the argument about defending modesty by litigation could be used both ways.

Litigation did not provide a predictable, guaranteed result. If the case went to the judge, a final sentence was given which might impose a penance and a repayment of costs on the guilty party. But few slander cases got as far as this. Although most sentences were given in favour of the plaintiff, only one in five to one in three cases even called witnesses, and of these over 80 per cent were settled or abandoned long before their formal conclusion. The church courts always aimed to encourage reconciliation, more than confrontation. Ostensibly, slander suits enabled the regulation of disruptive speech and the reconciliation of dispute. Martin Ingram's work has shown how these functions might serve litigants who sought conciliation.[57] But the contexts of these cases suggest that the relationship between the court's aims and those of their clients might also be a less easy one. If litigants wanted conciliation, there were plenty of opportunities outside the court.[58] Many people mediated their disputes through older neighbours, gentry or ministers, making a formal settlement and sealing it with shared food, drink and forgiveness. Taking a case to court, litigants rejected all these informal methods and set in train instead a series of regular official confrontations between plaintiffs, defendants, witnesses and proctors. Invoking the process of litigation seems more likely to have perpetuated a dispute than to have ended it. It was in the light of this use of the courts to "maintain" local and personal disputes that contemporaries complained of the increase in slander litigation, noting a tendency to "flee to the Law out of malice and make the Courts of Justice maintainers of every small and vaine brabble".[59] Like slanderous speech, litigation could be a stage in the processes of social disruption. Increasingly in the seventeenth century it led not to conciliation, but to the spread of dispute, with defendants and witnesses starting new suits of their own in complex networks of litigation. Slander and its prosecution were occasions, not of regulation or reconciliation, but of disturbance and dysfunction.

The words and legal actions of slander were a familiar part of the fabric of local disputes. Sexual slander litigation was one of the main ways in which women in early modern London found themselves in contact with the courts: in the seventeenth century, even the smaller city parishes of 200 or so households sent one or two cases of defamation a year to the consistory court.[60] Other people were involved in presentments for disciplinary offences, or the different kinds of business that went to the other church courts and the secular law.[61] The mechanics and meanings of litigation and disciplinary justice were common currency in local dispute, and they were recognized as serving particular social purposes. In the exchanges and disputes that fill these records, men and women threaten each other with legal language, talking of citation and prosecution, presentments and defences, standing bail and giving witness; they refer often to other lawsuits in progress amongst other members of the neighbourhood; and they explain the kinds of tensions about friendliness, money or territory that were associated with such litigation. Women insist on their power over institutional sanctions, proclaiming their ability to get other women "carted" or sent to Bridewell; others complain that they have been cited, or presented, or fined "at the suit of" a woman.

As much as legitimate complaint, the processes of disciplinary justice were perceived and discussed as a means of pursuing personal grievances. In the summer of 1621, Ann Yarrington and Ann Croste fought each other through a combination of public rituals and formal actions. In August Ann Yarrington "unhosed" Ann Croste in the street, saying to her "I am shited [punning rudely on cited] to poules [St Pauls] with a shitacon and that at the sute of Ann Croste whoe is my husbands whore". She produced an old handkerchief from her pocket and continued "for this ould handkercher my husband . . . hath occupied her . . . seaven tymes".[62] In such disputes, legal processes were understood to be part of the armoury of weapons for local and personal confrontations. They were particularly significant weapons for women. The men who came to this court were increasingly likely to participate in local and parochial government, to be able to write and to have some form of contact with formal record keeping: but their wives could rarely sign their names, most often worked outside companies and were explicitly excluded from participation in local officialdom. Participation in litigation offered women a rare official, institutional weapon in the daily and occasional conflicts of their local lives.

It also presented the opportunity of establishing a permanent record of their words or actions. Witnesses and litigants at the court told stories of the contested events to a clerk who recorded them at length in an idiom that was partly shaped by court tradition but that also bore traces of the narrator. Once it was written down, they heard it repeated to the court's judge. For most women this was the only time their words would be recorded with such acute attention. It enabled them to rewrite the events of dispute in their own versions, in the context of their involvement. The resulting depositions can be long, detailed and original narratives.[63] Women told stories that focused on their part in the words and acts of dispute, describing the work they were doing, their relationship to the combatants and how they intervened: their statements focused on women's daily lives. They also repeated with care the offensive words of sexual insult, dwelling at length on the details that were meant to play no part in women's speech.

At every level, the occasions involved in defamation made it a verbal and legal process that enabled women to stake some specific claims to authority in the household and the community. While punishment for sexual crimes was enforced through the church courts and by men, women asserted their part through more informal confrontations and penalties. While men's adultery was rarely pursued through the courts as women's was, some women publicized their husbands' behaviour through the words of insult, centring the blame on other women in order to speak at loud and at length about their emotional and financial grievances. In the household, women used the vocabulary of insult to complain of their husbands' adultery; in the broader range of the neighbourhood they used their position as the figurehead of household honour to decide other women's honesty, buttressed by their traditional authority over pregnancy or the informal punishment of "whores". At the courts, litigation provided a way of shifting personal, semi-public disputes into a much broader, official sphere to which women rarely had access. And once at the courts, women were required to repeat in full, in a church, the sexual words of defamatory disputes and to tell personal stories that were preserved in the kind of written record with which early modern women, to our loss, only occasionally came into contact.

Notes

I am very grateful to the participants of the conference for their discussion of this paper, and to Lyndal Roper and Sarah Waters for their help in revising it.

1. T. E., *The lawes resolution of womens rights: or, the lawes provision for women* (London, 1632), pp. 6, 4.
2. Greater London RO DL/C 231 f. 40, Lewis con Record, 24/10/1628. All cases quoted are from the records of the London consistory and archdeaconry courts, held at the Greater London RO (series DL/C) and the Guildhall Library (MS. 9189), between 1566 and 1640, when this series of records ends. For clarity, in quotations from witness depositions I have expanded contractions; the omissions shown are mostly of repetitive legal formulae.
3. For studies of slander elsewhere see J. A. Sharpe, *Defamation and sexual slander in early modern England: the church courts at York*, Borthwick Papers, 58 (York, 1980); M. Ingram, *Church courts, sex and marriage in England, 1570–1640*

WOMEN, CRIME AND THE COURTS

(Cambridge, 1987) ch. 10; A. Gregory, Slander accusations and social control in late sixteenth and early seventeenth century England, with particular reference to Rye (Sussex), DPhil thesis, University of Sussex, 1984; J. A. Thompson, "Her good name and credit": the reputation of women in seventeenth-century Devon, PhD thesis, University of Cincinnati, 1987. The situation in London before the Reformation is covered briefly in R. Wunderli, *London church courts and society before the Reformation* (Cambridge MA, 1981); and slander in eighteenth-century London is discussed in A. Clark, Whores and gossips: sexual reputation in London 1770–1825, in *Current issues in women's history*, eds A. Angerman *et al.* (London, 1989), pp. 231–48 and T. Meldrum, Defamation at the church courts: women and community control in London 1700–1745, MSc thesis, London School of Economics and Political Science, 1990. For the particular pattern of gender and defamation shaped by a different sex ratio, see M. B. Norton, Gender and defamation in seventeenth-century Maryland, *William and Mary Quarterly*, third series, **36**, 1979, pp. 3–39.

4. DL/C 18 (1618), 22 (1624), 27 (1633).

5. In marriage cases at the consistory court (sued half the time by women), 36 per cent of witnesses were women; in defamation cases, 46 per cent were women, and in those cases fought between women, 60 per cent of witnesses were women. Figures obtained from consistory court deposition books, 1572–1640 (from a total of 5371 witnesses).

6. The set of records I am using, mostly relating to the consistory court but some to the archdeaconry court, runs from 1566 to 1640.

7. Sharpe, *Defamation and sexual slander*, pp. 24–6, 22; Ingram, *Church courts, sex and marriage*, pp. 165–6, 304–306, 313–16.

8. J. March, *Actions for slaunder, or, a methodicall collection under certain grounds of heads, of what words are actionable in the Law, and what not?* (London, 1647), especially p. 4. Legally, spiritual defamation was defined by the element of malice in an imputation: *Auctoritate dei Patris* (1222), quoted in R. H. Helmholz, *Select cases on defamation to 1600* (London, 1985), pp. xxxii–iv.

9. As a lesser London court the commissary, already did in the early sixteenth century, and as the consistory was to continue to do when it resumed business after the Civil War: Wunderli, *London church courts and society*, p. 76; Meldrum, Defamation at the church courts, p. 16.

10. On the experience of London in this period, see I. Archer, *The pursuit of stability: social relations in Elizabethan London* (Cambridge, 1991), ch. 4 and S. Rappaport, *Worlds within worlds: structures of life in sixteenth-century London* (Cambridge, 1989), ch. 3.

11. Calculated from the biographical information given by witnesses at this court, 1572–1640.

12. Many of these themes are common to slanderous language recorded elsewhere in Europe, in New England and in New France: see for comparison P. Burke,

The art of insult in early modern Italy, *Culture and History*, **2** (1987), pp. 68–79; M. B. Norton, Gender and defamation in seventeenth-century Maryland; P. N. Moogk, "Thieving buggers" and "stupid sluts": insults and popular culture in New France, *William and Mary Quarterly*, third series, **36** (1979), pp. 524–47.

13. For examples of the advice literature, see W. Gouge, *Of domesticall duties: eight treatises* (London, 1622); R. Clever, *A godlie form of household government: for the ordering of private families, according to the direction of Gods word* (London, 1598); and one of their principal sources, H. Bullinger *The christen state of matrimonye,* tr. Miles Coverdale (Antwerp, 1541). The best guide to this literature is K. M. Davies, Continuity and change in literary advice on marriage, in *Marriage and society: studies in the social history of marriage*, ed. R. B. Outhwaite (London, 1981), pp. 58–80. The book of Proverbs, in particular Proverbs 6. 12–19, is one of the few sources directly evident in the words of insult: one defamer referred explicitly to the words of Solomon. See DC/C 231, f. 236, Treat con Blyth, 22/10/1628.

14. DL/C 221, ff. 539v.–540, Gibbons con Stronge, 15/11/1613. A wittall is a contented cuckold.

15. I. Archer's map of London bawdy houses shows a concentration around this area: Archer, *The pursuit of stability*, p. 212.

16. On such regulations see R. M. Karras, The regulation of brothels in later medieval England, in *Sisters and workers in the Middle Ages*, eds J. M. Bennett *et al.* (Chicago, 1989), pp. 97–127.

17. DL/C 230, ff. 16, 17, Banbridge con Tilbie, 27/1/1626.

18. On the female rituals of childbirth, see A. Wright, The ceremony of childbirth and its interpretation, and on women's experience of motherhood, and P. Crawford, The construction and experience of maternity in seventeenth-century England, both in *Women as mothers in pre-industrial England*, ed. V. Fildes (London, 1990), pp. 68–107 & 3–38.

19. Guildhall MS 9189/1, f. 130v., Maskall con Pomeroy, 6/2/1624.

20. DL/C 630, f. 290v., Office ad promotionem Layton con Francis, 11/11/1634.

21. DL/C 222, f. 1290, Barwicke con Chaddocke, 19/4/1613; DL/C 221, f. 1319 *et seq.*, Pett con Chaddocke, 21/10/1613.

22. See for example DL/C 630, f. 330v., Bowles con Heale, 21/1/1634.

23. DL/C 233, f. 229, Wood con Fanch, 18/11/1631.

24. Mocking processions. D. Underdown, The taming of the scold: the enforcement of patriarchal authority in early modern England, in *Order and disorder in early modern England*, eds A. Fletcher & J. Stevenson (Cambridge, 1985), pp. 116–36; M. Ingram, Ridings, rough music and mocking rhymes in early modern England, in *Popular culture in seventeenth-century England* (London & Sydney, 1985), pp. 166–97.

25. DL/C 231, f. 28v., Brosse con Ripon, 7/7/1628.

26. DL/C 220, ff. 540v.–48v., Alsop con Fullham, 15/6/1611.

27. See for example the ballad "Have among you good women", *The Roxburghe Ballads* I, no. 146, ed. W. Chappell & J. W. Ebsworth (London & Hertford, 1871–95); DL/C 225, f. 351, Berry con Squire et alios, 16/11/1618.

28. DL/C 226/III, ff. 41–2, Bird con Hickman, 17/11/1619.

29. Syphilis, for example, was perceived as affecting men's penises, but women's noses; many sexual insults go into exact detail about infection and damage.

30. DL/C 221, f. 1189v., Cartwright con Hixwell, 8/6/1613.

31. DL/C 226/IV, f. 28, Clerke con Lee, 26/1/1620.

32. These different kinds of response existed uncomfortably together, as M. Ingram points out (*Church courts, sex and marriage*, p. 163); nevertheless, they relied on similar kinds of symbolism and were equated by a number of these defamers.

33. DL/C 230, f. 225v., Hosegood con Marwent, 24/11/1626. Prudence also called Joan a whore, either earlier, or in retaliation: *ibid.*, f. 240v., Marwent con Hosegood, 6/12/1626.

34. Guildhall MS. 9057/1, f. 12, Eddis con Sadd, 1/12/1632.

35. DL/C 231, ff. 321–2, White con Townsend, 4/2/1629.

36. J. A. Sharpe, *Defamation and sexual slander*, p. 19; M. B. Norton, Gender and defamation in seventeenth-century Maryland, pp. 35–9; R. Thompson, "Holy watchfulness" and communal conformism: the functions of defamation in early New England communities, *New England Quarterly*, **56**, 1983, pp. 504–522: pp. 520–22.

37. No London slanders mention homosexuality at all; in the case of men this may have been because sodomy was a temporal more than a spiritual crime, and allegations of it were punishable at the secular courts.

38. J. Butler, *Gender trouble: feminism and the subversion of identity* (London, 1991), pp. 139–41.

39. C. A. Bowler, Carted whores and white shrouded apologies: slander in the county courts of seventeenth-century Virginia, *The Virginia Magazine of History and Biography*, **85**, 1977, pp. 411–26: p. 413.

40. Pulling them about, mishandling them.

41. DL/C 229, ff. 89, 90, Holmes con Turton, 3/12/1624.

42. DL/C 232, f. 156v., Garrad con Newton, 1630 [n.d.]; *ibid.*, f. 286, Garrad con Gilder, 2/2/1630.

43. N. Bashar, Rape in England between 1550 and 1700, in *The sexual dynamics of history*, ed. London Feminist History Group (London, 1983), pp. 28–42.

44. DL/C 213, p. 154, Banbury con Harman, 15/6/1587.

45. See also Norton, Gender and defamation in seventeenth-century Maryland.

46. J. Godolphin, *Reportorium canonicum* (London, 1678), p. 516.

47. Godolphin, *Reportorium canonicum*, p. 517; W. Vaughan, *The spirit of detraction, coniured and convicted in seven circles* (London, 1611), p. 346.

48. DL/C 227, f. 175, Matthewe con Brittanne, 26/10/1620.

49. DL/C 219, ff. 245–6v., Fanne con Smith, 31/10/1610.

50. DL/C 228, f. 71, Ashley con Gibbes, 8/11/1621; DL/C 214, pp. 95, 83, Holstead con Wharton, 25 and 13/11/1591. "Producent" is the church courts' term for plaintiff, i.e. the woman who was slandered.

51. DL/C 214, pp. 18–19, More con Dymsdale, 12/6/1591. The dispute was continued in a subsequent case, Elizabeth Dymcross con John More (*ibid.*, p. 21), in which Susan's husband was accused of attacking Elizabeth Dymsdale both physically and verbally and she of throwing a pail of burning coals at him.

52. DL/C 213, pp. 432, 445, Pridgen con Thompson, 9 and 12/11/1588. "Fleering" means sneering.

53. Sharpe, *Defamation and sexual slander*, pp. 3, 24–8; S. D. Amussen, *An ordered society: gender and class in early modern England* (Oxford, 1988), pp. 130–31; Ingram, *Church courts, sex and marriage*, pp. 166, 303; R. A. Houlbrooke, *Church courts and the people during the English Reformation, 1520–1570* (Oxford, 1979), p. 87.

54. A. Clark's work on eighteenth-century London shows women defining to a certain extent their own codes of sexual morality: Clark, Whores and gossips.

55. DL/C 211/1, f. 105, Aldeworth con Mortimer, 13/11/1572.

56. DL/C219, f. 174v., Greenrise con Pinge, 15/6/1610.

57. Ingram, *Church courts, sex and marriage*, p. 317–18.

58. See J. A. Sharpe, "Such disagreement betwyx neighbours": litigation and human relations in early modern England, in *Disputes and settlements: law and human relations in the West*, ed. J. Bossy (Cambridge, 1983), pp. 167–87.

59. J. March, *Actions for slaunder* (London, 1647), p. 4.

60. Calculated from the books and deposition books for 1631–40, GLRO DL/C 27, 232–35.

61. On involvement in the secular law, see C. Herrup, *The common peace: participation and the criminal law in seventeenth-century England* (Cambridge, 1987), and R. B. Shoemaker, *Prosecution and punishment: petty crime and the law in London and rural Middlesex, c. 1660–1725* (Cambridge, 1991), chs 2, 8.

62. DL/C 228, ff. 95v.–96, Croste con Yarrington, 23/11/1621.

63. On these narratives and their meanings see L. Gowing, Women, sex and honour: the London church courts, 1572–1640, PhD thesis, University of London, 1993, pp. 172–207.

Chapter Three

"Scolding women cucked or washed": a crisis in gender relations in early modern England?[1]

Martin Ingram

The words "scold" and "to scold" mean little to us nowadays. We all know the verb, but assign it to a nursery context: we get scolded for not eating our cabbage or spoiling our nice new clothes. The noun "scold" is effectively obsolete, though if pressed most of us find that we "know" that in the olden days sharp-tongued women were ducked in the village pond. In Tudor and Stuart times, in contrast, "scold" was a strongly negative term, in destructive impact second only to "whore" (and its equivalents such as "drab", "jade" and "quean") as a pejorative label applied to women. Yet it was also redolent of female strength and power, since it was traditionally supposed that a scold was capable of outfacing the devil. At the same time the scold was in some sense a figure of fun: the best way to taunt a scolding woman was to offer her a "wisp", "bottle" or "wad" of hay as an object to rail at, since this was universally recognized as the "perfect token" of a scold.[2] The concept of the scold thus offers an intriguing avenue for the exploration of some aspects of the lives of women in early modern England. It is that pathway that this paper follows, concentrating (in accord with the theme of the collection) on legal issues – the punishment of scolding as a crime.

I

Recent and not so recent work has gone a long way towards establishing a framework for understanding relations between the sexes in Tudor and Stuart England. It is accepted that the society was broadly speaking patriarchal, though there is much debate about what this meant in actual practice in terms of relations between husbands and wives, parents and children within the household.[3] Contemporary social commentators invariably assigned dependent, home-based rôles to women, in contrast to the more active, extra-domestic functions of the male. Historians have shown that in certain respects such prescriptions had little relation to reality – for example, women were in practice often found working in the fields, or out and about to buy and sell in the market – but female activities were undoubtedly restricted in many ways in the spheres of both work and leisure.[4] Certainly women were almost entirely excluded from positions of public authority; they could not hold office and played little part in the legal process. Reputation or "credit" – a matter of vital importance for all sections of Tudor and Stuart society – likewise had different implications for the two sexes; the good name of women was more fragile than that of men, and female "honesty" centred primarily on sexual behaviour whereas the characters of men were judged on a broader range of criteria, among which probity in business dealings and "honesty" in something like its modern sense were most important.[6] Studies of female criminal activity have also revealed marked gender differences. Then, as now, far fewer women came before the courts than men. Females were under represented most markedly in crimes involving physical violence, major larcenies or, more generally, activities that required a high degree of initiative and self assertion. When they were in trouble for criminal behaviour it was more likely to be as perpetrators of petty theft in household, workshop or market and of offences involving verbal rather than physical abuse, or as mere aiders and abettors of more serious crimes.[7] Witchcraft – still the most intensively studied gender related crime – is the exception that proves the rule. In contemporary society it was perceived as highly dangerous and destructive, a serious affront to God and mankind. Modern historians, however, have usually explained it in terms of the tragic dependence of needy women in a male-dominated society that was experiencing rapid social and economic change – as at most a fantasy of power.[8] Nonetheless, women in early modern England did enjoy some degree of quasi-public power; as brokers of gossip, makers and breakers of reputation, sharers in the process whereby both men and women could be reported to the ecclesiastical and secular courts for sexual misbehaviour and other offences.[9] But these female activities, socially significant though they might be, were regarded by men with some ambivalence if not hostility. The stock male view was that women were unduly addicted to "tittle-tattle", which was subversive, distracted women from their rightful duties, and easily led to strife (Plate 1).[10]

This brings us to scolds and scolding. Interest in these themes is by no means entirely new: Victorian antiquaries, in particular, were predictably fascinated by the history of the "unruly-tongued fair one" and the instruments used to punish her.[11] But the whole subject, like so many others, has gained new relevance in the light of the concerns of the women's movement. Rosalind Miles and other popularizers of feminist theory have seized on the figure of the persecuted scold as a powerful symbol of patriarchal oppression. A more circumspect approach is illustrated by the work of the social historians Miranda Chaytor and Jane Lewis, who nonetheless refer to "the continual repression of specifically female sources of power and protest", including "cursing, . . . mocking and scolding". The implication is that the figure of the "scold" and the offence of "scolding" were male constructs which served to restrict women's powers of expression and keep them in subjection.[12]

A fuller treatment of related themes is David Underdown's essay "The taming of the scold", which argues that contemporary action against scolds and scolding was the symptom of nothing less than a "crisis in gender relations" in early modern England. In the period 1560–1640, he suggests, local court records "disclose an intense preoccupation with women who are a visible threat to the patriarchal system", notably females who scolded and brawled with their neighbours and against their social superiors. Penalties for this offence were stepped up; cases multiplied; there was a veritable "epidemic of scolding". Underdown links this with the contemporaneous phenomenon of witch-hunting, and, more generally, with the cluster of socio-economic changes associated with the population rise and price inflation of the sixteenth and early seventeenth centuries. Scolding, he argues, was a "natural psychological outlet for the frustrations of the poor and the alienated"; or, in other terms, a symptom of "the decline in the habits of good neighbourhood and social harmony that accompanied the spread of capitalism". In Underdown's view it was a phenomenon particularly characteristic of towns and, in rural areas, of "wood-pasture" regions rather than corn-growing areas. Fielden villages, which Underdown sees as more hierarchical, more stable economically, more traditional in ethos, were relatively immune from the epidemic of scolding. But in urban areas and in the pasture lands there were "more poor people, less social cohesion, more individualistic attitudes on the part of the governing elite" – social features that generated real tensions in gender relations and fuelled the contemporary "obsession with scolds".

Underdown's paper is replete with stimulating ideas and interesting information, and some of the arguments are convincing. At the same time, the article is open to objection at many points – not least on the grounds that the forest/fielden dichotomy is at best a blunt tool of sociological analysis – and the overall thesis is in my view exaggerated.[13] The following discussion will first review some of the issues and suggest modifications and corrections. The later parts of the chapter will break new ground, delving a little deeper into the actual circumstances of scolds and scolding in order to get closer to the reality of the lives both of women and of men in the past. But what follows is by no means intended to be the last word on the subject, since many issues remain obscure and require a good deal of further investigation. Suggestions for such research are made throughout this chapter.

II

Let us start with some basic terms and definitions. As has already been noted, the verb *to scold* had a much stronger meaning than it does today: it meant to chide and to brawl and had undertones of violence and uncontrolled rage. A *scold* was a turbulent, chiding, brawling person. The term could apply to either sex, but from the fourteenth century it was characteristically used of women and by about 1700 had become virtually exclusive to them.[14] It should be noted also that, while the words *scold* and *to scold* could be used in a variety of social contexts – for example to refer to a nagging wife – they did have strong *legal* connotations. This was especially true of the noun: the phrase *common scold* was a technical term in common law, and meant an individual liable to prosecution and punishment as a nuisance for continually disturbing the neighbours by contentious behaviour (Plate 2). This point will be developed later, but it is worth emphasizing at the outset that in criminal terms "scolding" meant much more than mere female loquacity or assertiveness.[15]

Terms that invite comparison are *barrator* and *barratry*. These are the inverse of "scold" and "scolding", in the sense that although they could refer to either sex they were, in practice, applied mostly to men. In other respects barratry and scolding seem at first sight to have had much in common, since the basic definition of a barrator was "a common wrangler, that setteth men at odds, and is himself never quiet but at brawl with one or other". However, the term often carried much stronger implications of legal chicanery and the stirring up of unjust lawsuits.[16] Actual cases, on investigation, lead rapidly into the world of shady lawyers and crooked jus-

tices, corrupt bailiffs and constables, extortion rackets run by common informers, wars of litigation waged by vindictive yeomen and minor gentry.
In brief, barratry prosecutions were redolent of the wider public world
from which women were largely (if not entirely) excluded. Barrators were
commonly described on indictments as "oppressors" of their country, a
telling indication that they wielded power beyond the reach of most
women.[17] That said, it remains true that *some* barratry indictments related
to disruptive behaviour not dissimilar to that imputed to female scolds.
Moreover, court records reveal many cases where men, without necessarily
being labelled either as barrators or scolds, were accused of "railing" or
other verbal abuse. Often this was associated with drunkenness or physical
violence, in which case inebriety or assault might well be the main charge
brought against them; while railers of the male sex were, more often than
women, in trouble for abusing figures of authority, such as justices or local
officers.[18] But it is certainly not the case that "scolding" in the sense of a
certain type of behaviour was peculiar to females, nor that women were
prosecuted for behaviour that men could indulge in without penalty.
Rather the key points are that chiding, brawling and verbal abuse were
particularly though not exclusively associated with females because the latter
tended to eschew physical violence and did not ordinarily have easy access
to effective substitutes such as manipulation of the legal system; and that
such verbal aggression, when perpetrated by women, had come to be
labelled as a specific category of female offence with (as will be seen) peculiar modes of punishment.

III

The keystone of Underdown's argument is that there was an upsurge in the
prosecution of scolds in the eighty years or so between 1560 and 1640; in
contrast, prosecutions were markedly fewer before the mid-sixteenth century and after the mid-seventeenth. There is no disagreement on the last of
these points. Expressions of concern about scolds can certainly be found in
the late seventeenth century and even into the eighteenth,[19] but actual legal
proceedings against scolds were on the decline to such an extent that by
about 1700 formal prosecutions were becoming something of a curiosity.[20]
To explain why – and to address the more general issue of how "scolding"
declined into a nursery term – are important questions in their own right
and beyond the scope of this chapter, though some clues will emerge from
the discussion.

The idea of a marked rise in scolding cases after 1560, analogous to the well documented increase in witchcraft prosecutions, is harder to sustain. Detailed comparisons between the periods before and after 1560 are difficult because of important differences in the nature and survival of court records, coupled with shifts in jurisdictional patterns and major changes in population levels that make crude figures hard to interpret. What can be said with certainty is that prosecutions for scolding were commonplace in many jurisdictions in the late fourteenth, fifteenth and early sixteenth centuries, especially in the church courts, in city and borough tribunals and (with many variations in incidence) in manor courts serving rural communities.[21] Moreover, there survive some fifteenth-century expressions of communal concern about scolding not unlike those that Underdown cites for the period 1560–1640. Thus the borough ordinances of Leicester, promulgated in 1467, prescribed punishment for "all manner of scolds that are dwelling within this town"; while at Hereford in 1486 female scolds were the subject of a lengthy ordinance on the grounds that "much mischief arose in the city through such persons".[22]

How great was the incidence of scolding prosecutions in the period 1560–1640? Underdown never commits himself to any figures, but the vocabulary he uses implies brisk dealing in scolds in the courts of Elizabethan and early Stuart England. Again this proposition is not easy to test, not least since so many overlapping jurisdictions had cognizance of the offence of scolding. To establish statistics also raises problems of definition, especially with regard to prosecutions in the church courts which dealt with a wide range of quarrellers, brawlers and defamers (both male and female) in a variety of contexts and in which the common law category of "common scold" had no particular status. Despite these difficulties it is possible to determine figures that give at least a rough idea of the intensity of prosecution.

To this end Table 3.1 presents a selection of statistics for more or less randomly chosen periods and areas in various parts of England.[23] The figures relate primarily to women who were specifically accused of being scolds or common scolds, of scolding, or of offences which seem to amount to the same thing. (Of course the charges were often made in Latin: the terms most often used to denote the English "scold" were *rixatrix*, *garrulatrix*, *obiurgatrix*, *calumniatrix*, *litigatrix*, and *perturbatrix pacis*.) Males identified in closely similar ways have been included in the totals, but their numbers are separately identified in the bracketed figures. The totals *exclude* offences described as barratry, specific acts of defamation or abuse against individu-

Table 3.1 Prosecutions for scolding or being a common scold in selected periods and locations.

County quarter sessions (indictments and presentments)

Lancashire		Wiltshire	
1590–92	0	1615–29	7 (1)
1601–6	2		
		Yorkshire: West Riding	
Yorkshire: North Riding		1598–1602	1
1605–12	6 (1)	1637–42	4

City and borough courts

Devizes Borough Court		Dorchester Borough Court	
1580–1600	4	1631–5	30 (1)
Norwich Court of Mayoralty		Nottingham Borough Sessions*	
1630–35	14	1601–3	15 (1)
		1612–14	39 (1)
		1623–5	43 (1)

Manorial courts

Acomb, Yorks		Earls Colne, Essex (includes	
1550–1600	33 (4)	Colne Priory from 1604)	
		1560–99	4 (3)
Gillingham, Dorset		1604–40	1 (1)
1620–40	6 (1)		
		Henley in Arden, Warks.	
Manchester, Lancs.		1592–1647 (33 courts)	19
1552–1618	0		
1618–41	18		

Church courts

Diocese of Ely		Archdeaconry of Leicester	
Michaelmas 1590–	28 (2)	Michaelmas 1615–	7 (3)
Easter 1591		Michaelmas 1616	
Archdeaconry of Wiltshire		Diocese of York	
1586–99	37 (9)	Visitation, 1575	33 (14)

Middlesex, London and Westminster courts

Middlesex Sessions		Westminster Court of Burgesses	
1613–17	15	1610–16	52
[7 recognizances, 8 indictments]			
		St Katherine's Precinct	
Cornhill Wardmote Inquest		(Constables' Accounts)	
1571–1651	12 (4)	1598–1625	6

*Years commencing at Michaelmas: e.g. "1601" covers the period September 1601 to September 1602.

Note: Figures relate to persons prosecuted; bracketed figures indicate how many males (if any) are included in the totals. *Sources:* see *n*23.

Table 3.2 Prosecutions for scolding or being a common scold in selected Wiltshire manors.

Bremhill, Bromham, Rowden and Stanley		Brinkworth, Brokenborough, Charlton and Hankerton	
1565–1609	8 (4)	1572–86	1
1612–38	2	1625–45	0
Castle Combe		Mere with Kingston, Knoyle, Zeals and Stourton	
1569–96*	0		
1602–39	2	1566–1612	8 (1)
Nettleton		Stockton	
1561–94*	0	1616–26	0
1611–39	4		

* Occasional years missing from record.

Note: Figures relate to persons prosecuted (that for Mere, etc. includes two daughters presented with their mother); bracketed figures indicate how many males (if any) are included in the totals. *Sources:* see n25.

als (including office holders such as constables) when there is no indication that the offender was an habitual quarreller, pew disputes in churches, and various other miscellaneous quarrels and brawls in church, churchyard or elsewhere. To have included these sorts of cases, many of which involved men and which overlap heavily in kind with party-and-party suits for slander in both the ecclesiastical and the secular courts, would have altogether destroyed the coherence of the figures. Suffice to say that these miscellaneous brawls and abuses would together far outnumber the cases of female scolding.[24] The figures that do appear in Table 3.1 are arranged by type of court, and a wide range of jurisdictions has deliberately been sampled to illustrate the variety of legal contexts in which scolding cases could appear. Table 3.2, in contrast, focuses specifically on courts leet and on a particular area: the manors in the sample, chosen for the relative completeness, fullness and accessibility of their records, are all located in the western half of Wiltshire. This county is one of the three that feature most prominently in Underdown's study, so a close look at a portion of the region should facilitate the testing of his theories, particularly in relation to the topographical distribution of prosecutions in rural areas.[25]

The data in Tables 3.1 and 3.2 need to be interpreted carefully, bearing in mind the considerable periods to which some of the figures relate and the large areas and substantial populations covered by many of the sample jurisdictions. In this light it emerges that the prosecution of scolds was a very patchy phenomenon – regionally, locally and chronologically – but that the overall incidence was lower than Underdown's use of such terms as "crisis", "obsession" and "epidemic" would surely lead us to expect. To take an example, Underdown states that the manor of Gillingham in Dorset, a very large and populous jurisdiction including not only the market town of Gillingham but also the townships of Bourton and East and West Stour and the village of Motcombe, was "regularly ducking scolds in the 1620s and '30s".[26] In fact in the period October 1620 to September 1640 there was a total of five presentments for scolding, involving only three separate women (two were presented twice, and one of these repeaters was on one occasion named with her husband).[27] Many other places failed to match even this modest incidence of prosecutions. Even taking into account the aggregative effect of legal proceedings in overlapping jurisdictions, it would appear that numerous villages and even some towns must have gone for years, if not decades, without witnessing the prosecution of a single scold. On the other hand, there were some hotspots, such as Nottingham, where prosecutions were relatively numerous, while some expanding towns such as Manchester clearly stepped up prosecutions in the early seventeenth century.[28] Predictably, women predominated in scolding cases, though a few men were specifically described as scolds, while males who were not so labelled, but were prosecuted for what appears to have been essentially the same offence, made up a significant minority of cases in some ecclesiastical and manorial courts.

To some extent the prosecution figures were affected by legal conventions. For example, the presentments of manor courts were technically "verdicts" or statements of guilt (accusations rejected by the jury were simply omitted from the formal court rolls), whereas some borough courts included in their records all the cases that came to their attention, whether or not the accused person was convicted. Obviously this complicates comparisons between different localities. Nonetheless, it would seem that urban areas were, in general, more fertile ground for action against scolds than country districts. In part this was simply a function of the crowded conditions found in many towns and of the intensity of social regulation characteristic of well governed cities and boroughs. But it was also a reflection of the rather more prominent rôle played by women in urban as opposed to rural society, for example in marketing.[29] Regional and local variations in the prosecution of scolds in the countryside would bear more research. However, neither Table 3.1 nor Table 3.2 offers much support for Underdown's emphasis on wood-pasture areas. The limited number of prosecutions in the populous forest manor of Gillingham (Dorset) have already been noticed. Table 3.2 includes the manors of Mere, Bromham, Bremhill, Stanley, Rowden, Brinkworth, Charlton and Hankerton, which were all in (or partly in) the cheese and butter countries of Wiltshire and which should, according to Underdown's theory, have been teeming with scolds. While there were occasional prosecutions, overall the evidence of their court leet records suggests that concern about the subject was distinctly muted. In contrast, in this period the leets dealt with numerous prosecutions for a variety of trading offences, unlawful games, the illegal taking of inmates and subtenants, hedgebreaking, woodstealing and other petty pilfering, assault, affray and bloodshed, and a vast range of nuisances and neglect of communal obligations. It is plain that these matters, the bulk of which were perpetrated by men, were of much more persistent concern and interest than scolding women.[30]

Underdown is on much stronger ground in arguing that the *punishment* of convicted scolds, which in the late middle ages had commonly taken the form of a modest fine, became more severe in the century after 1550. However, corporal punishments or banishment from the community were by no means unknown in the earlier period,[31] and in so far as there was subsequently a shift towards more draconian penalties it was in line with a general trend in the punishment of all manner of crimes, not merely those that were characteristic of women.[32] In other respects, too, the matter is less clear cut than Underdown makes out. He is inclined to assume that the form and severity of punishments simply reflected levels of anxiety about the offences to which they were applied. This may have been a factor, but penal policy (like other aspects of the judicial process) was shaped also by specifically legal and jurisdictional concerns and, more generally, by a variety of cultural influences.

Changes in the legal sanctions applied to scolds were really confined to the temporal jurisdiction, since throughout the period the church courts continued to punish scolders and quarrellers with admonition and penance.[33] One striking development was the introduction of the "branks" or "scold's bridle" in parts of the north and west. Some of the surviving instruments identified as such by nineteenth-century antiquaries were in fact of foreign provenance and/or were used for penal purposes other than the punishment of scolds. However, it is certainly the case that the branks — sometimes of wood and leather, but often of iron and of cruel construction — was in use in such towns as Bridgnorth, Chester, Preston, Manchester and Newcastle upon Tyne by the seventeenth century (Plate 3).[34] Just how commonly the branks was employed, and what the motives for its introduction were, are matters on which further research is needed. The device may have been imported from Scotland, and it may therefore be significant that references to its use in English towns mostly cluster in the mid-seventeenth century when Scottish and English affairs became so closely intertwined.[35] More generally, the symbolism of taming a wild or unruly beast was obviously important; at a more mundane level, the branks may have been considered cheaper and more effective than other forms of punishment. In any event it is plain that the scold's bridle had a very brief history and was never used at all in most parts of England. Robert Plot, describing a specimen from Newcastle-under-Lyme (Staffordshire) in 1686, referred to it as "an instrument scarce heard of, much less seen".[36]

Scolds were sometimes punished in the stocks, by being incarcerated in the town "cage" or, occasionally, by being carted or paraded round the town with basins ringing before them.[37] But by the early seventeenth century the characteristic instrument for the punishment of scolds was the cucking-stool or, as it was increasingly referred to, the ducking stool (Plate 4).[38] The process whereby ducking became the stock punishment for this offence was a complex one. No doubt in symbolic terms the penalty was thought to be particularly appropriate for cooling the immoderate heat of the tongue,[39] while more generally the misogynistic tone of late Tudor and Stuart culture may have inclined law enforcers away from more lenient alternatives. But on close examination the evidence suggests that the development owed as much to a general trend towards legal definition, aided by the increase of printed materials, as to any demonstrable wish for greater severity towards scolds. Sixteenth- and seventeenth-century legal codifiers found that they had inherited from the judicial practice of the middle ages a wide range of terms denoting shame punishments that could be used against scolds. They included pillory, tumbrel, trebuchet, castigatory, thew, gumstool and cucking-stool. All had a fearsome ring but by the late sixteenth century the precise meaning of some of these terms had become uncertain. Some were thought to imply ducking, but this was not true of all.

Modern research into the early history of the cucking-stool has revealed that, in fact, there was great variety of usage in different manors, boroughs and cities. In some places the aim was primarily to exhibit the offenders to public ridicule, which might be achieved either by placing them in a fixed position in some prominent place or by carrying them about the town. Elsewhere the emphasis was on the ducking of the culprits, the effect of which might be simply to soak them or, more brutally, to defile them with mud or filth. These objects were achieved by means of a wide variety of engines and contraptions, not always chair-like in form, their precise nature depending on local traditions and available resources. To add to the confusion, up to the early sixteenth century, these multifarious penalties had been applied not only to scolds – instead of or as an alternative to fines – but also to bakers, brewers and other tradespeople who sold underweight or adulterated goods, and to other offenders such as bawds, prostitutes, cheats and cozeners.[40]

Faced with all these complexities, Tudor and Stuart legal commentators resolved the issues into the simple dictum that "scolds are to be ducked over head and ears into the water in a ducking-stool".[41] At the same time, widely distributed legal handbooks, notably John Kitchin's *Court leet, et court baron* (1580 and later editions), emphasized the duty of every manor and similar jurisdiction to provide, and maintain in good repair, a cucking-stool or "tumbrel" along with stocks and pillory. Some authorities even took the view that for lack of these vital aids to "bon government" the liberty was liable to seizure by the crown.[42] The principle that scolds should be ducked was reinforced by other influential texts, such as the official homily "against contention and brawling" (1547) and William Harrison's "Description of England", included in Holinshed's *Chronicles* (1577 and later editions).[43] At the popular level, the association of scolds, ducking and cucking-stools was cemented by an increasingly standardized message conveyed in almanacs, ballads and chapbooks. Thus *The cucking of a scold* (c.1615) invited the audience to imagine the ducking of seventeen-year-old wife "stripped naked to her smock", while George a Greene, the mythical hero of *The pinder of Wakefield* (1632), was credited with the invention, among so many other things, of "a new engine . . . the cucking-stool, which is used to this day for all scolds".[44]

IV

These processes of definition were bad news for scolds in that they clearly fixed on them a liability to corporal punishment and ensured that everyone who had responsibility for a court leet would at least consider the possibility of erecting a cucking-stool. Arguably, indeed, they were to the detriment of all women, in that the existence of harsh punishments, specifically associated with female assertiveness, reinforced the gendered concept of scolding and could intimidate women into acceptance of a submissive rôle. However, there were several reasons why the impact of these developments was more restricted than might at first sight be thought. On the legal front, the definition of the proper mode of shame punishments was tempered by injunctions to be circumspect in their use. "Now for that the judgement of the pillory or tumbrel . . .", warned Lord Chief Justice Coke, "doth make the delinquent infamous . . . justices . . . would be well advised before they give judgement . . . unless they have good warrant".[45] Such strictures may have done something to restrain the use of the cucking-stool, by the end of the seventeenth century if not earlier. In any case there were other, more practical considerations which even at an earlier date tended to limit the number of cases in which scolds were subjected to ducking.

One was financial. The administration of early modern justice, especially its penal aspects, was heavily influenced by the hardest of hard-nosed concepts of value for money. Cucking-stools were fairly elaborate instruments of punishment and hence expensive. They were also singularly liable to rot. It may be surmised that this was a major reason why, as Underdown notes, many smaller communities never provided a cucking-stool, and indeed were sometimes prepared to incur repeated fines rather than going to the expense of doing so.[46] But the point can be reinforced, since even populous and relatively wealthy boroughs or other substantial communities were not always convinced of the need to make the investment. To take an example, Southampton had a cucking-stool in the late fifteenth century; an elaborate wheeled specimen constructed in 1475 at a cost of 5s 4d. However, by Elizabeth's reign this had apparently disintegrated. Repeated presentments to this effect in the court leet culminated in 1601 in a sharp exchange of views on costs and benefits. A marginal note records the upshot: "something to be devised to be kept dry and to be used at the crane at full sea; it rots and is broken standing abroad; half a hogshead [a cask] will serve as well as anything". Despite the apparent ingenuity of this solution, the matter was not resolved and succeeding years saw repeated references to the lack of a cucking-stool. In many other places the instrument existed but was repeatedly out of commission, as frequent presentments of decay and often fruitless orders for repair abundantly testify.[47]

Apart from cost there were other restraints on the use of cucking-stools. Among these was humanity. Of course early modern England was not particularly squeamish in its use of physical punishments. If hanging was less common than historians once thought, it was by no means a rare phenomenon; while lesser punishments, especially whipping and the stocks, were commonplace and were applied not only to men but sometimes also to women for offences such as petty larceny and sexual immorality. However, it has been established that contemporaries were often reluctant to put close neighbours in danger of physical punishment.[48] Now it is clear that, although the penalty of ducking was probably thought to be less severe than a whipping or even exposure in the stocks for several hours, it was nonetheless an extremely disagreeable experience. Henri Misson, a French visitor to England in the 1690s, described the process as "rather amusing" (*assez plaisante*), but he was of course referring to the sensations of the spectators. Contrary to what some modern writers have suggested, there are virtually no reports of actual deaths, though a number of accounts point to physical injury of some sort. Unquestionably more usual was bitter humiliation. The Middlesex Grand Jury nostalgically requested in 1683 the more frequent use of "the old legal way of a ducking stool" in the hope that "shame may do that which we find other punishment will not", and the emphasis on discredit is corroborated in earlier accounts. A victim at Leeds in 1619 complained that the constables who came for her were accompanied by "a great rabble or multitude of base people" who, when she was ducked, "made great jollity and laughter". As a result, she claimed, she and her husband were utterly "disgraced [and] defamed".[49]

The reference in this case to a "rabble" of "base people" points to another possible objection to ducking: it was indecorous for all concerned. By definition scolds were not easily cowed and were prone to defend themselves against being punished. Even when the victims were secured it was hard to stop their tongues. The sixteenth-century antiquary John Stow quotes the interesting case of a woman who, for hooting at the bishop of London during the vestiarian controversy of 1566–7, was "set upon two ladders like a cucking-stool". Far from being repentant, she "sat [there] the space of one hour, greatly rejoicing in that her lewd behaviour". Of course this was an unusual case, but some commentators recognized that even for ordinary scolds the punishment could be counterproductive. Lord Chief Justice Holt remarked in Foxby's case in 1704 that "ducking would rather harden than cure her, and if she were once ducked, she would scold on all the days of her life".[50] A further hazard was that the scold or her husband would attempt revenge and that as a result proceedings would simply exacerbate community tensions. This certainly did occur in some instances, and the resulting feuds and enmities can occasionally be traced in prosecutions in the Star Chamber. Thus at Nettleton in Wiltshire, Agnes Davis and Margaret Davis (apparently not closely related) were involved in long-standing quarrels and eventually in 1614 both were presented as common scolds. Agnes managed to secure remission of the penalty, but Margaret was ducked. In revenge her supporters invaded the house of Agnes Davis on Christmas night and proceeded to make a nuisance of themselves: "having found out two minced pies they suddenly devoured them" and "in a brutish and uncivil fashion" urinated in a pottage pot. Then at first light on St Stephen's Day they dragged Agnes to the cucking-stool and did "dip and plunge . . . [her] in the . . . river seven several times". A legal penalty had degenerated into dangerous mob action; and this was by no means the worst case of its kind.[51]

The hazards of ducking both for the scold herself and for the peace of the community at large encouraged a less draconian approach. Probably many cases of scolding never led to formal proceedings: the culprits were dealt with by recognizance, or by admonition from local ministers, justices of the peace, or respected neighbours. Even when scolds were convicted in court they did not necessarily suffer the penalty of ducking. Some courts continued the medieval tradition of simply fining the culprits small sums: this was true, for example, in the Yorkshire manor of Acomb, and probably helps to explain why prosecutions for scolding and quarrelling were brought there with relative frequency (Table 3.1).

Often scolds were notionally sentenced to the cucking-stool, but formal or informal arrangements were made which allowed the penalty to be commuted to a money payment: this was done, for example, at Henley-in-Arden (Warwickshire) in 1635, when an exceptionally large crop of eleven scolds was presented.[52] Sometimes it was ordered that a sentence of ducking should only be carried out if the offence were subsequently repeated.[53] Quite commonly in the case of first offenders, the cucking-stool was simply set against the culprit's door as a warning, or the scold was ordered to ride or be carried home in the stool without actually undergoing a ducking.[54] When the authorities insisted on immersion, they sometimes took care nonetheless to ensure that the punishment was carried out with moderation. Spargo thought that duckings were mostly confined to the summer months, mere exhibition being preferred in winter. Though it is doubtful if such a policy was ever consistently followed, concern about the temperature is certainly discernible in individual instances. Thus at Dorchester (Dorset) in early May 1631, a certain Mary Tuxbery was "ordered to be plounced when the weather is warmer".[55] Whether or not scolds were actually ducked, great efforts were often made to secure their submission if not their reconciliation with their neighbours, so as to heal as far as possible the breach in community relations. Thus at Exeter in 1561, Agnes Jones "was upon her submission released of the punishment of the cucking-stool" on condition that any repetition of her offence would be severely punished. To complete the reconciliation, the people whom Agnes had most offended were called before the mayor and justices, and "by order taken the said Agnes asked forgiveness and desired their good will, as also the said parties asked her good will".[56]

There were thus numerous ways of dealing with scolds and different communities varied widely in the approach they adopted. In certain places any inhibitions that might have existed simply broke down, and the ducking of scolds became a routine occurrence. A number of factors may be identified which, in combination, were likely to promote such a development: first, the possession by a particular community of independent jurisdiction and the ability to impose corporal punishments without reference to outside authorities such as county justices; secondly, a long tradition of prosecuting scolds; thirdly, the existence within the jurisdiction of populous areas where scolding between neighbours was likely to be perceived as a problem; fourthly, marked social distance between the dispensers of justice and its victims, so that the former would not be inhibited in their treatment of the latter by neighbourly sentiments and other mitigating influences; and fifthly, a tradition of firm action, or an emergent crusade, against immorality and petty disorder, of the kind that was often (but not necessarily) associated with puritan groups in this period.

The clearest example of the operation of these factors that has so far come to light is Jacobean and Caroline Nottingham. There scolds had been regularly prosecuted, and in considerable numbers, since at least the fourteenth century, and the borough had a cucking-stool from the sixteenth century if not before. Nonetheless, culprits were generally punished with fines till the early years of the seventeenth century, when a change in penal policy rapidly became evident. In the legal year 1603–4, convicted scolds were ordered "to be carted" or "to ride" (an exhibition punishment used in London and many other cities and towns for sexual offenders), and the constables of the borough requested "a scold cart for scolds and to carry cripples in". Probably in 1605–6, and certainly in 1606–7, the punishment of carting was again employed, but from 1610 the characteristic penalty was to be ducked or, in some instances, "cucked" – the latter term may denote a lesser form of punishment involving exhibition without actual immersion. Indeed, for the next three decades or so the cucking-stool was used regularly and without mercy. In 1619–20, for example, the constables and jurors presented twelve women and two men as scolds; eleven were ordered to be ducked and three to be cucked. In *January* 1621 three scolds were sentenced to be ducked; in April 1624 another half dozen suffered the same fate; there were twelve more in July 1624; another fourteen in 1624–5; and so the dismal sequence continued. A place like this comes closest to Underdown's stereotype.[57]

In certain other places, experiments with ducking failed to establish a tradition. For example, the borough of Devizes in Wiltshire acquired a cucking-stool in or around 1582, and used it to exhibit one female slanderer in 1583 and to duck two scolds in 1589; thereafter the instrument was kept up but there is no further record of its use. Similarly in St Katherine by the Tower, one of the semi-independent London liberties with perhaps 490 households, a cucking-stool was constructed in 1606 by one "Giles the carpenter" at a cost of £1 12s 6d. The following year four women were ducked and two cucked. Soon the apparatus needed mending at an additional cost of 2s 3d, but the constables' accounts record no further indication of its use.[58]

Probably the norm in places that recognized ducking as the appropriate punishment for scolds was neither constant use nor complete disuse but occasional recourse to the cucking-stool. In puritan Dorchester, not only common scolds but also women who slandered or otherwise abused a single individual were liable to be "plounced"; but mostly the penalty was used as a threat. Admittedly in 1633 as many as eight women – two groups of four – were ducked, but this was quite exceptional: the offenders' book shows that an annual average of only one scold was so punished in the remaining four years of the quinquennium 1631–5. Similarly the Westminster Court of Burgesses threatened, on average, about one woman a month with the cucking-stool, but in the period 1610–16 only three women were actually ducked. (However, one of these was punished twice, the second time not in the cucking-stool but by being tied to a boat and dragged across the Thames, while another woman was made to "wear the mortars about her neck home to her house"). Even a large city such as Norwich, despite its reputation for puritanism and a firm commitment to law and order on the part of its magistrates, was in the early 1630s ducking only a few women a year.[59] In smaller communities the incidence was proportionately lower; indeed, sometimes the ducking of a scold was so rare that when it occurred a cucking-stool had to be specially constructed to meet the occasion.[60] This brings us back to the central message conveyed by Tables 3.1 and 3.2 and the discussions that have ensued – that the prosecution and punishment of scolds was in most places highly selective. How then were the victims singled out for legal action?

V

Purely in terms of social standing there seems to have been little to distinguish them. It is not always easy to determine marital status, but the indications are that in most places wives easily predominated among convicted scolds, with only a sprinkling of widows and single women. Of 42 female scolds prosecuted in the borough of Nottingham in the years 1623–6, 32 were specifically said to be married while only one was identified as a widow. The situation was roughly the same in Henley-in-Arden (Warwickshire): of 19 scolds named in the period 1616–47, 14 were positively identified as wives.[61] Married status implies that many of them were in the prime of life, as indeed one might expect from their robust behaviour, and perhaps had a certain standing in the community. As regards economic condition there were a few well-heeled scolds, the wives of yeomen or substantial traders and even the occasional gentlewoman.[62] At the other extreme there were almswomen and others who were clearly in a state of extreme poverty, such as "Widow Tutyn of the beadhouse" in Nottingham in 1639.[63] But most of these women were drawn from the broad, lower-middling ranks to which the bulk of the population belonged. In country areas there were the wives of labourers, cottagers, and husbandmen; but since most prosecuted scolds lived in towns or other populous settlements, many of them were the wives of tradesmen – butchers, bakers, weavers, and so forth. Such people are very familiar from the related context of plaintiffs and defendants in church court defamation suits.[64]

Some women accused of scolding had fallen foul of magistrates or legal officers, or were in contention with figures far above them in status or authority. Thus Isabel, the wife of Francis Rydings of Manchester, was charged in 1638 with "scolding upon an officer in the execution of his office"; Joan Clearke the elder of Lyme Regis in 1635 was said to be "a noted scolding railer and intemperate of her tongue, abusing some of the best of the town"; while Mary Stracke of Hempnall in Norfolk, accused in 1597 of being a sower of discord and breaker of Christian charity, alleged in her defence that "she have [sic] three children and is very poor, and when she spoke for her relief . . . they say she scoldeth".[65] However, most accused scolds appear to have been in contention not with the leaders of their societies, but with their immediate neighbours who were little, if anything, above them in social status. In this, again, the context of scolding cases was similar to that of slander suits; and like them, they must be understood in terms of the micro-politics and sometimes tense relationships of people living cheek-by-jowl in tiny communities.[66] In this sense Underdown seems wrong to relate scolding prosecutions to the *breakdown* of community; on the contrary, they were of its essence.

Prosecutions against scolds invoked communal values in claiming that they were a "common nuisance", and in formal terms they were normally instigated by public officers such as constables, or by presentment juries that supposedly represented the whole community. In practice they were frequently initiated by small groups of people, sometimes even particular individuals, who felt especially aggrieved and had determined to bring the culprit to book. Some cases were pursued as tactical legal moves in long-standing quarrels rooted in a variety of issues such as land, status and money, and complainants exploited the powerful symbolism of the scold in order to discredit their opponents. In this sense, some alleged "scolds" were probably more sinned against than sinning.[67] But wholly fabricated charges or outright malicious prosecutions were probably rare, since to convict someone of being a scold it was necessary to show that there had been repeated disturbance not just of individuals but of neighbours generally.

As the court remarked in *Regina* v. *Foxby* (1704), "scolding once or twice is no great matter; for scolding alone is not the offence, but it is the frequent repetition of it to the disturbance of the neighbourhood . . . ".[68] Hence the prime mover or movers of legal action had to bid for support among a wider circle. A common method was for them to make an initial complaint to a local minister or justice, who would thereupon circulate a petition against the alleged scold and invite supporting signatures. Sometimes the accused would respond by trying to procure a counter-petition signed by well-wishers, certifying to her "honesty" and "good behaviour". Depending on the results of these proceedings, a prosecution might or might not go forward.[69] It should be observed that the bulk of the prosecutors (as recorded in formal proceedings) were men, but given that the legal system was almost entirely operated by males this is hardly surprising. More worthy of note is that some of the accusers, including certain of the prime movers, were women; and that some of the male accusers were in fact acting on behalf of their wives who felt themselves injured by the alleged scold.[70] The late Christina Larner was right to assert that "a patriarchal social structure divides women. Dependent for their livelihood on the goodwill of men, most women will not only conform, but also attack women who by their nonconformity threaten the security of conformist women".[71] But the presence of women among accusers does alert us to the possibility that the behaviour of scolds was obnoxious in ways that cannot be construed merely in terms of a threat to the patriarchal order.

J. A. Sharpe has remarked of scolding cases in Essex that the crime was not uncommonly "associated with other offences".[72] In fact, this appears to have been a general pattern and often helps to explain why particular women were singled out for prosecution. A connection between witchcraft and scolding is, of course, well known, but the point should not be laboured. Reginald Scot may have been right to assert that the "chief fault" of witches "is that they are scolds". But the converse was not true; it was actually only a small minority of accused scolds who were charged with having magical powers or even of ritual cursing.[73] More usually alleged scolds were simultaneously accused of one or more mundane neighbourhood offences or breaches of personal morality: petty theft; hedgebreaking; sexual immorality; swearing and blaspheming; drunkenness; unlicensed aleselling; or, more generally, "lewd", "wicked" or "evil" behaviour.[74] When it is possible to trace individuals through a lengthy series of court records it emerges that some women had a long history of troublesome behaviour; sometimes their husbands and other members of their families were likewise delinquent, a circumstance which may have been beyond their control but was unlikely to make them any more popular among their neighbours.[75]

Whatever the other delinquencies of the women in question, they were prosecuted for being scolds or for scolding. Exactly what kind of the behaviour was implied by these words? The point is crucial for determining whether scolding prosecutions should be seen as an attempt to impose tight controls on women's speech, or whether they were directed at disruptive behaviour well beyond the normal range. It is in the first place clear from depositions and other supporting evidence that contemporaries were by no means undiscriminating in their appraisal of female behaviour. Of course they started from the premise that certain kinds of demeanour were inappropriate for women. Some witnesses spoke of "uncivil and unwomanly" behaviour, "far unfit for any sober woman"; while the wives who were ducked after taking part in an enclosure riot in 1597 were castigated for being "not women", on the grounds that in the course of the dispute they had pitilessly injured some ewes.[76] Often women accused of being scolds were denounced as "disordered", "disorderly", "unquiet", "unruly", "turbulent", or "of a contentious spirit".[77] It should be noted that such epithets were often applied also to troublesome men, but these characteristics were thought to be particularly reprehensible in women.

Since verbal abuse was close to the heart of the offence of scolding, accused individuals were also commonly described as "busy with her tongue" or "unruly tongued".[78]

However, it is clear that men did not set down any loquacious, vociferous, or sharp-tongued woman as a scold, and far less did they try, in the normal course of events, to keep women quiet by threatening them with prosecution. On the contrary, it appears that men were realistically tolerant (if also rather patronizing) of some degree of verbal assertiveness, and on those grounds sometimes willing to speak in the defence of women accused of scolding. A Wiltshire man seems to have expressed a widespread view when he stated in 1621 that "an honest woman may have some froward qualities". Another man, commenting on an accusation in 1622, would admit only that the alleged scold "will talk when she is angry as other women and no otherwise . . . ". In the same vein an innkeeper from Andover in Hampshire commented in 1602 that a certain Elizabeth Ayers "is froward as other women are when they are angry, and one time the cucking-stool was set against her door, but yet she is accounted to be an honest woman".[79] These statements, which distinguish between the acceptable or even legitimate use of language and the offence of scolding, echo the words that some accused women themselves used to justify their behaviour. Rebecca Bingham of Islington, for example, in 1636 denied scolding save that "when she hath been urged [i.e. provoked] by . . . one of her neighbours by slanderous and reproachful speeches she hath used her tongue for her own defence".[80] Such pleas were sometimes convincing to the courts: of eight alleged scolds whom the Westminster Court of Burgesses formally tried by jury in the period 1610–16, five secured an acquittal.[81]

What brought most scolds to court was not mere assertiveness, loquacity, or even ill language, but much more specific forms of objectionable behaviour. It is true that some courts were willing to entertain charges when the offence was simply that of loud and prolonged quarrelling, sometimes involving foul language, which took place in the open street or otherwise in public, "disturbing and disquieting their neighbours".[82] But charges of being a "common scold" that were likely to bring women to the cucking-stool usually involved not merely brawling and abuse but also such offences as indiscriminate slander, tale-bearing, the stirring up of strife, the deliberate sowing of discord between neighbours, and sometimes also the pursuit of quarrels through needless lawsuits and legal chicanery.[83] When detailed supporting evidence is available it reveals that the misbehaviour ascribed to scolds was indeed often blatant, seriously hurtful to the immediate victims, and likely to disrupt the whole neighbourhood. The modern word that best captures the sense of scolding is *harassment*, involving insult and abuse that might well be repeated day after day and expressed with great verbal or even physical violence. The case of Catherine Barnaby of St Alban Wood Street in London, recounted in detail in a series of depositions in the archdeaconry court of London in 1637, may serve as a type.[84]

The chief prosecutor was John Dickenson, currently serving as church-warden in the parish and by trade a girdler. He was supported by eight other witnesses, most of whom can be traced in the 1638 listing of London inhabitants and appear to have been of roughly equal status to the accused.[85] Dickenson claimed that, for the seven years he had known her, Catherine Barnaby "hath been and still is a very troublesome and disquiet woman amongst her neighbours by calling them out of their names, and especially . . . [his] wife whom she hath very much abused in these terms . . . 'Thou . . . art a drunken quean and a coppernosed quean and thou goest a drinking from house to house every day'." At various times she had pointed to his wife when she stood in the shop in the presence of other people, and said that "that drunken quean hath murdered my child and smothered it in a rug". She had also proclaimed that "that drunken quean . . . hath made my husband spend £500 and hath now sent him beyond sea, and that she keeps company with none but pedlars, rogues and thieves".

Of Dickenson himself she "reporteth upon [*sic*] and down that he . . . keepeth pretty wenches in his house and that he hath coaches coming and going at his back door at all hours in the night, and that he hath such fid-dling and singing and hallooing in his house that she cannot sleep for it". Furthermore she had proclaimed that "he is a cheating knave and a cozen-ing knave and that he getteth his living by cheating, bribing, cozening and buying of stolen goods, and that he brought a piece of stolen stuff to make his wife a gown". It must be recognized that in early seventeenth-century conditions, these charges could have been seriously harmful to Dickenson: they traduced his moral character, his probity in business dealings, and his honesty as a citizen, and no respectable tradesman could afford to let such slanders pass. Likewise, the aspersions on his wife were highly offensive and defamatory. However, what made them particularly difficult to deal with was their *variety*: to seek redress for defamation of character would have required a number of lawsuits in different courts. Moreover, Dickenson and his wife were not alone in being abused. It was claimed that Catherine

Barnaby had "abused most part of her neighbours by filthy speeches", and to add insult to injury tried to make out that her neighbours, not she, were guilty of scolding. Thus it was said that she

> will fall a scolding with her neighbours daily, and if that any of them
> do give her an answer she presently runneth and fetcheth a bottle of
> hay [the traditional emblem of a scold] and setteth it up and says she
> cannot be quiet for these rogues and rascals, and therefore she sets it
> up for them to scold at.

When the local minister and other witnesses were brought against her at the sessions to indict her as a scold, she called them "perjured knaves and perjured rogues" and threatened to get them all put in the pillory for bearing false witness; apparently she meant what she said, for she had commenced three lawsuits against various of the inhabitants, including a prosecution in the Star Chamber.[86]

Cases like this raise questions about the personality and state of mind of women accused of being scolds. Just why were they so disruptive? The general social factors suggested by Underdown do not appear to be relevant to many cases; it is therefore probably to personal circumstances and individual psychology that we should look for an explanation. Inevitably this is a highly speculative area, that in any case requires further research on the basis of a larger dossier of detailed cases; nonetheless, a few comments are possible here. Underlying many cases, no doubt, was a great deal of pent-up anger, envy and frustration arising from quarrels with neighbours, unsatisfactory domestic circumstances, or disappointed hopes. Some women, it is known, were under severe pressure. Mary Hooper, repeatedly in trouble in Dorchester for scolding and other offences, was bitterly at odds with her father-in-law, whom she upbraided for drunkenness, while her husband was a man of violent disposition who eventually tried to sexually abuse his 18-year-old stepdaughter. In the case of Catherine Barnaby there are even stronger indications of difficult personal circumstances, and even tragedy, underlying the tangle of litigation and mutual recrimination in which she was embroiled with her neighbours. It appears that her husband faced financial ruin and was forced to emigrate, and had in any case disowned her; and that she had suffered the death of a child. It is only too easy to see how experiences such as these could have translated into aggressive behaviour.[87]

It is possible, however, that some of the most extreme cases involved something more – what the nineteenth-century churchman and antiquary

Archdeacon Hale described as insanity and which would now be interpreted as mental illness. Catherine Barnaby's actions and utterances suggest
that she may have become seriously disturbed, while Mary Hooper's behaviour had an erratic quality that led her father-in-law to demand
"whether she . . . would never leave her mad-headed tricks". Even more
suggestive is the case of Margaret Betts of Westminster. One of the half-
dozen witnesses and accusers claimed that "upon Sunday morning at service time, he saw her sweep the kennel [i.e. gutter] against her door and
swore that if any did sweep down the dirt to her door she would strike him
over the face with her broom"; another witness, a woman, claimed that
Margaret Betts had "threatened to cut her throat and in violent manner
pulled down the seat at her door to get into the house". Such apparently
irrational, obsessive and violent behaviour seems hard to explain without
reference to mental disturbance. In a case from Islington in 1636 the
connection was made explicit: when a widow called Ann Pennell was presented "for a railer, a scold and a lascivious talker", one of the churchwardens appeared on her behalf and certified under the hand of the parish
minister that she was *non compos mentis*.[88]

This last case was, however, a rarity, in that witnesses and prosecutors
normally eschewed this and other expressions (such as "lunatic" or "distracted") which might have implied that the scold was not responsible for
her behaviour.[89] Indeed the assumptions underlying legal action were quite
the contrary. As the language of presentments and court proceedings indicates, the behaviour of the alleged scold was usually seen not merely as
unreasonable but deliberately so – as an outrageous breach of "manners", a
complete disregard for the rules of "civil and orderly demeanour and
behaviour" which both men and women expected of their neighbours.
Thus contemporaries, rightly or wrongly, perceived the accused as *wilfully
refusing* to accommodate herself. In such circumstances the use of the
cucking-stool or other penalty was intended not merely to punish but also
to achieve "reformation", to "work . . . good" both for the culprit's "own
instruction" and for "admonition to others".[90]

In short, it is difficult to see scolding cases as evidence of a "crisis of gender relations". In the sixteenth and seventeenth centuries, as is the case
today, males were responsible for the majority of breaches of the peace.
Scolding women did, however, represent a significant undercurrent of disorder, especially in towns. But concern about them was muted in many
areas and prosecution was very selective. Close examination of well documented cases reveals how the women who did end up in court had aroused

the wrath of their neighbours. Whether or not they were mentally disturbed, and whatever abuses or disasters they themselves had suffered, they were invariably dismal negotiators of social relationships. Hot tempered and sharp tongued, they were quick to give and to take offence, temperamentally inclined to confrontation rather than to compromise, and hence liable to get locked into a spiral of deteriorating relationships. In these tiny worlds of village and town streets, peace, quiet and mutual forbearance were at a premium, and people who could not or would not conform to at least the minimum standards of co-operation were a major nuisance. Neighbours – whether men or women – sometimes made determined efforts to resolve the situation by recourse to the various formal and informal mechanisms of mediation and arbitration that were so widely used in early modern English society, but these could only work if the culprit was amenable.[91] A number of witnesses against Catherine Barnaby claimed that "the parishioners would be willing to remit all suits and to be quiet if she . . . would consent thereto, but . . . she refused it". Such women became liable to the cucking-stool when the patience of neighbours finally snapped. The exasperated John Dickenson told Catherine Barnaby that "if she did not mend her manners" he "would have her ducked" – and eventually he did just that.[92]

Notes

1. The quotation in the title is taken from Wilts RO, D5/28/35, no. 73. (In this and other quotations, spelling and punctuation have been modernized.) The paper was originally prepared for Sir Keith Thomas's seminar on "Problems in early modern history", held at Oxford on 27 April 1989, and was subsequently presented at a variety of seminars and meetings. I am grateful to the participants for their helpful suggestions.

2. L. de Bruyn, *Woman and the devil in sixteenth-century literature* (Tisbury, 1979), pp. 139–40; *Poor Robin's true character of a scold: or, the shrews looking-glass* (London, 1678); H. E. Rollins (ed.), *A Pepysian garland: black-letter broadside ballads of the years 1595–1639* (Cambridge MA, 1922), p. 76; Constantia Munda, *The worming of a mad dogge* (London, 1617), p. 16; Wilts RO, D5/22/7, f. 106v. (where the object to scold at is a napkin on a rolling pin).

3. For a variety of different viewpoints, see L. Stone, *The family, sex and marriage in England 1500–1800* (London, 1977), esp. ch. 5; K. Wrightson, *English society, 1580–1680* (London, 1982), ch. 4; R. Houlbrooke, *The English family 1450–1700* (London, 1984), esp. chs 5–7; S. Amussen, *An ordered society: gender and class in early modern England* (Oxford, 1988).

4. K. M. Davies, Continuity and change in literary advice on marriage, in *Mar-*

riage and society: studies in the social history of marriage, ed. R. B. Outhwaite (London, 1981), pp. 66–7; A. Clark, *Working life of women in the seventeenth century*, eds M. Chaytor & J. Lewis (London, 1982), pp. xxix–xxxviii; Amussen, *Ordered society*, pp. 68–9 and *passim*; M. Roberts, Women and work in sixteenth-century English towns, in *Work in towns, 850–1850*, eds P. J. Corfield & D. Keene (Leicester, 1990), pp. 86–102.

5. Sir Thomas Smith, *De republica anglorum*, ed. M. Dewar (Cambridge, 1982), pp. 64–5.

6. J. A. Sharpe, *Defamation and sexual slander in early modern England: the church courts at York*, Borthwick Papers, no. 58 (York, 1980); M. Ingram, *Church courts, sex and marriage in England, 1570–1640* (Cambridge, 1987), pp. 301–3 and ch. 10 *passim*; Amussen, *Ordered society*, pp. 98–104; L. Gowing, Gender and the language of insult in early modern London, *History Workshop Journal*, **35**, 1993, pp. 1–21.

7. C. Z. Wiener, Sex roles and crime in late Elizabethan Hertfordshire, *Journal of Social History*, **8**, 1974–5, pp. 38–60; J. M. Beattie, The criminality of women in eighteenth-century England, *ibid.*, pp. 80–116.

8. A. Macfarlane, *Witchcraft in Tudor and Stuart England: a regional and comparative study* (London, 1970), esp. chs 10–16; K. Thomas, *Religion and the decline of magic: studies in popular beliefs in sixteenth and seventeenth century England* (London, 1971), chs 14–18.

9. Ingram, *Church courts, sex and marriage*, pp. 163–5, 242–5, 305–6; Amussen, *Ordered society*, pp. 98–104.

10. British Museum, Satires, 61, "Tittle-tattle; or, the severall branches of gossipping". Note, however, that the images are based on a French print of *c.* 1560, "Le caquet des femmes", reproduced in N. Z. Davis, *Fiction in the archives: pardon tales and their tellers in sixteenth-century France* (Cambridge, 1987), pp. 90–1. They cannot therefore be taken as evidence of English customs.

11. T. N. Brushfield, On obsolete punishments, with particular reference to those of Cheshire: part I. the brank, or scold's bridle; part II. the cucking stool and allied punishments, *Journal of the Architectural, Archaeological and Historic Society . . . of Chester . . . December 1855 to December 1862*, II, 1864, pp. 31–48, 203–34; F. A. Carrington, On certain ancient Wiltshire customs, *Wiltshire Archaeological and Natural History Magazine*, I, 1854, pp. 68–79. For a more recent approach see J. W. Spargo, *Juridical folklore in England illustrated by the cucking-stool* (Durham NC, 1944).

12. R. Miles, *The women's history of the world* (London, 1988), pp. 79–80; Clark, *Working life of women*, p. xxxvi; cf. A. Fraser, *The weaker vessel: women's lot in seventeenth-century England* (London, 1985 edn), p. 114.

13. D. Underdown, The taming of the scold: the enforcement of patriarchal authority in early modern England, in *Order and disorder in early modern England*, eds A. Fletcher & J. Stevenson (Cambridge, 1985), pp. 116–36 (for the quotations see pp. 119, 120, 122, 126, 135). Note that the essay deals not only with

prosecutions for scolding but also with skimmington rides and the use of cuckold's horns, issues that are not addressed here. Underdown's argument is set in wider context in his *Revel, riot and rebellion: popular politics and culture in England 1603–1660* (Oxford, 1985). For a critique of the fielden/forest model, see N. Davie, Chalk and cheese? "Fielden" and "forest" communities in early modern England, *Journal of Historical Sociology*, IV (1991), pp. 1–31.

14. *Oxford English Dictionary* [OED], s.v. "scold"; Spargo, *Juridical folklore*, ch. 5.

15. W. Sheppard, *A grand abridgment of the common and statute law of England*, 4 parts (London, 1675), III, p. 267; W. Hawkins, *A treatise of the pleas of the crown*, 2 vols (London, 1716–21), I, pp. 198, 200.

16. Sheppard, *Grand abridgment*, I, p. 300; Hawkins, *Pleas of the crown*, pp. 243–4.

17. For some examples, see M. Ingram, Communities and courts: law and disorder in early seventeenth-century Wiltshire, in *Crime in England, 1550–1800*, ed. J. S. Cockburn (London, 1977), pp. 122–4; Ingram, *Church courts, sex and marriage*, p. 316; J. A. Sharpe, *Crime in seventeenth-century England: a county study* (Cambridge & Paris, 1983), pp. 158–9. See also Sheppard, *Grand abridgment*, I, p. 300; *West Riding sessions records*, ed. J. Lister, 2 vols, Yorkshire Archaeological Society, Records Series **3**, 54 (Worksop & Leeds, 1888–1915), II, pp. 112, 121, 171 and *passim*.

18. E.g. BL, Add. MS 37270, ff. 19, 22v., 38, 76; Wilts RO, 88/2/21 (unfoliated), Brinkworth, View of Frankpledge, 3 Sept. 21 Eliz. I (1579).

19. *Kentish sources: VI. crime and punishment*, ed. E. Melling (Maidstone, 1969), p. 193.

20. Inferred from the comments of the judges in *Foxby's case* (1704): *Modern reports, or select cases adjudged in the courts of King's Bench, Chancery, Common-pleas, and Exchequer, since the restauration of . . . Charles II*, 12 vols (1682–1738), VI, pp. 11, 178, 213, 239. (It appears from the indictment that the woman's name was really Saxby: see Carrington, Ancient Wiltshire customs, pp. 75–6.)

21. For some examples, see *The Register of John Chandler, Dean of Salisbury, 1404–17*, ed. T. C. B. Timmins, Wiltshire Record Society, **39** (Devizes, 1984), pp. 3, 4, 16, 77, 80 and *passim*; London Corporation RO, 242A: Portsoken Ward Presentments; Guildhall [Library, London], MS 9064/5, ff. 11v., 12, 16v., 19, 28v., 29 and *passim*, MS 9065J/1, ff. 44, 113v., 114, 128v., 133v. and *passim*; Leics RO, 1 D 41/13/1, ff. 16, 27v. ; *Records of the borough of Nottingham*, ed. W. H. Stevenson *et al.*, 9 vols. (London and Nottingham, 1882–1956), I, pp. 294, 304, 308, II, pp. 48, 106, 240, 268, 270, 338, III, p. 353; Notts RO, CA 5, no. 2, CA 7a, no. 4, CA 7b, no. 6, CA 8a, no. 5, CA 8b, no. 7, CA 9d, nos. 4, 7–9, and CA 10a–47c *passim*; *The municipal records of the borough of Shaftesbury*, ed. Charles Herbert Mayo (Sherborne, 1889), p. 21; Dorset RO, D/FAN, Gillingham Court Rolls (uncatalogued), Lawday 17 Oct. 8 Edw. IV (1468), Lawday with View of Frankpledge, 25 May 16 Hen. VII (1501), Manor Court, 7 Sept. 17 Hen. VII (1501), Manor Court, 7 Dec. 17 Hen. VII (1501); Wilts RO, 906/SC/14, Court with View of Frankpledge, 26 October 1475; F. H. Fenton

et al. (eds), *Manor of Tottenham series . . . court rolls*, 6 vols, in progress (London, 1956–), VI, pp. 15, 104, 142, 233, VII, pp. 4–5, 51; M. K. McIntosh, Local change and community control in England, 1465–1500, *Huntington Library Quarterly*, XLIX, 1986, p. 232.

22. *Leicester borough records*, ed. M. Bateson *et al.*, 7 vols (London, Cambridge & Leicester, 1899–1974), p. 291; M. Bateson (ed.) *Borough customs*, 2 vols, Selden Society, 18, 21 (London, 1904–6), I, pp. 79–80. Cf. Spargo, *Juridical folklore*, p. 68.

23. The sources used were as follows. County quarter sessions: *Quarter sessions records*, ed. J. C. Atkinson, 9 vols, North Riding Record Society, 1–9 (London, 1884–92), I, *1605–12*; *West Riding sessions records*, ed. Lister; *Lancashire quarter sessions records: vol. I. quarter sessions rolls, 1590–1606*, ed. J. Tait, Chetham Society, new series, 77 (Manchester, 1917); Wilts RO, A1/110/1615H–1629M. City and borough courts: Wilts RO, G20/1/12–16; Dorset RO, DC/DOB 8/1; W. L. Sachse (ed.), *Minutes of the Norwich Court of Mayoralty*, I, *1630–1631* [*recte* 1630–1632], II, *1632–1635*, Norfolk Record Society 15, 36 (London and Fakenham, 1942–67); Notts RO, CA 57–9, 65–7, 72–4. Manorial courts: H. Richardson (ed.), *Court rolls of the manor of Acomb*, Yorkshire Archaeological Society: Record Series, 131 (York, 1969); A. Macfarlane *et al.* (eds), *Records of an English village: Earls Colne, 1400–1750* [microfiche] (Cambridge, 1980–1); Dorset RO, D/FAN, Gillingham Court Rolls (uncatalogued); F. C. Wellstood (ed.) *Records of the manor of Henley in Arden, Warwickshire* (Stratford-upon-Avon, 1919); J. P. Earwaker (ed.), *The court leet records of the manor of Manchester*, 12 vols. (Manchester, 1884–90). Church courts: Cambridge University Library [Camb UL], Ely Diocesan Records, B/2/11, ff. 42–110v. ; Leics RO, 1 D 41/13/40; Wilts RO, D3/7/1; W. J. Sheils (ed.), *Archbishop Grindal's visitation, 1575: comperta et detecta book,* Borthwick text and calendars: records of the northern province, 4 (York, 1977).

London, Middlesex and Westminster courts. W. Le Hardy (ed.), *Calendar to the Middlesex sessions records*, 4 vols (London, 1935–41); Guildhall, MS 4069/1 (Cornhill Ward: Wardmote Inquest Book), MS 9680 (St Katherine by the Tower Constables' Accounts); Westminster Public Library [West PL], WCB 1–2 (Records of the Court of Burgesses; I am grateful to Dr J. Merritt for references to scolds from this record).

24. A good impression of the immense range of cases of quarrelling and brawling can be derived from F. G. Emmison, *Elizabethan life: disorder* (Chelmsford, 1970) and *idem*, *Elizabethan life: morals and the church courts* (Chelmsford, 1973), *passim*.

25. The sources used were as follows. Bremhill, Bromham, Rowden, Stanley: BL, Add. MS 37270; Wilts RO, 122/1. Brinkworth, Brokenborough, Charlton, Hankerton: Wilts RO, 88/2/21, 22, 24. Castle Combe: BL, Add. Ch. 18503–5, 18507–15; Wilts RO, 777/1–2. Mere with Kingston, Knoyle, Zeals Clevedon, Chaddenwick, Zeals Ailesbury, Stourton, Woodlands. PRO, SC 2/19–37.

Nettleton: BL, Add. Ch. 15020–3, 15025–6, 15028–32, 15034–6, 15038–43, 15045–6, 15048, 15050–60, 15243, 15307, 15244–6; Add. MS 23151. Stockton: Wilts RO, 906/SC/25–8. Cf. Underdown, Taming of the scold, pp. 125, 129, 136 and *passim*; Underdown, *Revel, riot and rebellion*, pp. 4–8, 16–17, 38–40 and *passim* (Underdown's other sample counties are Dorset and Somerset).

26. Underdown, Taming of the scold, p. 125. On the manor of Gillingham, see J. H. Bettey, The revolts over the enclosure of the royal forest at Gillingham 1626–1630, *Proceedings of the Dorset Natural History and Archaeological Society*, XCVII, 1976, p. 21.

27. Dorset RO, D/FAN, Gillingham Court Rolls (uncatalogued), Courts with Views of Frankpledge, 21 Oct. 20 Jas I (1622), 22 Apr. 4 Chas I (1628), 4 Apr. 8 Chas I (1632), 2 Oct. 8 Chas I (1632), 17 April 13 Chas I (1637). For some years in the 1620s the cucking-stool or "tumbrel" appears to have been lacking: *ibid.*, 11 Oct. 22 Jas I (1624), 28 Apr. 1 Chas I (1625), 3 Oct. 2 Chas I (1626), 1 Oct. 4 Chas I (1628).

28. On the expansion of Manchester see T. S. Willan, *Elizabethan Manchester*, Chetham Society, third series, 27 (Manchester, 1980), pp. 38–9 and *passim*.

29. Roberts, Women and work, *passim*; cf. Beattie, Criminality of women, *passim*.

30. The precise pattern varied from manor to manor, reflecting not only local social and economic conditions but also administrative traditions.

31. E.g. Guildhall, MS 9065, f.70v.; Fenton *et al.* (eds), *Manor of Tottenham series . . . court rolls*, VI, pp. 233–4, VII, pp. 4–5, 51; Greater London RO, Acc. 518/80, pp. 4, 6, 7, 10 (I am grateful to Mr Faramerz Dabhoiwala for this reference).

32. J. A. Sharpe, *Judicial punishment in England* (London, 1990), pp. 19–30. Sharpe has little to say about local jurisdictions, but the increasing resort to corporal punishments emerges clearly in the court proceedings of many manors and boroughs for which long series of records survive, such as Castle Combe (Wiltshire), Gillingham (Dorset) and Nottingham.

33. For examples of penances, see H. Hall, Some Elizabethan penances in the diocese of Ely, *Transactions of the Royal Historical Society*, third series, I, 1907, pp. 272, 273.

34. Brushfield, Obsolete punishments, pp. 35–46; *Historical Manuscripts Commision, tenth report, appendix, part IV. The manuscripts of the earl of Westmorland . . . and others* (London, 1885), p. 437; Earwaker (ed.), *Court leet records of the manor of Manchester*, III, p. 283; Anthony Hewitson (ed.), *Preston court leet records: extracts and notes*, (Preston, 1905), p. 89; R. Plot, *The natural history of Staffordshire* (Oxford, 1686), p. 389; R. Gardiner, *England's grievance discovered, in relation to the coal-trade* (London, 1655), pp. 110–11.

35. There are, however, a few earlier references: G. B. Richardson (ed.), *Extracts from the municipal accounts of Newcastle-upon-Tyne*, (Newcastle, 1848), p. 41; Brushfield, Obsolete punishments, p. 35.

36. Plot, *The natural history of Stafford-shire*, p. 389.

37. BL, Add. MS 37270, ff. 19, 56; Wilts RO, 88/2/21 (unfoliated), Brinkworth, View of Frankpledge and Court Baron, 20 Sept. 17 Eliz. I (1575); Sachse (ed.), *Minutes of the Norwich court of mayoralty 1632–1635*, pp. 14, 40, 168, 225; Lister (ed.), *West Riding sessions records*, II, p. 18.

38. The etymology of the term "cucking-stool" is uncertain, but the most plausible explanation is that the first element derives from "coquean": cf. *OED, s.v.*

39. H. Misson, *Memoires et observations faites par un voyageur en Angleterre* (The Hague, 1698), p. 41; Spargo, *Juridical folklore*, ch. 5 *passim*.

40. *Ibid.*, ch. 1.

41. Gardiner, *England's grievance discovered*, p. 111.

42. J. Kitchin, *Le court leet, et court baron* (London, 1580), ff. 12v., 15, 25, 55; Sir John Comyns, *A digest of the laws of England*, 5 vols (London, 1762–7), V, p. 547.

43. J. Griffiths (ed.), *The two books of homilies appointed to be read in churches* (Oxford, 1859), pp. 145–6; W. Harrison, *The description of England*, ed. F. J. Furnivall, 3 parts, New Shakspere Society, series VI, 1, 5, 8 (London, 1877–81), I, p. 228.

44. Rollins (ed.), *Pepysian garland*, pp. 72–7; E. A. Horsman (ed.), *The pinder of Wakefield*, English Reprints Series, 12 (Liverpool, 1956), p. 17. See also H. E. Rollins (ed.), *The Pepys ballads*, 8 vols (Cambridge MA, 1929–32), I, p. 193; J. Swetnam, *The arraignment of lewd, idle, froward, and unconstant women* (London, 1615), sig. A3; B. Capp, *Astrology and the popular press: English almanacs 1500–1800* (London and Boston, 1979), p. 125.

45. Sir Edward Coke, *The third part of the institutes of the laws of England* (London, 1660), p. 219; *Modern reports*, VI, pp. 11, 213, 239.

46. Underdown, Taming of the scold, pp. 124–5; Spargo, *Juridical folklore*, pp. 45–6.

47. Spargo, *Juridical folklore*, p. 27; F. J. C. Hearnshaw & D. M. Hearnshaw (eds), *Court leet records*, [3 parts consecutively paginated and supplement], Southampton Record Society, 1, 2, 4, 6 (Southampton, 1905–1908), pp. 141, 162, 174, 345, 381, 401.

48. Sharpe, *Judicial punishment*, pp. 19–30; Ingram, Communities and courts, pp. 127–34.

49. Misson, *Memoires et observations*, p. 40; R. B. Shoemaker, *Prosecution and punishment: petty crime and the law in London and rural Middlesex, c. 1660–1725* (Cambridge, 1991), p. 162; PRO, STAC 8/266/29, m. 2; see also STAC 8/123/16, m. 3; G. von Bülow & W. Powell (eds), Diary of the journey of Philip Julius, duke of Stettin-Pomerania, through England in the year 1602, *Transactions of the Royal Historical Society*, new series, VI, 1892, p. 65. Cf. Miles, *Women's history of the world*, p. 80.

50. J. Gairdner (ed.), *Three fifteenth-century chronicles, with historical memoranda by John Stowe*, Camden Society, new series, 28 (London, 1880), p. 140; *Modern reports*, VI, p. 213.

51. PRO, STAC 8/123/16, m. 3; BL, Add. MS 23151, ff. 48v., 50, 52; Wilts RO, D3/

4/5, f. 106v. (The case is discussed in Underdown, Taming of the scold, p. 125; idem, Revel, riot and rebellion, pp. 16–17.) For a worse instance of mob action, see B. H. Cunnington (ed.) Records of the county of Wilts (Devizes, 1932), pp. 65–6.

52. Wellstood (ed.), Records of the manor of Henley in Arden, p. 107; see also J. W. Horrocks (ed.), The Assembly Books of Southampton, 2 vols, Southampton Record Society, 19, 21 (Southampton, 1917–20), II, p. 94; R. Collyer & J. H. Turner, Ilkley: ancient and modern (Leeds, 1885), pp. 127, 131; Spargo, Juridical folklore, p. 14.

53. E.g. W. H. Manchée, The Westminster city fathers (the Burgess Court of Westminster) 1585–1901 (London, 1924), pp. 118–19; Dorset RO, DC/DOB 8/1, ff. 16v., 18v., 59, 81v., 157, 199v., 204v., 227v.

54. E.g. A. J. Willis (ed.), Winchester consistory court depositions, 1561–1602 (Hambleden, Lyminge and Folkestone, 1960), p. 52; B. H. Cunnington (ed.), Some annals of the borough of Devizes, 3 parts in 2 vols (Devizes, 1925–6), I, pt 2, p. 2; Spargo, Juridical folklore, pp. 24–6.

55. Spargo, Juridical folklore, p. 22n; Dorset RO, DC/DOB 8/1, f. 79.

56. W. J. Harte, Illustrations of municipal history from the act book of the Chamber of the city of Exeter, 1559–1588, Reports and Transactions of the Devonshire Association for the Advancement of Science, Literature and Art, XLIV, 1912, p. 221; see also Walter Rye (ed.), Depositions taken before the mayor and aldermen of Norwich, 1549–1567, Norfolk and Norwich Archaeological Society (Norwich, 1905), p. 73; Atkinson (ed.), Quarter sessions records, V, p. 262; J. Wake & S. A. Peyton (eds), Quarter sessions records of the county of Northampton, Northants Record Society, 1 (Hereford, 1924), p. 99.

57. For the context and a sample of cases, see Stevenson et al. (eds), Nottingham borough records, I–V passim; see also G. Nuttall, The emergence of nonconformity, in The beginnings of nonconformity, eds Geoffrey Nuttall et al. (London, 1964), pp. 13–32; C. J. Sisson, Lost plays of Shakespeare's age (Cambridge, 1936), pp. 196–203. The changes in penal policy and subsequent treatment of scolds can be traced in Notts RO, CA 59, nos. 8, 51; CA 60, nos. 9, 28, 47; CA 61, no. 2; CA 62, nos. 14, 30, 33; CA 69, nos. 6, 29, 74, 80; CA 70, nos. 2, 25; CA 72, nos. 37, 63, 64; CA 73, nos. 27, 52, 77; and CA 63–79 passim.

58. Wilts RO, G 20/1/16, ff. 58, 79 (I assume that the four women listed at the end of the latter entry, reproduced in Plate 2, are the witnesses mentioned in the proceedings; it is unlikely that they were additional victims of the cuckingstool – as is implied by the inaccurate and incomplete transcript printed in Cunnington (ed.), Some annals of the borough of Devizes, I, pt 2, p. 12 – but even if this was the case it would not significantly affect my argument); Guildhall, MS 9680, ff. 15, 16, 20v. (for the number of households in the liberty of St Katherine by the Tower, see I. Archer, The pursuit of stability: social relations in Elizabethan London (Cambridge, 1991), p. 225).

59. Dorset RO, DC/DOB 8/1, passim; West PL, WCB 1, pp. 76–7, 81 and passim,

WCB 2, pp. 18, 124, 127 and *passim* (carrying or wearing mortars or a mortar – a vessel of wood or metal – as a punishment for scolding was not confined to Westminster but was occasionally found elsewhere: see *OED, s.v.*); Sachse (ed.), *Minutes of the Norwich court of mayoralty, passim*. Dr P. Griffiths (personal communication) has found a total of only 123 scolding cases prosecuted in the Norwich Mayor's Court over the period 1562–1640; two or three cases a year was the normal pattern.

60. BL, Add. MS 23151, f. 52v. ; Underdown, Taming of the scold, p. 125.
61. Based on search of Notts RO, CA 72–4; Wellstood (ed.), *Records of the manor of Henley in Arden*, pp. 83–117. Cf. F. G. Emmison, *Elizabethan life: home, work and land* (Chelmsford and Plymouth MA, 1976), p. 235.
62. E.g. PRO, STAC 8/123/16, m. 3; STAC 8/151/12, m. 3; Sheils (ed.), *Archbishop Grindal's visitation*, p. 39.
63. Notts RO, CA 80a, no. 71; see also Dorset RO, DC/DOB 8/1, ff. 199v., 218, 281v.
64. Ingram, *Church courts, sex and marriage*, p. 304.
65. Earwaker (ed.), *Court leet records of the manor of Manchester*, III, p. 268; Wilts RO, D5/28/35, no. 73; J. F. Williams (ed.), *Diocese of Norwich: Bishop Redman's visitation, 1597. Presentments in the archdeaconries of Norwich, Norfolk and Suffolk*, Norfolk Record Society, 18 (Fakenham & London, 1946), p. 105; see also Dorset RO, DC/DOB 8/1, f. 79.
66. Ingram, *Church courts, sex and marriage*, pp. 303–19.
67. E.g. Wilts RO, A1/110/1648H/209; Cunnington (ed.), *Records of the county of Wilts*, pp. 188–9, but cf. *ibid.*, p. 199.
68. *Modern reports*, VI, p. 213.
69. E.g. Wilts RO, D1/42/38, f. 135v.; Guildhall, MS 9057/1, ff. 160, 163v.
70. E.g. PRO, STAC 8/266/29, m. 2 (referring to the examinations of Anne Eastborne, Margaret Tailor, Elizabeth Walker and Margaret Watler alias Watlers); Wilts RO, D1/42/38, f. 135v.; Manchée, *Westminster city fathers*, p. 118.
71. C. Larner, *Witchcraft and religion: the politics of popular belief*, ed. A. Macfarlane (Oxford, 1984), p. 86.
72. Sharpe, *Crime in seventeenth-century England*, p. 156.
73. R. Scot, *The discoverie of witchcraft* (London, 1584), p. 34. For a striking case see Wilts RO, D5/21/1/1 (unnumbered file), Peter Gwynne to John James, 14 July 1563 (I am grateful to Mr Steven Hobbs for this reference); see also *Quarter sessions records*, ed. Atkinson, I, p. 213.
74. E.g. PRO, SC 2/209/21, Lawday and View of Frankpledge, 21 Oct. 14 Eliz. I (1572) (theft; blasphemy); SC 2/209/30, 8 Oct. 36 Elizabeth I (hedgebreaking); STAC 8/266/29, m. 1 ("lewd"); Williams (ed.), *Diocese of Norwich: Bishop Redman's visitation*, pp. 45 (swearing and cursing), 94 (blasphemy), 105 (drunkenness), 107 (sexual immorality); Atkinson (ed.), *Quarter sessions records*, I, pp. 55–6 (drunkenness, unlicensed aleselling, etc.); H. Hampton Copnall (ed.), *Nottinghamshire county records: notes and extracts from . . . the seventeenth century*,

(Nottingham, 1915), p. 32 (drunkenness); Emmison, *Elizabethan life: morals and the church courts*, pp. 24 (sexual immorality), 47 (drunkenness and obscene behaviour).

75. See, for example, the case of Mary Hooper of Dorchester: Dorset RO, DC/ DOB 8/1, ff. 52v., 91, 102, 102v., 103, 125v., 160v., 203v., 220v., 221, 231, 233v. –234v., 267. See also D. Underdown, *Fire from heaven: the life of an English town in the seventeenth century* (London, 1992), pp. 64, 70, 98, 100.

76. Wake & Peyton (eds), *Quarter sessions records of the county of Northampton*, p. 99; PRO, STAC 8/123/16, m. 3; PRO, STAC 5/K5/23.

77. Notts RO, CA 72, no. 37; Hearnshaw & Hearnshaw (eds), *Court leet records*, I, p. 345; Atkinson (ed.), *Quarter sessions records*, p. 168; Copnall (ed.), *Nottinghamshire county records*, p. 33.

78. E.g. BL, Add. MS 23151, f. 52; Wilts RO, D1/42/39, f. 82v.

79. Wilts RO, D1/42/37, f. 107v., D1/42/38, f. 133; Willis (ed.), *Winchester consistory court depositions*, p. 52.

80. Guildhall, MS 9057/1, f. 105v.

81. West PL, WCB 1, pp. 8, 76–7, 81, 245, WCB 2, p. 22.

82. *Ibid.*, WCB 1, p. 98 and *passim*, WCB 2, *passim*.

83. E.g. Guildhall, MS 9057/1, ff. 114v. –15v., 122–4v.; Williams (ed.) *Diocese of Norwich: Bishop Redman's visitation*, pp. 107, 110; Copnall (ed.), *Nottinghamshire county records*, p. 33; Manchée, *Westminster city fathers*, pp. 118–19; Lister (ed.), *West Riding sessions records*, II, p. 228.

84. Guildhall, MS 9057/1, ff. 157v. –65v., 170–5v.

85. T. C. Dale (ed.), *The inhabitants of London in 1638*, 2 vols (London, 1931), I, pp. 1–2.

86. Guildhall, MS 9057/1, ff. 163, 170, 171, 173v.–5.

87. Dorset RO, DC/DOB, ff. 125v., 203v., 220v., 221, 267; Guildhall, MS 9057/1, ff. 160v., 161v. –2, 170, 174.

88. Dorset RO, DC/DOB 8/1, f. 125v. ; West PL, WCB 1, pp. 172–3; Guildhall MS 9059/1, f. 54v; Hale's observation is quoted in Brushfield, Obsolete punishments, p. 48.

89. On contemporary ideas about violent madness and the treatment of those afflicted with it, see M. MacDonald, *Mystical bedlam: madness, anxiety and healing in seventeenth-century England* (Cambridge, 1981), pp. 121–32; cf. Dorset RO, DC/DOB 8/1, ff. 265v., 269v. ; Cunnington (ed.), *Records of the county of Wilts*, p. 94.

90. BL, Add. MS 23151, f. 52v.; PRO, STAC 8/266/29, m.1; Wilts RO, D5/28/35, nos. 50, 51.

91. Ingram, Communities and courts, pp. 125–7; J. A. Sharpe, "Such disagreement betwyx neighbours": litigation and human relations in early modern England, in *Disputes and settlements: law and human relations in the West*, ed. J. Bossy (Cambridge, 1983), pp. 173–8.

92. Guildhall, MS 9057/1, ff. 173v., 175v., cf. ff. 158v., 162, 164v., 165v.

Chapter Four

Women, theft and the world of stolen goods

Garthine Walker

WHY?, cause & effect.

Although offences against property constituted the most common type of prosecution for serious crime in early modern England,[1] we know very little about the involvement of women. Analysis of the records of Cheshire county and Chester city courts[2] suggests that we can move closer to an understanding of the experiences of women relative to men by confronting a number of difficulties inherent in the conceptual and methodological frameworks that have been commonly employed by historians.

Table 4.1 shows that, as with most other offences, a minority of defendants in Cheshire were women.[3] Because men have always comprised the majority of persons prosecuted, the concepts and methodologies of historians have been biased accordingly. They have rarely been concerned with gender *per se*, and thus offer little illumination of the experience of criminal women. For instance, studies which have examined jury behaviour with regard to the suspect's social status have tended to define women as an homogenous category, and at most have created female subgroups of wives, widows and spinsters. Yet it is largely impossible to discern the social status of widows and spinsters and, given the unreliability of additions noted on indictments, that of wives must be treated with some scepticism.[4] This means that comparing the judicial treatment of women to that of men in various status categories tells us very little. If, as has been argued, jurors had differing responses according to the status of male defendants, it is unlikely that they had a uniform response to women.[5] Furthermore, whilst social status was clearly relevant to judicial decision making, it has been noted that "it is impossible to measure precisely the influence of such considerations".[6] The same is surely true of gender in this regard.

I have shown elsewhere that the judicial treatment of women, as of men,

81

** we know this!
married women more likely to get off infanticide than single girls*

Table 4.1   Men and women prosecuted for property offences.[a]

Offence	1590s		1620s		1660s	
	Men	Women	Men	Women	Men	Women
Larceny	108	26	229	59	76	29
Housebreaking	–	–	23	18	7	3
Burglary[b]	47	13	74	29	8	3
Cutpursing	3	3	14	7	1	2
Robbery	9	–	6	–	8	–
Horse theft	23	–	31	–	13	1
Total (%)	190 (82)	42 (18)	377 (77)	113 (23)	113 (75)	38 (25)
Grand total	**232**		**490**		**151**	

[a]Prosecutions at the courts of Great Sessions and Quarter Sessions.[b]For the 1590s burglary and housebreaking prosecutions have been compounded. It is not possible to distinguish between the two offences in many cases due to the poor state of the Gaol Files.

was complex. A crude differential based simply upon the sex of offenders is often misleading if less tangible influences as well as other equally quantifiable factors are not considered. Indeed, by broadening the field of indeterminacy and by sharpening the focus of the enquiry to specifics rather than relying on an overview based on aggregate figures, it is clear that, in Cheshire, women were not general recipients of judicial clemency as is commonly assumed. Stastically, they were in fact subject to more severe treatment by the courts than their male counterparts. But this cannot be taken as a reflection of a monolithic trend in the attitudes of juries and judges towards women: the jury itself was not, after all, an homogenous entity.[7] However, the purpose of this chapter is not to consider the fate of male and female defendants, but to explore the dynamics of property crime and related activites such as receiving stolen goods in the light of gendered experience.

Assumptions made about female criminals include notions that they were not as brave as male criminals, were less likely to operate as solitary agents and more likely to be accomplices to men; that they stole items of less value and more immediate use than men did; that they were on the whole less criminally inclined and were therefore less likely to be considered criminally dangerous by contemporaries; and, consequently, that women were the recipients of generous treatment and clemency within the criminal justice system.[8] Such views have been used as evidence for a binary model of sexual difference, in which women are inherently passive and men inherently assertive.[9] More convincingly, it has been argued that

* Can see this from
Old Bailey rec's.

WHY?

the constraints of women's social and economic position in early modern society precluded, minimized and concealed female criminality to varying degrees. Although some fruitful attempts to contextualize gendered experience have been made, the ways in which gender is conceptualized as an historical category have not been challenged.[10]

The social realities of gender are often obscured by legal formulations. Legal definitions of property, for instance, especially those of the common law, have generally been taken at face value by historians.[11] Yet, although in legal terms the ownership of property was weighted towards men, popular perceptions of ownership did not strictly adhere to legal definitions. Women clearly felt uninhibited in claiming the right to protect goods and chattels which they deemed to be theirs, either as their own personal possessions or as the property of the household of which they were a part. A common manifestation of this was in disputes over inheritance, and in the many cases in which women physically fought bailiffs and constables who attempted to serve warrants on their goods and chattels.[12]

The rôle of gender in characterizing theft and related activities can be considered if contextual and discursive evidence such as that contained within examinations is used in conjunction with quantifiable sources such as indictments, and the conceptual parameters of the enquiry are modified to allow new questions to be posed. It seems that women's experience of illegal ventures was not exactly the same as men's, but was certainly significant. In order to demonstrate this, the criminal associations of men and women, the value and nature of goods they stole, and the networks of exchange and interaction which typify women's involvement in the world of stolen goods will be considered in turn.

* * *

Women have been seen as dependent criminals in accordance with their supposed social rôle – dependent, that is, largely upon the guidance of men in illegal activity.[13] Yet the Cheshire evidence suggests that this was not universal. Female participation in burglary and housebreaking, activities that involved a higher incidence of premeditation and were more likely to involve groups of people working together than simple theft, might be expected to show a large proportion of women working as accomplices to male principals. At first sight, this appears to be the case. Of 97 men prosecuted in the 1620s, almost a third were solitary agents. Of 47 women, only six were acting alone.

But Figure 4.1 reveals that men and women had gender orientated

83

(* many groups in O.B solely female)

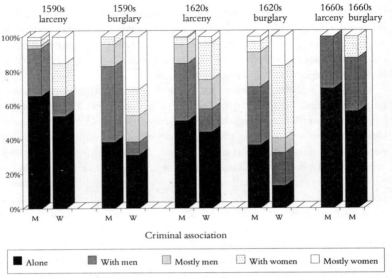

1590s larceny   1590s burglary   1620s larceny   1620s burglary   1660s larceny   1660s burglary

Criminal association

■ Alone   ▩ With men   ▨ Mostly men   ⊡ With women   ☐ Mostly women

Figure 4.1 Criminal association in Cheshire, 1590s to 1660s.

This figure is based on the following data (percentages are given in parentheses).

1590s Larceny, men acting alone 71 (65.7); with men 30 (27.8); with mostly men 2 (1.9); with women 3 (2.8); with mostly women 2 (1.9). Burglary, men acting alone 18 (38.3); with men 21 (44.7); with mostly men 6 (12.7); with women 2 (4.3). Larceny, women acting alone 14 (53.8); with men 3 (11.5); with women 5 (19.2); with mostly women 4 (15.4). Burglary, women acting alone 4 (30.8); with men 1 (7.7); with mostly men 2 (15.4); with women 2 (15.4); with mostly women 4 (30.8).

1620s Larceny, men acting alone 92 (50.8); with men 61 (33.7); with mostly men 20 (11); with women 7 (3.9); with mostly women 1 (0.6). Burglary, men acting alone 36 (36.4); with men 34 (34.3); with mostly men 20 (20.2); with women 6 (6.1); with mostly women 3 (3). Larceny, women acting alone 23 (44.2); with men 7 (13.5); with mostly men 9 (17.3); with women 11 (21.2); with mostly women 2 (3.8). Burglary, women acting alone 6 (12.8); with men 9 (19.1); with mostly men 4 (8.5); with women 20 (42.5); with mostly women 8 (17).

1660s Larceny, men acting alone 23 (69.7); with men 10 (30.3). Burglary men acting alone 9 (56.3); with men 5 (31.3); with women 2 (12.5). Larceny, women acting alone 7 (100). Burglary, women acting alone 2 (33.3); with men 2 (33.3); with women 2 (33.3).

patterns of criminal association. Men were far more likely to work either alone or with other men than with women: in the 1620s fewer than 10 per cent of male burglars[14] took part in operations where women were actively involved. In contrast, nearly half of female burglars chose to work exclusively with other women, mainly in pairs; if we include those operating in groups in which women outnumbered men, almost two-thirds worked with women, or mostly women. Only a quarter were apparently in league with a male partner or in a group in which men outnumbered women. Likewise, in both the 1590s and the 1660s most women committed burglaries either alone or in league with other women, whereas most men evidently chose to work alone or with male partners.[15] Larceny prosecutions similarly show that most women did not engage in criminal activity as accomplices to men. In the 1620s only a third did so. In the 1590s, this pattern was even more acute: only a tenth were prosecuted solely with men. Again, men and women tended to be prosecuted either alone or with members of their own sex. Women who were prosecuted for various types of theft appear to have been involved in a predominantly female culture of dishonest activity.

This is also suggested by the qualitative material of depositions. A common excuse given by men and women when caught red-handed with stolen goods, was that they had unwittingly received them from a stranger.[16] Some of these tales were probably true, but certainly some were fabricated in often futile attempts to avoid prosecution. The sex of suspects appears to have been a decisive factor in the construction of such stories: men tended to blame unknown men; women tended to blame unknown women. When Alice Mannerall was apprehended in 1628, she explained her possession of stolen linens by the following story. After arriving in Chester that afternoon,

> she came into . . . a cellar, but does not know what street [it was in], and in there came a woman who was a stranger to her, and they drank together and spend 2d a peece and she told the woman the occasion of her coming there to look for service, and thereupon they went both together into the Castle lane and as they were going the woman told her that she had left her clothes where she did dwell before and wished her to stay while she went back for them . . . [and] the woman came back shortly with a little fardell under her arme. And then the woman said she had forgotten something, and told [Alice] to stay by the fardell while she went for them.

*Recieving stolen goods,
found not guilty
may of time*

Alice was apprehended before the anonymous woman returned. Her tale was not believed: she was subsequently tried, convicted and branded for the theft. Evidence given by a witness suggested that she was lying, and her own examination was inconsistent and suspicious, including her inability to name a woman with whom she had allegedly spent enough time to have drunk two quarts of ale, and in whose company she presumably intended to spend longer.[17]

Whether such mysterious women thieves were real or not, suspected women's narratives reveal no tension in locating criminality within the sphere of female experience. This is also true of the many examinations by women in which other named women predominate. Women constructed tales involving female criminal personae These two points alone – that women worked alone or predominantly with other women rather than with men, and that the protagonists of their narratives were female – indicate that female criminality cannot be seen merely as a subsidiary of male criminality.

If we look at the value of goods stolen by men and women in Cheshire, shown in Table 4.2, it is clear that women were not necessarily prone to stealing goods of lower value than were men, as is regularly assumed.[18] In grand larceny cases prosecuted in the 1620s, for example, over three-quarters of both the men and the women were prosecuted for thefts of items worth up to 40s. This may in part be a reflection of goods being undervalued to allow men to plead benefit of clergy if they were found guilty. It does not, however, explain why women were in fact more likely

Table 4.2 **Proportionate value of goods stolen by men and women: 1620s.**[a]

Grand larceny			Burglary	
M %	W %	Value	M %	W %
30.7	19.2	Less than 5s	17.9	19.4
16.0	23.1	5s–10s	17.9	9.7
33.3	38.5	10s–40s	30.3	38.8
16.0	19.2	40s–£5	17.9	19.4
2.7	–	£5–£10	1.8	6.4
1.3	–	Over £10	14.3	6.4
76	26	Gender total (N)	56	31
	101	Grand total		87

[a]As given on indictments at Great Sessions. The totals are smaller than the number of defendants overall as not all prosecutions resulted in indictments.

than men to be prosecuted for goods valued within each of the three categories between 5*s* and £5, and less likely to be accused of taking goods worth less than 5*s*. The remaining fifth of female felons stole items valued at between 40*s* and £5. This is a very similar pattern to male felons, the remainder of whom were also mostly in that category. Only three of the 76 men stole goods valued at over £5. Neither does the value of goods stolen during burglaries indicate that women were more timid or less concerned with profit-making than men. About two-thirds of both men and women were accused of taking items valued at up to 40*s*. Only in the highest bracket do men predominate. But the discrepancy is not so great overall as to suggest that men and women had overwhelmingly different patterns of criminality in terms of the value of their spoils.[19]

There are, however, perceivable differences in *what* men and women stole and in the gendered meanings of those items. Table 4.3 shows that although clothes and household linens were the most popular goods stolen by both sexes, women had a far greater propensity than men to steal these items over others.[20] Proportionately, household goods such as pewter dishes and cooking utensils, and cloth, wool and yarn were also particularly female targets.[21] This is consistently so in each of the courts and in every decade studied here. Furthermore, women were disproportionately prosecuted for clothes and linens: in the 1620s, for example, women were involved in over a third of larcenies in which these items were stolen, even though only one defendant in five was female.

Women's thefts, especially burglaries, also tended to be more piecemeal than men's. Margaret Foster took a child's coat, a pewter dish and four herrings when she committed a burglary on a butcher's house in 1624. When Elizabeth Chaddock and her two female partners stole many items of clothing from a husbandman's dwelling, they also took a remnant of new flaxen cloth, a purse valued at merely a penny, a pair of scissors which belonged to the maidservant and a bunch of keys which belonged to the husbandman's wife. Although men did sometimes steal items in a similar fashion, it was usually when at least one woman was involved. Three women and a man supplemented their main booty of soft furnishings worth more than £10 by their taking a picture, a blanket, a brass pot and some gift boxes. In another incident involving five women and two men, all that was taken were two pewter dishes, three brass candlesticks and a pair of boots.[22] Women were prone to stealing more than one type of item at a time, drawn from a smaller range of possible targets. The pattern of female theft was eclectic but clearly defined.

87

Table 4.3 Goods stolen by men and women.[a]

Category of goods	1590s				1620s				1660s			
	M	%	W	%	M	%	W	%	M	%	W	%
Clothes & linens	49	21.4	25	36.8	99	26.9	55	39.0	18	16.8	14	34.1
Cloth, wool, etc.	11	4.8	5	7.3	31	8.4	20	14.2	4	3.7	7	17.1
Money	16	7.0	8	11.8	43	11.7	18	12.8	17	15.9	5	12.2
Household goods	4	1.7	7	10.3	9	2.4	10	7.1	1	0.9	2	4.9
Food[b]	11	4.8	2	2.9	23	6.3	7	5.0	12	11.2	6	14.6
Corn, grain, etc.	19	8.4	2	2.9	22	6.0	6	4.3	5	4.7	2	4.9
Industrial materials	9	3.9	4	5.9	12	3.3	5	3.5	3	2.8	2	4.9
Large livestock	24	10.5	3	4.4	35	9.5	3	2.1	9	8.4	–	–
Small livestock	14	6.1	1	1.5	28	7.6	4	2.8	6	5.6	–	–
Silver, plate, etc.[c]	11	4.8	5	7.4	15	4.1	6	4.3	1	0.9	2	4.9
Horses	23	10.0	–	–	29	7.9	–	–	13	12.1	1	2.4
Tools	4	1.7	1	1.5	7	1.9	–	–	5	4.7	–	–
Firewood, timber	29	12.7	3	4.4	11	3.0	2	1.4	6	5.6	–	–
Books	1	0.4	1	1.5	–	–	1	0.7	4	3.7	–	–
Miscellaneous	4	1.7	1	1.5	4	1.1	4	2.8	3	2.8	–	–
Gender total	229		68		368		141		107		41	
Grand total	297				509				148			

[a]Prosecutions at Cheshire Great Sessions, Quarter Sessions and City of Chester Quarter Sessions and Crownmote. [b]Includes fowl. [c]Includes jewellery.

The female concern with the theft of clothes, household linens and other household goods has been dismissed in various ways. Historians of crime have tended to associate it with opportunist and petty criminality: women's thefts of clothing have been presented as both the evidence for and the result of their place among "the less terrifying criminal elements".[23] Historians of consumption have relied heavily upon a model of emulation to explain women's motives for the legal acquisition of clothing in the late seventeenth and eighteenth centuries, following on from contemporary commentators who supposed that a labouring woman would starve herself and her family in order to acquire a secondhand gown and petticoat of a type worn by those above her station.[24] If this were true, female felons might also have been driven by such a desire, thus demonstrating that women were indeed "obsessed with petty materialism and ostentation".[25] agree?)

However, both of the above approaches are misleading. In the early modern period, clothes were valuable. Not only did they have a remarket-

Tittle-Tattle; Or, the feveral Branches of Gofsipping.

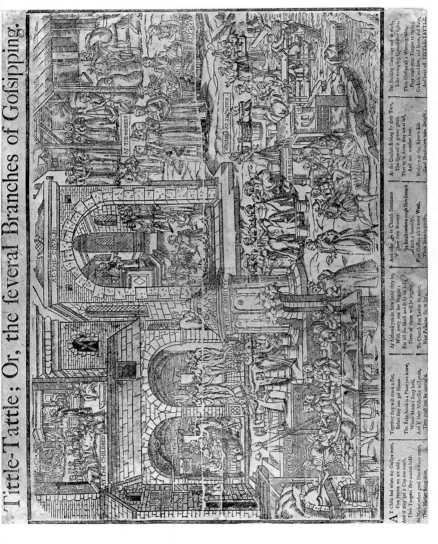

A T Child-bed when the Gofsips meet,
Fine Stories we are told,
And if they get a Cup too much,
Their Tongues they cannot hold.
At Market when good Houfewives meet,
Their Market being done,

Together they will crack a Pot,
Before they can get Home.
The Bake-houfe is a Place you know,
Where Maids a Story hold,
And if their Miftrefs will prate,
They muft not be controul'd.

At Although you fee how jovial they be,
With every one her Noggin;
For till the Staff and Billy be faft,
None of them will be jogging.
To Church fine Ladies do refort,
New Fafhions for to fpy.

And alfo go to Church fometimes
I hear their Prayers:
Yet bouffe makes a rough Skin forgath,
at both it beautifies.
Wife Gofsips uf it every Week,
Their Skins to purify.

At the Conduit ftriving for their Turn,
The Quarrel it grows great,
That up by Arms they are at laft,
And one another beat.
Wedding at the River's fide
Good Houfewives take Delight,

But fcolding Slats cap not at work,
Like wrangling Queans they fight.
Then Gofsips all a Warning take,
Pray curb your Tongue to prate;
Go kim, and brew, and bare, and bake,
And leave of TITTLE-TATTLE.

1. Tittle-tattle, c.1603. (By permission of the Trustees of the British Museum.)

2. Proceedings against scolds in the borough court of Devizes, Wiltshire, 1589. (By permission of the Wiltshire Record Office. Photo: Derek Parker.)

A. Robert Sharp.   B. Ann Bidleſtone.

3. Anne Bidlestone punished with the branks in Newcastle upon Tyne, c.1655. From Ralph Gardiner, *England's grievance discovered, in relation to the coal-trade* (London, 1655), p. 110. Bodleian Library, 4° S21. Jur. (By permission of the Bodleian Library).

4. A cucking-stool in operation, *c.*1700. From G. F. Townsend, *The town and borough of Leominster* (Leominster [1863]), p. 317, originally printed in *A strange and wonderful relation of the old woman who was drowned at Ratcliff-highway* (London, n.d.).

5. A henpecked husband and his punishment. From *Halfe a dozen good wives: all for a penny* (London, 1635?), in *The Roxburghe ballads*, eds W. Chappell & J. W. Ebsworth, 9 vols (London and Hertford, 1869–99), vol. 1, p. 451.

6. Matthew Hopkins Witch Finder General. From *The discoverie of witches*, 1647.

7. The Chelmsford witches. From *The apprehension and confessions of three notorious witches. Arreigned . . . at Chelmesforde,* 1589.

8. The Lancashire witches, 1612. From J. Ashton, The history of Mother Shipton, in *Chapbooks of the eighteenth century*, 1882.

9. Hanged woman. From J. Ashton, The whole life and adventures of Miss Davis, *Chapbooks of the eighteenth century*, 1882.

able value akin to that of video and compact disc players today, but they constituted the largest single category of lawful household expenditure after food (and food production); in contrast, household goods were more durable and therefore less of the household finance was spent on replacing them.[26] Moreover, clothing expressed both social status and individuality for both sexes;[27] apparel was, after all, a primary means of identification in criminal cases.

One Charles Brown was prosecuted for burglary upon leaving his hat at the scene of the crime. The hat in question was a black felt with a twisted band wrought with silver thread, upon which Brown had been complimented in an alehouse. He had, he said, "silver thread of his owne with which he made up the hatband himself", and added that the present company "would little thinke that I had made it myself".[28] It is not suggested here that women had a monopoly of interest over the cultural value of clothing, as Brown's pride in his lovely hat demonstrates. But recent research on early modern wills, household accounts and diaries suggests that women had a more self-conscious, emotional investment in clothing, household goods, and personal effects, even when these were humble in origin and of little monetary value.[29]

It is perhaps not surprising, then, that female victims appear to have furnished their narratives with a fuller description of colours and adornment than men did, even when the property in question had been retrieved, making this type of detail superfluous. Dorothy Woods, for example, described among other things her red petticoat, her laced riding safeguard, her shoes "with polonie heels and blew silk ties" and her silk caul with a gold lace. Even her stolen Bible was, she said, covered with green cloth.[30] Women's acquisition by theft is not adequately explained either by drawing on the supposed petty nature of their activities, or purely in terms of a consumer impulse, any more than is their purchase of new and secondhand goods.

There are far more tangible factors which provide a framework for female theft. The goods which women commonly stole were those which concerned them in the normal run of things. The conversion of household linens and old clothes into other garments and linens was common practice for most women. In households of middling status, women presided over day-to-day purchasing.[31] There is no reason to suppose that in poorer households this type of provision was any less a female concern, although the money or exchange value would have been less and the choice of commodities more limited. Women were more likely to steal household goods, perhaps, because they would have known the value invested in them in a more immediate sense than most men. When such items were stolen, wives and female servants often reported the theft to JPs, gave evidence at trials, and sometimes entered into recognizances to prosecute, even though their husbands and masters were legally required to be named as official owners of the goods. Maidservants added small lists of their stolen garments and effects to those of their masters and mistresses, and being *femes sole* sometimes entered into joint prosecution. Thus in the prosecution of Mary Smith, two indictments exist for one burglary: one was prosecuted by the householder, William Brereton, husbandman, and lists all the goods therein as his, although the recognizance lists over half of them as "belonging to and in the custody of Margaret Brereton his wife". The other was prosecuted by Brereton's servant, Margaret Olton, spinster, for several items of clothing, a remnant of new cloth, and a pair of scissors, "being her goods".[32]

Amy Erickson has shown that clothing and household goods comprised the mainstay of ordinary women's marriage portions, and on their husbands' deaths women often got back those goods. As Erickson says, women were likely to continue to regard such property as theirs for the duration of the marriage.[33] This is clear in disputes over inheritance where moveable property rather than land was the issue: women played out their grievances in the kitchen, and focused their attacks on other women; men were likely to become protagonists only when recourse to the courts was taken, and not always even then.[34] Discrepancies in probate documents that survive for both spouses are also instructive. One husbandman's inventory in 1682 amounted to £36, and included only 8s in household goods; that of his wife, who died just three weeks later, came to £66, and although it included all of her husband's goods valued at a slightly higher rate, her household goods were valued at £18.[35] Concerns and rights regarding property were not exclusively male, but were rooted in the family or household; yet neither the ideology of household ownership nor the legal framework of the common law precluded a popular understanding that some property belonged to women and some other to men.[36]

The mundane aspect of the pattern of female targets for theft should not, therefore, be interpreted in terms of lack of bravado or initiative. Nor is this suggested by the high incidence of women involved in burglaries and housebreakings, especially given their patterns of criminal association. Moreover, many women as well as men appear to have shown initiative and courage in their unlawful practices. The odd example of feminine boldness cannot of course be taken as evidence of an absence of gendered behaviour, yet it is foolhardy to argue that women's criminal activity shows them to have been particularly timid and faint of heart.[37] The pattern of women's theft should be seen in its wider context. Women stole the types of goods of which they had knowledge and a means of disposal.

An important and obvious ramification of theft was the existence of a market in which to sell stolen goods. Clothing was particularly easy to dispose of due to the ubiquity of both pawnbroking, which provided a credit system for a great part of the population, and a thriving market in used clothes. But most objects could be similarly exchanged.[38] By the mid-eighteenth century, one commentator was able to remark that pawnbrokers were so necessary to the labouring poor that "I cannot comprehend almost how they live without the Pawnbroker"; another claimed that "the Thief disposes of his Goodes with almost as much Safety as the honest Tradesman".[39] Whilst this market was not restricted to women, as suppliers, traders or consumers, many of those who dealt in secondhand goods, who are visible in the depositional evidence of the Cheshire courts, were female. This is unlikely to be solely the result of contemporary bias as the accounts of female involvement are often incidental rather than judgemental or troubled. Nevertheless, as Michael Roberts has noted, "everywhere there was a struggle to reconcile the ideal of the household with the wayward but necessary improvizations of working women".[40]

Women's rôle as receivers of stolen property has been noted by historians, but has been delegated to a subsidiary position. As studies of criminality have focused so heavily upon formal court proceedings, the lack of discussion is partly the result of the infrequency with which the offence was formally prosecuted: there was no effective statute against receiving stolen goods until 1691, and it remained an offence that was notoriously difficult to prosecute.[41] It was, however, taken seriously by contemporaries. Ellen Hutchins defended herself against a charge of defamation at the consistory court by claiming that she had called Margaret Grice "the Egge of a whore and a Cuckolde birde" having been "provoked thereto by . . . [Margaret's] scandalouse and injurous speeches" against her. For, according to Ellen, Margaret had called her

a Receipter and her children Thieves, and Ellen being so provoked replied in defence of her own Credit and the Credit of her said children and in her heat and choller said and spoke the words of defamation.[42]

Although the legal definition of receiving theives was ambiguous, and did not necessarily include the receiving of stolen property, the two acts are linked by contemporary legal commentators. Receiving the goods was often synonomous with receiving the culprit.[43] Despite fundamental problems of sources and of definition, female involvement has been misrepresented and discussed as if it were peripheral to "real", that is, male criminality. Women's rôle as receivers has been linked to their position within the household, yet the association has largely been with notions of female dependence and familial obligation rather than with their own economic activities or their interactive social position within the community.[44]

(The participation of women in pawnbroking and receiving and selling stolen goods should not be underestimated, even when they were not officially prosecuted. Historians have recognized the important rôle that many women played in businesses registered in their husbands' names. This was especially true of alehouses and inns, where small-scale pawning was commonplace, and the retail trades which dealt in textiles and clothing, as well as small-wares and food.[45] Women traditionally turned to hawking and peddling goods on the streets for a living, and were active dealers in every capacity.[46] At a time when transactions in cash and kind were still a common feature of the marketplace, it is axiomatic that "in the management of the associated pawns and credit dealings women were the experts".[47] Women's involvement in the secondhand trade should not, then, come as a surprise.)

When, in the summer of 1669, Aurelia Savage had clothes and linens to the value of 9s stolen, she had a good idea where they might be, even though she did not initially suspect Jane Care, the bricklayer's wife who took them. The following day she went to Arthur Fisher's alehouse, and found some of her goods in the possession of Fisher's wife, Elizabeth, and two of her maidservants. Elizabeth promised to compensate Aurelia for two aprons and a napkin no longer in her custody – presumably sold. Although Arthur was hovering about in the background, evidently aware of what was going on, Elizabeth was clearly the dealer. It was she who was prosecuted by recognizance for her part in this case; and when the Fishers refused to give Jane Care "some relief for to entertain her in prison" after her arrest, Care told the constable "she would open such a doore against . . . Elizabeth Fisher as should not please them". Other incidents tell a similar story. Having heard of Aurelia's success in recovering her goods, Ellen Sadler asked Elizabeth Fisher whether Care had taken her stolen yarn there. Although Elizabeth protested ignorance, yet another woman, Anne Wilkinson, later took it upon herself to make a search; she discovered the yarn, and returned it to Ellen Sadler.[48]

There are other cases in which mistresses and their female servants seem to have been involved in independent and disreputable economic relationships. Ellen Cowper and her maids were all implicated when stolen clothes were allegedly pawned at her house, despite the male culprit's insistence that he only went there to buy a penny loaf. The extent of the female involvement is clear: the house in question was Robert Cowper's alehouse in the city of Chester, yet witnesses and magistrates were interested only in the activities of his wife and the maidservants. In addition, all of the several witnesses were female, and although one Thomas Lindopp was named on the indictment as the owner of the goods and prosecutor, it was his wife Margaret who went to the justices and was bound over to prosecute the bill.[49]

In addition to their involvement as victims, suspects and agents in the disposal of stolen goods, the social and economic rôle of women placed them in a strong position to detect and deal with thefts — especially those by other women. Many women as well as men acted on their own authority before informing officials and male and female victims of thefts they believed they had uncovered. Elizabeth Welsh was visiting her neighbour Ellen Thomas when she observed the suspicious behaviour of another visitor, Elizabeth Johnson. Perceiving that Johnson had something in her apron which "she desired to keep close", Welsh forced open the apron and uncovered some yarn. Demanding to know how Johnson had got it, she was told that it belonged to Johnson's master although, in fact, Johnson was out of service at the time of the incident. Being unhappy with this explanation after leaving the house, Welsh returned to find the the door locked, which aroused her suspicions further. Eventually readmitted, she found Ellen Thomas and Johnson together in a chamber, at which point Johnson left the room. Elizabeth Welsh remained determined to discover any misdeeds, and being told by a little boy that there was a "false loft" in the house, she "caused Thomas Welsh a boy that [her] husband keeps to make serch with a candle"; Johnson was discovered lying down between the slates and the roof, and was dragged out. Having secured the audience of the two women, Welsh then demanded to know the whereabouts of the yarn. Both denied all knowledge of it, Johnson now saying that she had brought none into the house, so Welsh herself made a search, and found the yarn hidden in a cradle. Consequently, Ellen Thomas was to be prosecuted for receiving along with Johnson, although in the event only the latter was indicted, found guilty and branded. The offence was prosecuted by the male owner of the goods but female involvement in detection was of paramount importance.[50]

Anne Stockton's theft of Mistress Tannat's four hens and silver spoons similarly came to light through the agency of women. Anne asked Alice Buckley to sell the hens for her, bringing her a silver spoon – perhaps for her trouble. Having sent her sons to Chester to sell the hens, Alice asked Anne Alcocke and Mary Llewellen, servants to Mistress Tannat, whether some hens and spoons had been missed. When Mary said that they had, Alice replied, "Get Anne Stockton out of the house . . . for [Mistress Tannat] is wronged by her". Alice claimed that she spoke to the two women "to the end they might acquaint [their] Mistress . . . therewith to prevent any further mischief", which they did. Tannat evidently chose to deal with Anne Stockton informally, which was probably commonplace in thefts by servants of both sexes. However, female involvement as thief, receiver, and informer is masked by the formal court records – only Alice's son was bound by recognizance for his part in selling the stolen poultry.

That women were so involved in cases where clothes, linens and household goods were stolen reflects the preoccupations and concerns of women in early modern social and economic life. Such disputes were often played out within female circles, with their own structures of authority and responsibility, precisely because women often had a personal investment in such goods. Margaret Dod was indicted, along with her maidservant Mary Catharall, for stealing an iron mortar and pestle, a kettle, and a pewter dish from the house of her deceased husband's brother, William Brocke, in what appears to have been a dispute over inheritance. Brocke was the official plaintiff on the indictment, and the goods were, of course, listed as his. The legal status of goods informed the rhetoric with which such items were described: when his servant, Elizabeth Parsonage, confronted Margaret, she asked why she was taking "her Master's goods". Yet in Elizabeth's examination, both the verbal argument and the physical fight that ensued between the women placed the parameters of the disputed ownership very firmly within a female sphere. In reply, Margaret "swore they were her own and she would have them, and that she would go through the house and take what was her own". Why then, Elizabeth asked, "would [Margaret] not fetch her goods when *her mistress* [Anne Brocke] was at home";[52] whereupon Margaret replied she "would have the goods in spite of [Anne's] nose, giving her [Elizabeth] many ugly unseemly words".

The language is that of sexual slander: references to noses were associated with adultery in women, especially when made by the wronged wife about her husband's supposed mistress. Margaret's position was in part that of the injured wife, not through usurpation in a sexual sense, but in the material basis of her household. That Margaret's verbal abuse should take this form is not surprising in itself; the language of whoredom was of course the most common form of sexual insult. But in referring to Anne in this way, Margaret claims for herself the position of the honest woman which in the context of a dispute over the lawful possession of goods was entirely relevant. As Laura Gowing has said, such arguments between women are located within their own corpus of sanctions, "encompassing sexual sin in contexts as broad as the neighbourhood and as narrow as the household".[53] But they also indicate the areas of contention in which women felt an immediate investment, and in which they felt that their own authority and prerogatives were compromised and worth fighting for.[54]

In fact, this type of case is instructive as the women on both sides were claiming a legitimate position for themselves which was informed by their beliefs in their own property rights. Elizabeth Parsonage, Margaret Dod and Mary Catherall did have a fight over the goods. Elizabeth deposed that Margaret returned after taking the kettle out of the house, and "tooke up a greate Iron Morter with a Pessell, [Elizabeth] taking hold of one eare of it, and shee in the Black Bagge [Margaret] holding the other eare, [both] striving to get the mortar".

Whatever the reality of the incident, in her account to the justices Elizabeth undermined Margaret's claim of honesty. She was well aware of Margaret's name, and her relationship to William Brocke. Yet throughout her lengthy examination, she consistently referred to her as "she in the Black Bagge", after just such a bag into which Margaret was putting the seized goods. She mentions the fact that Margaret was the widow of Brocke's brother only when she was specifically asked about the relationship between them. She also described the fight in terms of Margaret's dishonesty. As notions of acceptable or "right" violence depended upon a fluid concept of social order, she portrayed Margaret's transgression of this by drawing upon common notions of injustice: she was overcome not only because Mary joined in the fracas, but also because Margaret stood on the stair above her, and was thus able to give her such a blow on the arm and wrist that she was forced to let go. Later, Anne Brock had Margaret Dod and Mary Catherall bound over to keep the peace towards her and her children, who were allegedly "so fearful of these two persons that they dare not stay in the house alone for feare of them". Mary Catherall countered this by claiming that Anne Brocke had assaulted her, deposing that Anne "has broken her head and still threatens her". Tales of women's violence had greater resonance when they were based upon their claims to property. And as in so many other incidents, the entire dispute over the rightful possession of these goods was played out between women – neither William Brocke nor Margaret Dod's new husband were apparently involved beyond the strictures of legal requirement. If they acted unofficially, it was presumably between themselves.[55]

The separate patterns of relationships between women them, were characterized by both conflict and co-operation as one might expect. Consequently, relationships between households could look very different through male and female eyes. It has recently been suggested that a study of women's visiting patterns in their neighbourhoods might provide evidence about sociability and obligation across class boundaries.[56] The same might be true as regards women's working patterns. Roger Bosson's relationship with his landlord, Edward Stockley, and Stockley's sisters was very different from that between the women in the respective households. Bosson repeatedly claimed to his neighbours that Anne and Elizabeth Stockley constantly stole his milk, apples, turves, coals and the fire "from under his pot". In making the accusations, he aligned himself with male order, implying that it was this that the Stockley women transgressed. He presented a picture of women conspiring together to rob not only him, but their own brother of his corn, "and if they stole of their brother they might as well steal of him". His own transgression in speaking of his landlord's sisters in this way is deflected by his insistence that whilst he had "a mind to leave Mr Stockley's house", no other tenant would stay long unless the women were removed from the house. The manner in which he described them compromises the acknowledgement of their rank by manipulating the language of deference: they were, he said, "light fingered Gentlewomen, and not fit to be called Gent, for there was nothing that was too hot or too heavy for them". Yet there is also a sense of powerlessness in his position.

> They did repeatedly steal his milk out of the eashers, and . . . they steale his turves and hide them in the buttery, and [he] swore by God, he knew not where to lay his Coales, for they would take them and rob him.

Bosson's relationship with Mr Stockley was of tenant and social inferior.

He said to witnesses and to Anne Stockley herself that "but for his landlord he would have had a warrant for her". It was in fact Edward Stockley who had Bosson bound over to keep the peace towards him, not his sisters. The relationship between Bosson's wife and the women in the Stockley household was rather different, however. Since the public face of the household was not dependent on women's work, their associated social and economic relationships were perhaps more easily interactive. Bosson's servant Alice Brindley explained that his milk was not stolen, nor was the remainder watered down to avoid detection as he claimed, but that his wife and Anne Stockley sometimes exchanged milk. Another witness deposed that when she had overheard Anne ask Bosson's wife whether she accused her of stealing her fire, the reply had been, "not she, for they [the Bossons] did burne Mr Stockley's fire when they first came, and [Mr Stockley and his sisters] might burne of her husband's fire now it was come". Moreover, Alice Brindley deposed that she had never seen either of the Stockley sisters take turves or other fire from Bosson, but that "she herself hath sometimes taken a turfe or twoe that lay in her way or some . . . stickes and lay them to Mr Stockley's fire".[57] Again, women were operating within female networks based on mutual concerns which did not necessarily correspond to those of their male counterparts.

The world of stolen clothes, linens and household goods was populated by women: women stealing, women receiving, women deposing, women searching, and women passing on information, as well as goods, to other women.[58] Although the husbands of those in the above cases appear not to have actively participated in the events cited, the rôle of men such as Arthur Fisher makes clear that we are not talking about "separate spheres" as such, but networks, and the distinction is an important one. These networks were not gender specific, but were gender related. Men too had networks which contributed to the detection of criminals. When the dyer Frederick Dukesell had newly dyed cloth stolen from him, William Pickering, a clothworker in the same town, informed him of its whereabouts upon recognizing Dukesell's mark when the cloth was taken to Pickering to be dressed.[59] Male affiliations are easier for the historian to detect as they often existed within visible occupational, institutional and economic structures, from whose public realm women were largely excluded. Male occupational identity has been recognized as a form of political and cultural display, in accordance with men's rôle as the public face of the household; as such, it could have little bearing on actual economic and non-public rôles.[60]

Conversely, the absence of women from public urban records belies the degree and nature of female economic activity. Women were largely excluded from the skilled, paid work defended by urban guilds. Their appearance in records was usually as transgressors of the guild and borough regulations which sustained the male monopoly. Women rarely claimed for themselves or were identified by an occupational ascription. As their work was more socially cohesive and interactive and less well defined, we have to reconsider how gender influenced constructions of "public" and "private" by contemporaries and historians, and not to assume, as some historians have done, that women's participation in public life involved stepping into the public rôles of men.[61] Michael Roberts has recently called for a redefinition of women's "work", based on the contemporary perception of work or labour according to its location: the crucial contribution of women lay in "the reproduction of social relations, through their management of household, kin and community interaction".[62] The "undoubted importance" of women in neighbourhoods argued by Patricia Crawford[63] was reflected in the networks within which women operated.

In view of this, historians of women's crime must practise a little lateral thinking, just as historians of women's work have done. By employing gender as an analytical tool, our definition of "criminality" must surely be redefined, as it is here, to include female participation in the various economic and social networks of exchange and interaction which provided the backdrop to prosecutions for property crime.[64] This is crucial if historians use the low incidence of female offenders prosecuted by indictment to contribute to theories about either the nature of women or their socioeconomic position in early modern society. Nor can we interpret female experience of the type described above as a kind of subculture of female agency. Whatever the rhetoric of female inferiority, women existed at the nub of social life alongside men, not in some segregated enclosure outside the village. Women were often engaged in quasi-official activity in the return or custody of stolen goods. Katherine Lopus claimed that the piece of Scotch cloth she tried to sell had been pawned with her by a chapman who afterwards told her to sell it on his having no money to redeem the cloth. Her story was not believed and the cloth was kept in the Sheriff's custody for two months, during which time it was not claimed. It was therefore to be delivered back to Lopus, "upon the word of Bridgitt Waynewright, widow, who doth undertake the said cloth to be forth coming or els answer for the value thereof".[65] In another case, Thomas Parre apprehended a woman whom he believed had stolen two carpets. Before taking her to the constable, he "delivered the carpets to William Rowends wife who dwells in the Nuns lane" for safe keeping.[66]

★ ★ ★

Studies of criminality belie the extent to which women were involved in theft and related activities, and the nature and importance of that involvement. A methodology that has leant so heavily upon the quantification of formal court records has masked the rôle which women played, and the problem has been exacerbated by the manner in which gender has often been considered simply as a binary model of comparison. A more fluid model increases our range of analysis and allows deeper insights into the rôle of gender in influencing criminal behaviour in early modern England. Examining the dynamics of gender relations and human interaction allows new questions to be asked and old ones to be answered more satisfactorily. Sweeping generalizations based on all too few studies have led to the marginalization of female criminality as an historical topic. Acknowledging that much of our historical understanding of female experience has been mediated through sources which reflect a public male world challenges the implicit assumption in much historical interpretation that the social and economic position of women in communities was entirely derived from the men to whom they were related. By shifting the focus of the analysis in a lateral manner, the dynamics of female criminality in early modern England reveal a far more complex and instructive view of gendered experience than historians of crime have hitherto acknowledged.

Notes

1. J. M. Beattie, The pattern of crime in England, *Past & Present*, **72**, 1974, pp. 73–8; J. S. Cockburn, The nature and incidence of crime in England 1559–1625, in *Crime in England 1500–1800*, ed J. S. Cockburn, (London, 1977), pp. 60–70; B. A. Hanawalt, *Crime and conflict in English communities 1300–1348*, (Cambridge, MA.,1979), pp. 66–7; B. A. Hanawalt, The female felon in fourteenth-century England, *Viator*, **5**, 1974, p. 261; C. B. Herrup, *The common peace: participation and the criminal law in seventeenth-century England* (Cambridge, 1987), pp. 45–47; J. A. Sharpe, *Crime in seventeenth-century England: a county study* (Cambridge, 1983), pp. 91–2.
2. The sources of this study are the records of the Cheshire Quarter Sessions, Palatinate of Chester Great Sessions (in criminal matters equivalent to the assizes in other counties), Chester City Quarter Sessions and Crownmote, and the Diocese of Chester Consistory Court, for alternate years in the 1590s,

1620s and 1660s.

3. For a description of the offences cited in Table 4.1, see Beattie, *Crime and the courts*, pp. 140–192; Sharpe, *County study*, ch. 7.

4. J. S. Cockburn, Early modern assize records as historical evidence, *Journal of the Society of Archivists*, **5**, 1975, pp. 215–31.

5. For the effects of the status of defendants and victims on jury behaviour, see Herrup, *Common peace*, pp. 115–18, 149–56, and Tables 5.4, 5.5, 6.4 & 6.5.

6. Herrup, *Common peace*, p. 118.

7. The bearing of gender on judicial decision-making is discussed in detail in G. Walker, Crime, gender, and social order in early modern Cheshire, PhD thesis, University of Liverpool, chs. 3 & 4.

8. J. M. Beattie, The criminality of women in eighteenth-century England, *Journal of Social History*, **8**, 1974–5, pp. 80–116, and *Crime and the courts in England 1660–1800* (Oxford, 1986), esp. pp. 237–43, 436–9; G. R. Elton, Introduction, see Cockburn (1977), p. 13; R. Gillespie, Women and crime in seventeenth-century Ireland, in *Women in early modern Ireland*, eds M. MacCurtain & M. O'Dowd (Edinburgh, 1991), pp. 43–53; Hanawalt, Female felon, p. 265; M. Ingram, "Scolding women cucked or washed", this volume, p. 49; Sharpe, *County study*, p. 101; Sharpe, *Crime in early modern England* (London & New York, 1984), pp. 108–109; R. B. Shoemaker, *Prosecution and punishment. Petty crime and the law in London and rural Middlesex, c. 1660–1725* (Cambridge, 1992), esp. pp. 207–16; C. Z. Wiener, Sex rôles and crime in late Elizabethan Hertfordshire, *Journal of Social History*, **8**, 1974–5, pp. 38–60.

9. Wiener, Sex-rôles, *passim*. Wiener continues to be cited in various sources as a useful introduction: A. L. Erickson, "Introduction" to A. Clark, *Working life of women in the seventeenth century* (London, 1992), p. xxix; Gillespie, Women and crime, p. 52 *n*19; Sharpe, *Crime in early modern England*, p. 207 *n*51.

10. J. M. Beattie, *Crime and the courts*, pp. 237–43; *idem*, Criminality of women, pp. 80–116; Gillespie, Women and crime, pp. 49–51; Shoemaker, *Prosecution and punishment*, pp. 207–16; Sharpe, *Crime in early modern England*, pp. 108–9. Extreme versions of the concealment theory are predicated on a spurious account of female sexuality which claims that the ability of women to fake orgasm leads to their greater propensity to deceive men in every other area of life, including criminal behaviour: O. Pollack, *The criminality of women* (Greenwood, Connecticut, 1950, reprinted 1978), p. 10. Such claims will be given no credence here.

11. M. Abbott, *Family ties. English families 1540–1920* (London, 1993), p. 34; R. A. Houlbrooke, *The English family 1450–1700* (London, 1984), pp. 229–47; L. Stone, *The family, sex and marriage in England 1500–1800* (London, 1977), pp. 136–9; L. A. Tilly & J. W. Scott, *Women, work and family* (New York, second edn, 1987), pp. 24–6. Cf. L. Roper, *The Holy household: women and morals in reformation Augsburg* (Oxford, 1989), pp. 173–6. For a critique of this view, see A. L. Erickson, Common law versus common practice: the use

of marriage settlements in early modern England, *The Economic History Review,* second series, **XLIII**, 1990, pp. 21–39: 24–5, and *Women and property in early modern England* (London, 1993), *passim.*

12. This is discussed in detail in Walker, Crime, gender and social order.

13. Beattie, Criminality of women, p. 92; Gillespie, Women and crime, pp. 48, 49; Hanawalt, Female felon, p. 262; Hanawalt, *Crime and conflict,* pp. 118–19; Sharpe, *Crime in early modern England,* p. 108–109.

14. Unless otherwise indicated, burglary and housebreaking are compounded in this discussion.

15. Beattie says that many of the female burglars in his study were associated with men, but provides no statistical evidence for comparison, Criminality of women, p. 92. Hanawalt states that 46.6 per cent of women prosecuted for burglary were acting with an accomplice, "usually a male" (Female felon, p. 262). As over half of the women in her study were thus acting alone, and not all of the accomplices were male, the majority of women were not working with men.

16. For a summary of common excuses given by defendants, see Herrup, *Common peace,* pp. 146–9.

17. Chester City Record Office [CRO], QSF 73/2 ff. 71, 72. Other examples are Chester CRO, QSF 73/1 f. 9; QSF 79/2 ff. 14, 63; QSF 73/1 ff. 11, 12; QSF 73/1 f. 21; QSF 73/2 f. 50; QSF 73/2 f. 52. For exceptions, see Chester CRO, QSF 73/2 f. 68, and Cheshire Record Office [Chesh RO], QJF 53/4 f. 3.

18. Cf. Beattie, *Crime and the courts,* pp. 183–4 and Table 4.8. Goods were sometimes devalued to less than 12*d* prior to or after the drafting of indictments. Women do not seem to have been the predominant beneficiaries of this practice in Cheshire. Cockburn, *Introduction,* pp. 66–9; Herrup, *Common peace,* p. 47 & *n*6; Sharpe, *County study,* pp. 10, 92, 146. In areas where large livestock constituted a larger proportion of male thefts, one would expect the relative value of male and female thefts to be less similar. See, for example, Hanawalt, *Crime and conflict,* p. 119.

19. Nor were women consistently prosecuted for less valuable thefts in the other decades analyzed.

20. This is true of other areas also: Beattie, *Crime and the courts,* pp. 186–9, and Table 4.9; Hanawalt, Female felon, pp. 262–3; Gillespie, Women and crime, pp. 48–9; Sharpe, *County study,* ch. 7, esp. Table 2. In Essex, clothing and household linens were the second largest category of stolen items after sheep. Sheep farming was not widespread in Cheshire which may explain why sheep were not a commonly stolen item.

21. See also Hanawalt, *Crime and conflict,* pp. 121–2; Sharpe, *County study,* p. 101.

22. PRO, CHES 21/3 f. 98v., CHES 24 [unfoliated] 117–2, Indictment and recognizance of Margaret Foster; CHES 21/3 f. 144, CHES 24 118–4, Indictment of Elizabeth Chaddock *et al.;* CHES 21/3 f. 97v., CHES 24 117–2, Indictment and recognizance of Mary Williamson *et al.;* CHES 21/3 f. 172v., CHES 24 119–3,

Indictment of Anne Deykyn *et al.*

23. See, for example, Sharpe, *County study*, p. 101; Hanawalt, however, does see the pattern of women's theft as a reflection of their economic interests, Female felon, pp. 262–3, 264. Cf. D. Hay, War, dearth and theft in the eighteenth century: the record of the English courts. *Past & Present*, **95**, 1982, pp. 117–59.

24. Mandeville, cited in A. Vickery, Women and the world of goods: a Lancashire consumer and her possessions, 1751–81, in *Consumption and the world of goods*, eds J. Brewer & R. Porter (London, 1991), p. 277.

25. For a critique of "social emulation" as a conceptual framework, see Vickery, World of goods, *passim*; quotation, p. 274.

26. L. Weatherill, Consumer behaviour, textiles and dress in the late seventeenth- and early eighteenth-centuries, *Textile History*, **22**, 1991, p. 298.

27. F. E. Baldwin, *Sumptuary legislation and personal regulation in England*, (Baltimore, 1926); N. B. Harte, State control of dress and social change in pre-industrial England, in *Trade, government and economy in pre-industrial England. Essays presented to F. J. Fisher*, eds D. C. Coleman & A. H. John (London, 1976).

28. Chester CRO, QSF 69/1, ff. 44, 45, 46, 47, 48. Other examples in which apparel was the primary means of identifying suspects include Chesh RO, QJF 53/4, f. 69; 95/3 f. 124; Chester CRO, QSF 69/1 f. 52; 69/2 f. 53; 73/1 f. 21; PRO, CHES 24 133/1, Examinations concerning Dorothy Meadowes.

29. Vickery, World of goods, pp. 276, 274, 294; A. L. Erickson, Introduction to Clark, *Working life of women*, pp. xxxix–xl; A. L. Erickson, Common law versus common practice, pp. 21–39; B. Lemire, Consumerism in pre-industrial and early industrial England: the trade in secondhand clothes, *Journal of British Studies*, **27**, 1988, pp. 1–2; L. Weatherill, Consumer behaviour, textiles and dress in the late seventeenth- and early eighteenth-centuries, pp. 298–301, 306–307.

30. Chester CRO, QSF 73/1 ff. 8, 13.

31. Vickery, World of goods, p. 291. The making of new clothes under the regulations of trade guilds was of course largely the domain of men. M. Prior, Women and the urban economy: Oxford 1500–1800, in *Women in English Society 1500–1800*, ed. M. Prior (Oxford, 1985), pp. 110–11.

32. For similar instances see, Chester CRO, QSF 73/1 ff. 11, 12, 17,18,19; PRO, CHES 21/3 f. 144; 24/118–4, Indictments and recognizances concerning Elizabeth Chaddock, Ann Bate and Mary Smith.

33. Erickson, *Women and property*, pp. 86, 162, 223, 226–7.

34. For example, Chesh RO, QJF 97/2 f. 158.

35. Cited in Erickson, Common law versus common practice, p. 35.

36. Erickson, *Women and property, passim*.; Roper, pp. 171–4.

37. In fourteenth-century England similar proportions of male and female felons to those in seventeenth-century Cheshire were involved in larcenies and burglaries. Hanawalt, Female felon, p. 261.

38. On the respectable side of the secondhand clothes trade see, Lemire, The trade in secondhand clothes, pp. 1–24; M. Ginsburg, Rags to riches: the second hand clothes trade, 1700–1978, *Costume*, 14, 1980; M. Spufford, *The great reclothing of rural England: petty chapmen and their wares in the seventeenth century* (London, 1984). On stolen clothes see, Beattie, *Crime and the courts*, pp. 189–90; A. Buck, Buying clothes in Bedfordshire: customers and tradesmen, 1700–1800, *Textile History*, **22**, 1991, p. 228; B. Lemire, Peddling fashion: salesmen, pawnbrokers, taylors, thieves and the second-hand clothes trade in England, *c.* 1700–1800, *Textile History*, **22**, 1991, pp. 67–82; J. L. McMullan, *The canting crew. London's criminal underworld 1550–1700* (Baltimore, 1984), pp. 23–5, 106; Roper, *Holy household*, p. 176.

39. Lemire, Peddling fashion, p. 78.

40. M. Roberts, Women and work in sixteenth-century English towns, in *Work in towns 850– 1850*, eds P. J. Corfield & D. Keene (Leicester, 1990), pp. 93–5; Beattie, Criminality of women, p. 93. For additional examples of female involvement in the secondhand and stolen clothes trade to those cited below, see Chesh RO, QJF 51/4 ff. 62, 42; 53/4 f. 4; Chester CRO, QSF 73/1 ff. 3, 9; 73/2 f. 45.

41. Beattie, *Crime and the courts*, pp. 189–90.

42. Chesh RO, Chester Diocesan Records, EDC 5(1624)5, Margaret Grice c. Ellen Hutchins. See also EDC 5(1624)37, John and Ellen Hollinworth c. Thomas and Margaret Hollinworth.

43. For example, see P. Leicester, *Formes of endictments. . . 1664*, Chesh RO Leicester-Warren of Tabley Collection, DLT/unlisted/16; M. Dalton, *Countrey justice* (London, 1635 edn), pp. 287–8.

44. Beattie, *Crime and the courts*, pp. 189–90; Gillespie, Women and crime, p. 49; Hanawalt, Female felon, pp. 256–7, 261, 266–7; Shoemaker, *Prosecution and punishment*, pp. 133, 171–2; J. S. Cockburn, Trial by the book, pp. 66–7; Dalton, *Countrey justice*, pp. 287–8; Herrup, *Common peace*, pp. 82, 152.

45. L. Charles, Introduction, in *Women and work in pre-industrial England*, eds L. Charles & L. Duffin (London, 1985), pp. 1–23; A. Clark, *The working life of women in the seventeenth century*, (London, 1919), pp. 197–209; P. Clark, *The English alehouse* (London, 1983), pp. 145–7, 138–9, 229; W. H. Crawford, Women in the domestic linen industry, see MacCurtain & O'Dowd (1991), pp. 255–64; N. Cullen, Women and the preparation of food in eighteenth-century Ireland, *ibid.*, pp. 265–75; P. Earle, *The making of the English middle class* (London, 1989), pp. 160–3, 166–74; P. Earle, The female labour market in London in the seventeenth and early eighteenth centuries, *The Economic History Review*, second series, **XLII**, pp. 328–53: 343, 350–1; Sharpe, *County study*, p. 112.

46. Spufford, *Great reclothing, passim*. Research in progress suggests that about 11 per cent of pawnbrokers and used clothes dealers were women; B. Lemire, Disorderly women and the consumer market: women's work and the second-

hand clothing trade in early modern England, paper presented to the Anglo-American Conference of Historians, Institute of Historical Research, 1993.

47. Roberts, Women and work, p. 95.
48. Chesh RO, QJF 97/2 ff. 82, 133.
49. Chester CRO, QSF 73/1 ff. 11, 12; Chesh RO, CDR, EDC 5(1620)1, Elizabeth Cowper c. William Heald.
50. Chester CRO, QSF 73/1 ff. 9, 10, 13.
51. Chesh RO, QJF 91/1 f. 119; QJB 3/1 f. 74v. For thefts by servants, see J. H. Baker, *An introduction to legal history* (London, third edn, 1990), p. 607; Beattie, Criminality of women, pp. 91–2; McMullan, *Canting crew*, p. 23. See also Chesh RO, CDR, EDC 5(1626)49, Margaret Hanford c. Eleanor Johnson, for an example of how theft by servants could be played out in other jurisdictions.
52. My emphasis.
53. Gowing, Women, power and the law, this volume, pp. 26–47; quotation, p. 32 ; *idem*, Gender and the language of insult in early modern London, *History Workshop Journal*, **35**, 1993, p. 10; For other examples see Chesh RO, QJF 89/3 ff. 196, 184; QJF 23/3 f. 47; QJF 23/1 ff. 16, 30, QJB 2/4 f. 7.
54. The parameters of women's perception of their own authority regarding the household can also be found in Chesh RO, QJF 89/1 ff. 90, 91, 92, 114, 105–9, 222; 89/2 ff. 29, 45; 93/1 f. 69. It is interesting that the cases in which this is most explicit are found in the 1660s. For a discussion of changes in female self-perception during the seventeenth century see Walker, Crime, gender and social order.
55. Chesh RO, QJF 97/2 ff. 35, 87, 158, 159, 160. Non-lethal violence is discussed in detail in Walker, Crime, gender and social order, ch. 2.
56. P. Crawford, Review of I. Archer's The pursuit of stability: social relations in Elizabethan London, in *Continuity and Change*, **8**, 1993, pp. 130–31.
57. Chesh RO, QJF 89/3 ff. 133, 194.
58. The same is apparent in trial pamphlets. See, for example, the nature of the female involvement, in *A true and impartiall account of the arraignment, tryal, examination, confession and condemnation of Col. James Turner* . . . (London, 1663).
59. Chesh RO, QJF 53/4 f. 2.
60. Roberts, Women and work in sixteenth-century English towns, pp. 88–9.
61. For example, Abbott, *Family ties*, pp. 93–4.
62. Roberts, Women and work in sixteenth-century English towns, pp. 87–90. See also, Roper, *Holy household*, pp. 179–180; Weatherill, Consumer behaviour, textiles and dress, p. 307.
63. Crawford, Review, p. 130. Examples of the importance of female community networks may also be seen in Chesh RO, CDR, EDC 5(1620)3, Mary Griffiths c. Edward Stones, EDC 5(1620)16, Joane Stockton c. Robert Whittingham, EDC 5(1620)23, Jane Leadbetter c. Elizabeth Sutton, EDC 5(1624)2, William & Anne Blanchard c. John & Margaret Blanchard.

64. Merely stating, as R. Gillespie does, that activities such as receiving and selling stolen goods "much depended on the perception of contemporaries as to what was criminal and what was not" does not go far enough, Women and crime, p. 49.
65. Chester CRO, QSF 73/2 f. 68.
66. Chester CRO, QSF 73/2 f. 71.

Chapter Five

Women, witchcraft and the legal process

Jim Sharpe

The problem of gender is one that has only recently begun to attract the attention of historians of crime, of the law, and of the operation of legal systems. There have, of course, been a number of works that have demonstrated the potential fruitfulness of various lines of approach: the different participation rates of the two sexes in various types of offence; male and female involvement in litigation, perhaps most notably in church court slander cases; and on such gender related (or indeed gender specific) matters as infanticide and scolding.[1] Yet it remains clear that considerable work needs to be done both in charting the statistical contours of such matters as prosecutions brought against men and women, and the punishments inflicted upon them, as well as in using court records to help to understand gender as a social construct, as a bundle of assumptions or attitudes about how men and women should behave.[2] The difficulties in following such a course are, unfortunately, more severe when women are under consideration. The English legal system was run by men, the statutes it enforced were drawn up and promulgated by men, and the English common law seemed designed to constrain the rights of women as much as possible.[3] At first sight then, it would seem that historians studying the relationship between women and the legal process in the past have had their task restricted to doing little more than cataloguing the ways in which women were disadvantaged.

Nowhere would this premise, again at first sight, seem more conspicuously true than when considering the prosecution of witchcraft in Tudor and Stuart courts. As is well known, around 90 per cent of persons indicted for witchcraft at the Home Circuit assizes between the passing of the Elizabethan statute in 1563 and the abolition of laws against witchcraft in 1736

106

were women.[4] Work on comparable sources suggests that this rate was fairly usual for the indictment of malefic witchcraft in England.[5] Yet even the first step that might be taken beyond this simple counting exercise exposes complications. Reworking the figures for Essex, we discover that the 236 presentments for witchcraft or related matters made before the Archdeacons of Essex and Colchester between the 1560s and the 1630s reveal a male participation rate of 29 per cent.[6] Further complications arise when we examine cunning men and women, those "good" witches who attracted so much hostility from the writers of English demonological tracts, but whose services were so eagerly sought by the population at large. Whereas over 90 per cent of those accused at the Essex assizes for witchcraft were female, two-thirds of the cunning folk whom Macfarlane was able to identify in his Essex study were men.[7] These figures suggest that we will have to refine our standard notions of the connection between women and witchcraft at some future point. For the present, however, it seems safe to take as our starting point that the overwhelming majority of persons accused of malefic witchcraft were women, and that a study of witchcraft cases could offer a potentially fruitful approach to the study of women's involvement in the legal process in early modern England.

We must, however, pause to consider what we mean by the term "legal process". To understand the operation of the law in its full context, it is necessary to go beyond the courtroom and the strict rules of legal procedure, and even to speculate about what was going on outside areas covered by the legal record. The English criminal legal system was an accusatory one, and, in large measure, the prosecution of witches, along with other felons, was dependent on the initiative of the person offended against – the victim. As I have argued elsewhere, on the strength of Northern Circuit assize depositions, women showed no reluctance in accusing other women of being witches, or of giving evidence against alleged witches.[8] Indeed, in both these areas female participation in the legal system seemed to be at least equal to that of men. In this chapter I should like to take things further, and seek other points at which we can delineate a distinctive female contribution to the prosecution of witches: the rôle of women in searching for the witch's mark; wider evidence about female involvement as witnesses in witchcraft cases; the behaviour of both witches and their accusers in court; and the subsequent behaviour of condemned witches on the gallows. A consideration of these topics, based as it must be on imperfect and at times contradictory materials, can only lead to very tentative conclusions. What it does demonstrate is that witchcraft prosecutions cannot be interpreted purely as the oppression of women by a male dominated legal system.

★ ★ ★

One area where women were of unique importance in the judicial trial of witchcraft was in their being used to search for the witch's mark. The mark was seen as a method of establishing guilt in some fifteenth-century Continental trials, although the then current custom of shaving body hair from suspects to facilitate the search does not seem to have been followed in England.[9] The first pamphlet account of a witchcraft trial in England, published in 1566, stressed the importance of the mark as a means of establishing proof,[10] and as English trials progressed its importance remained central. It also seems that it gradually became accepted that the mark, with women, most commonly took the form of a teat-like growth in the pudenda, from which it was thought that the witch's familiar sucked blood. Contemporary usage dictated that if the discovery of such a mark was thought vital for proving witchcraft, the search for it should be made by women. The earliest known reference to appointing women for this task comes, perhaps a little unexpectedly, from the court leet of Southampton in 1579. The wording of the relevant order suggests that the practice was already a familiar one. The leet jury directed that half a dozen honest matrons should be appointed to strip widow Walker and to determine if she had "eny bludie marke on hir bodie which is a comon token to know all witches by".[11] That the practice was widely known at this time is confirmed by a tract describing the prosecution of several women in Essex in 1582. This incident involved the searching of a number of suspected witches by local women, including the alleged victims of witchcraft, one such group of searchers being described as "women of credite".[12]

The actual mechanics by which women were appointed to search witches varied enormously. Edward Fairfax, a Yorkshire gentleman who thought two of his daughters were being bewitched, recorded how in 1621 the suspected women were "by appointment, at the house of widow Pullens, at Fuystone, searched for marks upon their bodies", which suggests a degree of official sanctioning of the process. Some years later, in another Yorkshire case, Dorothy Rodes, another parent who thought her child to be bewitched, noted how the suspected witch, Mary Sikes, was "searched by weomen appointed by a justice of peace". A male witness recorded how he went with one of Rodes' sons to Henry Tempest, a West Riding justice who seems to have been much involved in witchcraft cases, "to procure a warrant for searching the said Mary Sikes and Susan Beaumont". Six women, three married and three widows, were appointed. Another Yorkshire witness, Alice Purston, told in 1655 how she and other women were appointed to search Katherine Earle on the direction of the constable of their township who was himself acting under direction from a justice. Four years earlier, in another Yorkshire case, the direction seems to have come simply from the local constable.[13] The decision to search seems, therefore, to have involved an interplay between official attitudes and the demands of the local community, whose members were aware of the need to search for the mark. This suggests that the legitimation for searching operated at both an official and a popular level.

Perhaps the most remarkable evidence we have of the dynamics of the search for the mark comes from the case of Elizabeth Sawyer, executed after trial at the Middlesex Sessions in 1621. Sawyer's trial was rather hanging fire, with neither the judge nor the jury apparently having much idea of what to make of the evidence before them. At that point a Justice who had taken considerable interest in the case, Arthur Robinson, intervened. He told the court that "information was given unto him by some of her neighbours, that this Elizabeth Sawyer had a private and strange marke on her body, by which suspition was confirmed against her". "The Bench", we are told, "commanded officers appointed for those purposes, to fetch in three women to search the body of Elizabeth Sawyer". One of these was Margaret Weaver, "that keepes the Session House for the City of London, a widdow of honest reputation". She was joined by "two grave matrons, brought in by the officer out of the streete, passing there by chance". Sawyer resisted the searchers, behaving "most sluttish and loathsomely towards them, intending thereby to prevent their search of her", but the women continued in their efforts, each of them deposing separately to court about the results of the exercise. They found a teat "the bignesse of the little finger, and the length of halfe a finger", which looked as though it had recently been sucked. This evidence proved decisive, and swung the jury against Sawyer.[14]

As this case suggests, the credentials needed by women searchers were those resulting from good character rather than technical expertise. Some other cases, however, suggested that women with some type of knowledge might be favoured. Midwives were, of course, uniquely qualified to comment on irregularities in the female genitals. The exceptionally rich documentation provided by the Matthew Hopkins trials of 1645–7 shows a number of them in action. A midwife named Bridget Reynolds searched one of the Essex witches, Elizabeth Harvey. Five women gave evidence against Joan Salter, one of those accused on the Isle of Ely, and deposed how they found three teats in her privy parts "which the midwife and the rest of these informants have not seen the like on the body of any other woman".[15] Later in the century, again in Essex, we find a midwife being appointed to search the body of a suspected witch "in the presence of some sober women". This she did, and informed the author of the narration of the case

> that she never saw the like in her life: that her fundament was open like a mouse hole, and that in it were two long biggs, out of which being pressed issued blood: that they were neither piles nor emrods (for she knew both) but excressences like to biggs with nipples which seemed as if they had been frequently sucked.[16]

Some midwives clearly felt themselves able to give expert evidence in witchcraft cases.[17]

Others might claim a more general expertise. Hence, again during the Hopkins trials, Anne the wife of Thomas Savory of Upwell in Norfolk was examined by "some that were there who p[re]tended to have skill in the discovery of witches" who "sayd that some of the divles impes had sucked her".[18] The Hopkins episode also saw the emergence of a woman who clearly attained a regional reputation as a searcher for the witch's mark, Mary Philips. Philips was involved as a witness in some of the early Essex trials in the spring of 1645 and, for reasons which remain elusive, seems to have acquired a wider repute as a finder of the witch's mark. Certainly, she was brought in by the authorities of Aldeburgh in Suffolk to supervise other women searching suspected witches there, and was paid for such duties and also received expenses.[19]

Not all of the women searched, as the case of Elizabeth Sawyer suggests, submitted willingly, while several of them offered those searching them explanations for those physical peculiarities which risked being identified as the witch's mark. Joan Salter explained to an investigating justice that "the markes that she hath about her are not the markes of a witch but caused as it pleaseth God she beleaveth by child bearing". Mary Armitage, a Yorkshire witch, was searched by four women in 1658, and a suspicious hole a quarter of an inch deep was found on her right shoulder. The suspected witch attributed this to an injury sustained while carrying a bundle of thorns, one of which penetrated her shoulder. She explained that the thorn "continewed there about a yeare before itt could be gott out &

caused a great swelling & since that tyme there hath beene a little hole upon her shoulder". Something of the experience of the search for the witch's mark is conveyed in the examination of another Yorkshire witch, Katherine Earle. Earle, asked

> why she did not tell the woemen that searched . . . of a marke betweene here thighs as well as that of behind her eare she at first a-nswered that she did not know of it, whereat the women laughing she p[re]sently after said it came by a burne and she had it 36 yeares.[20]

The frequency of references in surviving depositions to women search-ing for the mark suggests that the practice, existing as it did on the periph-eries of the legal process, was widespread and culturally familiar. This point is reinforced by a remarkable case from Oxfordshire in 1687. Joan Walker of Bicester, the widow of a gentleman, petitioned the bench in that year, to the effect that despite her good reputation and good conduct,

> severall wicked & mallicious persons enveing the good name, fame, credit & reputacon of your peti[tioner] have uniustly & without any ground or collo[u]r of reason given out in speeches that your peti[tioner] is a witch which odious name yo[u]r peti[tioner] utterly abhors & detests & all the works of the devill.

To clear herself, widow Walker requested that the bench should order that she "may be searched by foure & twenty honest sober iudicious matrons & make report of their opinions at next sessions", and that the persons abus-ing her should be bound over to appear there. By this time, and at this social level, the attention of the jury of women searchers was clearly recog-nized, while Walker's suggestion that she should be searched by "foure & twenty" women is instructive. A criminal accusation at the sessions or assizes typically would be screened by a grand jury of twelve or so men, and then tried by a trial jury of another twelve. Walker obviously desired that the search that was intended to clear her name should mirror proper legal process as far as possible.[21]

This last case reminds us that the female searchers officially sanctioned to search women were but one of a number of types of juries, or near juries, of female experts who were called in to adjudicate in a number of legal matters, both criminal and civil. The English medieval ecclesiastical courts had sought female assistance in cases of annulment of marriage on the grounds of the husband's impotence, when the accuracy of the plea was

tested by "honest women" who, by baring their breasts and kissing or fon-
dling the man, attempted to arouse him sexually.[22] This practice seems to
have been discontinued by the sixteenth century, but the operation of the
church courts still made occasional use of women as experts in sexual cases.
Thus when, in 1595, a man from Barking in Essex was presented for incest
with his daughter, it was reported that the suspicion was not founded
merely on "common report", but also "upon the assertion of honest
women, who have had the examincion of the young wench".[23] Although
the point needs further investigation, it seems certain that similar searches,
sometimes with official sanction, would be made by women in infanticide
and rape cases. Most familiar, perhaps, was the use made by female juries in
examining women who claimed to be pregnant after conviction for felony,
and who hence hoped to delay or evade being executed.[24] Together, this
use of female juries or less formal groups of female investigators constitutes
a part of the legal process that must modify the general assertion that
women were excluded from official participation in it. They did not serve
as magistrates or jurors but the authority derived from the crucial evidence
of their "special knowledge" was a dramatic reversal of their generally
powerless rôles as petitioners, witnesses or parties to litigation.

Women were also frequently involved as witnesses against witches. The
Home Circuit assize records reveal that there were 1207 calls for witnesses
at witch trials between 1600 and 1702. Of these, 631 (or 52 per cent)
involved men and 576 (or 48 per cent) women, a nearly even split. In isolated cases, there might be a heavy preponderance of women witnesses: 14
women to 3 men in Kent in 1657, 10 women to 5 men in Surrey in 1664,
8 women alone in Essex in 1650. Such cases would seem to support the
conclusion advanced elsewhere, on the strength of Northern Circuit assize
depositions, that women felt no qualms about giving evidence against female witches.[25] The Home Circuit records also suggest that the proportion
of women witnesses increased over the seventeenth century, from 46
women to 80 men in 1600–1609, to a preponderance of women witnesses
in the 1660s and 1670s. The importance of these figures is emphasized
when we compare them to the gender ratio of all witnesses called to give
evidence in felony cases in Hertfordshire between 1610 and 1619. In that
decade 572 men and 36 women were called to give evidence in felony
cases at the Hertfordshire assizes, a ratio of over twelve male witnesses to
each female.[26] In the same decade, taking the Home Circuit as a whole,
there 92 men and 82 women were called to give evidence in witchcraft
cases. On these figures, women were over 11 times more likely to act as

witnesses in witchcraft trials at the assizes than they were in all felony cases. We return to the notion that the connection between women and witchcraft lay not only in the gender of the accused, but also in a much wider, much more complex, and as yet barely investigated web of assumptions about gender, female power, and female interaction in early modern England.

* * *

It is possible to push beyond statistics occasionally, and to reconstruct something of the experience of women in the courtroom. Such instances throw light on what is still one of the problem areas of English legal history: the very basic issue of how trials were actually conducted, of what happened in the push and shove of a court in session. The official documentation engendered by an English criminal trial in this period rarely sheds much light on these matters. The indictment is a notoriously arid document, while depositions, although invaluable for illustrating other matters, were essentially pre-trial documents that by their very nature usually tell us nothing of what happened in court. Other sources can be more revealing and, as we shall see, something can be constructed from pamphlet accounts of trials, and from isolated references in letters, diaries, memoirs, and such like. The general point to be made is that court proceedings were more disorderly, more ramshackle, and less seemly than those obtaining in a modern court of law. Some notion of typical conditions can be gained from the case of Mary Spencer who, at her trial for witchcraft, complained that "the wind was so loud, and the throng so great, that she could not hear the evidence against her".[27] John Aubrey noted that at the trial of a witch in 1653 "the spectators made such a noise that the judge could not hear the prisoner nor the prisoner the judge, but the words were handed from one to the other by Mr R. Chandler, and sometimes not truly reported".[28] Sometimes the throng in the court during a witchcraft trial might be so oppressive, and demonstrate its hostility to the accused so forcefully, that, as Roger North recorded of one post-Restoration case in the south-west, the judge might be pressured into convicting against his inclinations.[29]

All this was bad enough for the accused, but even giving evidence could be a stressful experience. The century which witnessed the judicial style of Judge Jeffreys in 1685 was not one in which witnesses might usually expect indulgent attitudes from judges, and witnesses, male and female alike, were often browbeaten or ridiculed by the judiciary. In 1712 there occurred the last known assize trial for witchcraft in England, the accused being a Hertfordshire woman named Jane Wenham. One of those giving evidence against her was Elizabeth Field. She told how Wenham had bewitched a child of hers about nine years previously. The judge asked why she had not prosecuted Wenham immediately after this incident, to which she answered "she was a poor women, and the child had no friends able to bear the charges of such a prosecution". The judge, who was sceptical, and who was subsequently to reprieve Wenham after conviction, asked sarcastically if Field had now grown rich.[30] Conversely, there were signs of women witnesses being treated with politeness. In 1702 Richard Hathaway was tried as a cheat for accusing Sarah Morduck of witchcraft. Elizabeth Willoughby was one of those giving evidence on Hathaway's behalf before the sceptical Chief Justice Holt. Holt asked her what skill she had in matters of witchcraft, and she replied that she had been bewitched as a child, and that this experience had given her insight into such matters. An obviously unconvinced Judge Holt was very restrained in his subsequent questioning about this claim.[31]

If the treatment of women witnesses varied, so did that of the women accused of witchcraft. Low conviction rates at the assizes suggest that throughout the period of the operation of the English witch statutes, judges were, broadly speaking, sceptical about, if not the abstract possibility of witchcraft, at least of the guilt of the individual old women brought before them.[32] By the later seventeenth century, when convictions were very rare, judges must have played a major part in helping accused witches evade execution. Yet in other instances women accused of witchcraft in the confusing and hostile environment of the court might find themselves under heavy pressure. In many cases the accused were elderly women who had been cowed by the experiences of community hostility, examination by justices and mob pressure on the way to the place of trial. Such women were unlikely to mount much by way of a coherent defence against the charges levelled against them. Nevertheless, scattered evidence suggests that a few women were able to defend themselves in court. Thus in 1586 Joan Cason, a widow of Faversham in Kent, was tried at the borough sessions for invoking evil spirits and bewitching a child to death. Seven women and one man, poor people but her near neighbours, gave evidence against her. Cason, while admitting contact with what may have been familiars, denied bewitching the child to death, claiming that her adversaries were maliciously accusing her and that there were existing differences between them in which her accusers had already done her wrong. Her arguing convinced the Recorder of Faversham of her innocence, although a bungle over legal technicalities led to her execution.[33]

Other cases of what amounted almost to defiance were recorded. Anna Trapnel, the Interregnum religious visionary, recorded how during her travels in Cornwall she was investigated as a witch, and that a clergymen helped to frame an indictment against her, "but though he and the witch-trying woman looked steadfastly in my face, it did no way dismay me".[34] Margaret Landish, one of the Essex witches accused in 1645, alleged malice and an old grudge against her at her trial, and at one point made "a strange howling in the court to the great disturbance of the whole bench".[35] Temperance Lloyd, one of three witches executed at Exeter in 1682, although confessing her witchcraft at her trial, was "perfectly resolute, not minding what should become of her immortal soul, but rather impudently at, as well as after her tryal, so audacious".[36] Another distraction to the court was offered by Anne Ashby, tried at Maidstone in 1652. Ashby confessed to copulation with the devil, and in open court "fell into an extasie before the bench, and swelled into a monstrous and vast bigness, schreeching and crying out very dolefully", and on her recovery claimed that her familiar had entered her body.[37] *? WHY*

More commonly, the progress of witch trials was disturbed by sufferings of this last type on the part of the alleged victims of witchcraft. One of the recurring themes of English witchcraft was the possession of young people by spirits sent by a witch, or by curious diseases inflicted on them by witchcraft. The accounts of the sufferings of such possessed persons, frequently involving fits and convulsions, are some times very long and very harrowing. What is striking, however, is the number of occasions when such behaviour occurred in the courtroom, sometimes being regarded (at least by the accusers) as evidence of bewitchment. Although people of either sex might be possessed, it seems that most of the cases of fits and convulsions occurring in court of which details have come down to us involved young women. Frequently these took the form of dramatic interventions on the part of the alleged sufferer when the supposed witch entered the court or was first noticed by the supposedly possessed girl.

Thus in one well documented case we find Mary Glover, daughter of a London shopkeeper, who was thought to be bewitched in 1602, falling into a fit when she was called to give evidence in court. The three strong men who carried the girl out of court declared that they had "never carried a heavier burden". The Recorder of London and other officials tested the genuineness of her fit by burning her hand until it blistered: the girl remained insensible.[38] In another case, tried at the Berkshire assizes at almost the same time, Anne Gunter, a gentleman's daughter, similarly went into fits at the trial of two of the women who had allegedly bewitched her, one witness referring to the "gogling of hir heade & eyes, the turning of her armes and hands, the dubling & swelling of hir body" in court.[39] Two decades later two other daughters of the gentry, Helen and Elizabeth Fairfax, likewise "fell into a trance before the judge, and were carried out". Justices present followed the girls out, and "made experiments to prove if they counterfeited or not". The girls' father noted that "report said that it was not so civil as I expected from such men, yet their curiosity found nothing but sincerity in my children".[40]

The theme of the possession of adolescents is a major one in the history of English witchcraft in this period, and is too complex to go into here. What is obvious is that being possessed, whether in the courtroom or not, gave adolescents a unique opportunity to cast off their characteristically submissive and repressed rôle, and indulge in bad behaviour that was not only licensed, but also made them the centre of attention.[41] Given the probability that girls were more likely than boys to be deeply socialized into submissiveness, their behaviour when possessed attracted considerable comment from contemporary observers, and indeed may have been regarded as a deeper affront to social norms than that of young males. Something of the divergence in the normal expectations of a young woman's behaviour and that of the possessed adolescent girl in the presence of a judge can be glimpsed in the account of the sufferings of yet another daughter of the gentry, Margaret Muschamp. The girl and her mother were attempting to persuade a sceptical judge to prosecute the persons suspected of witchcraft, and the girl fell into fits before the judge, at one stage, as was typical in such cases, vomiting foreign bodies. But when she came out of her fits, she "did not know what was past, as all the beholders did see onely an innocent, bashfull girle, without any confidence at all when she was out of her fits".[42] When examining gender as an aspect of witchcraft, it is clear that being possessed and launching a witchcraft accusation gave many an "innocent, bashfull girle" the chance to become the centre of attention and to exercise power over adults.

After trial and condemnation the witch, like any other felon, would be prepared for death. Appropriately enough, this process would be entrusted to a clergyman. Hence Henry Goodcole worked on (to use the contemporary phrase) Elizabeth Sawyer in 1621 to accept her sinfulness and the death by hanging that it had drawn upon her, and to make a full confession. It was desirable that the condemned witch, like other convicted

116

felons, should "make a good end", and die penitently and with dignity. In Sawyer's case, Goodcole officiated at the execution, and at the gallows read to her the confession that she had made earlier, which she declared to be true "in the hearing of many hundreds".[43] Sometimes this sort of clerical pressure could be excessive. Joan Peterson, executed at Tyburn in 1652, was, at the place of execution, exhorted nine or more times to confess by the Ordinary of Newgate. At this point the executioner commented that "the Ordinary might be ashamed to trouble a dying woman so much", to which the clergyman responded that "he was commanded to do so, and durst do no otherwise". This story does at least demonstrate that convicted witches could be obdurate at the gallows.[44] Ideally, however, as with Elizabeth Sawyer, an execution would involve the convicted witch making a "good end" and behaving in an appropriately edifying fashion. Thus when Joan Cason died at Faversham in 1586 she made a gallows speech accepting that her fate was the result of divine justice, and made so godly an end that many who had previously been her enemies lamented her death.[45]

But not all died so edifyingly. Ann Bodenham, executed at Salisbury, was worked on by a minister named Foster, "who comforted her to bear death Christianly, boldly, and chearfully". He managed to bring her "to that pitch as to promise him she would goe a true penitent to her place of execution, and to die as a lamb". She refused, however, to confess the matters for which she had been convicted, adding "that she wrongfully suffered death, and did lament extremely, and desired to die quietly". Her execution was, in fact, less than edifying. According to the pamphlet account, she was "very desirous for drink, and had not Mr Undersheriff's prudence been such as to restrain her from it she would have died drunk". As she walked to the gallows, "by every house she went by, she went with a small piece of silver in her hand, calling for beer, and was very passionate when denied", while she was also, for unclear reasons, very annoyed when the sheriff told her she could not be buried at the gallows. In fact, at the gallows she refused to confess, and

> being asked whether she desired the prayers of any of the people; she answered, she had as many prayers already as she intended, and desired to have, but cursed those that detained her from her death, and was importunate to goe up the ladder.

She then tried to turn herself off on the gallows, but was restrained by the executioner, who asked her forgiveness, as was the custom. "She replyed forgive thee? A pox on thee, turn me off, which were the last words she spoke". "Thus", concluded the account of her trial, "you have her wicked life, her wofull death. Those that forsake God in their lives, shall be forsaken of him in their deaths". Those who have argued that witchcraft accusations were a means of controlling women can at least take consolation in Bodenham's case as one of hegemony's failures.[46]

★ ★ ★

This chapter has concentrated on witchcraft and the secular criminal law courts. But before moving to any conclusions on the evidence presented by this connection, we should remind ourselves that there were other tribunals involved with witchcraft cases, notably the ecclesiastical courts. Less serious forms of witchcraft, sorcery and charming might be presented before these courts, while, more importantly for our immediate purposes, defamation suits involving allegations of witchcraft might be pursued there. Ecclesiastical law gave women greater opportunities for litigating than did the common law, and some of the better documented cases reveal clearly how witchcraft accusations might form part of a wider body of tensions and conflicts between women.

One such case was tried before the Chester Consistory Court in 1662. It arose from problems between Mary Briscoe and Ann Wright. Wright's daughter, aged about twelve, had fallen ill, and "was very sadly afflicted and in a strange manner by fitts", during which time "she would many times say that Mary Briscoe pricked her to the heart with pins and would have her heart and the like, and she did swell much in the body and soe dyed". In consequence, as a witness named Cicely Winne deposed, "the said Mary Briscoe was suspected by many neighbours to be the cause both of her afflictinge and likewise of a brother of hers who was sadly afflicted before that & dyed in a strange manner".

Thus we have a case which resembles so many others: the strange death of a child, the allegation of witchcraft, the neighbourly evaluation, the focusing of suspicion, the defamation suit in defence of good name. Unusually, however, the surviving documentation allows us to piece together something of the background. Neither woman had an unblemished reputation. Briscoe was described as a "very troublesome and wrangling woman among her neighbours", or as a "very wilfull high spirited woman amongst her neighbours". Indeed, her husband, worried about the suspicion of witchcraft against his wife, had discussed the problem with Cicely Winne, and told her "he was much troubled at it but he could not rule her, and he was very much afraid that she would come to the same end as her moth[er] did". But Wright herself had given birth to an illegitimate child just after the Restoration, had refused to identify its father to the midwife and had refused to do penance for it. One witness, interestingly, deposed that Wright claimed Briscoe had bewitched her at the time of the child's conception. She also complained at about the same time of being compelled "to be a witness against her husband for speaking treason against the king". Another women, Margery Whishall, claimed that Wright had slandered her for adultery. With Wright and Briscoe we obviously have two rather contentious women, who had, in fact, already been locked into a dispute over a house in which Wright had dwelt, "which the said Mary had a great mind of". This dispute had already provoked a suit which had been arbitrated by a justice of the peace. This case, which ended in Wright performing public penance in her parish church, demonstrates how the ecclesiastical law helped women to become agents in legal matters. Wright and Briscoe were clearly not victims of a patriarchal legal system, but rather two women who were willing to use the law to pursue their own ends.[47]

This assertion reminds us of the problems of determining a specifically female experience before the courts and legal process. We are examining witchcraft, a crime which, correctly, has been regarded as having a peculiar connection with women. But much of what seems to have happened to women involved in witchcraft cases, whether as accused, accusers or witnesses, seems very similar to what happened to their male counterparts: men accused of felony, and male witnesses giving evidence in court, might be hectored or pressured by aggressive judges, and men convicted of felony, like women convicted of witchcraft, were "worked on" by clergymen before their execution in hopes that they might produce a model speech from the gallows. However, we must keep our minds open to the possibility that although women might have shared with men the experience of going through various stages of the judicial process, the quality of that experience and the reactions and emotions it might provoke could have been very different for them.

There were, however, aspects of the prosecution of felony which were either specific to or more marked in trials of witchcraft. The most obvious of these, as I have stressed, was the use of groups of women to search suspected witches for the mark. Another recurring theme in accounts of witchcraft cases was the frequent occurrence of something amounting to mob action, or at least popular pressure. Of course, the phenomenon of crowd action or popular attitudes towards criminals or at executions was not limited to witchcraft cases; but the frequency of references to hostile mobs is striking, especially since they were on the fringes of the legal process. Suspected witches might be subjected to swimming, scratching or other forms of popularly licensed violence. Further research into this issue might lead to some useful insights into attitudes to gender, given that most of the people towards whom such violence was directed were women.

The willingness of other women to act against alleged witches is also a constant theme. As I have suggested elsewhere, materials from Yorkshire demonstrate that witchcraft accusations were not simply foisted onto women by men, but rather were frequently generated from tensions between women, often arising from such traditional female concerns as childrearing, and were often formulated and refined in the world of female sociability, gossip among women, and female concern over reputation.[48] This creates problems for those investigating constraints on female behaviour in early modern England. Many witchcraft accusations, I would argue, reveal a social arena where channels of female force, female power, and female action could run. The high level of participation of women witnesses in witchcraft cases, and the ready participation of women in searching for the witch's mark, were areas in which women could enter the male dominated milieu of legal process, and in which women, perhaps within parameters dictated and maintained by men, could carve out some rôle for themselves in the public sphere. This would seem to be a line of investigation well worth pursuing.

This leads us to a final point. It is a commonplace that early modern England was a patriarchal society in which issues of gender, like everything else, were viewed in hierarchical terms, and in which women, not least in their status before the common law, were disadvantaged. This is especially relevant when we consider witchcraft, an offence which, even if we eschew some of the women's movement writings on the subject from the 1970s, is somehow connected with the male domination of women. Yet in the preceding pages we have seen women acting strongly: defying judges and executioners; accusing other women as witches; giving evidence against suspected women witches; and suing each other for defamation arising from allegations of witchcraft. Even though contemporary attitudes to gender probably made those experiences different for the women involved, they nonetheless establish women as active participants in the legal system. Like all of us, these women found themselves in a real world that imposed constraints upon them. Yet within those constraints and limitations, in the legal process and before the courts as elsewhere, they were historical actors.

Notes

1. For participation rates, see C. Z. Weiner, Sex roles and crime in late Eliza-bethan Hertfordshire, *Journal of Social History*, **8**, 1975, pp. 18–37, and J. M. Beattie, The criminality of women in eighteenth-century England, *ibid.*, pp. 80–116; for defamation litigation, J. A. Sharpe, *Defamation and sexual slander in early modern England: the church courts at York*, Borthwick Papers, 58 (York, 1980); for infanticide, P. C. Hoffer & N. E. Hull, *Murdering mothers: infanticide in England and New England 1558–1803* (New York, 1981); for scolding, D. E. Underdown, The taming of the scold, in *Order and disorder in early modern England*, eds A. Fletcher & J. Stevenson (Cambridge, 1985), pp. 116–36.

2. Gender as a social construct has so far received little attention from historians of early modern England. For an important preliminary discussion, see S. Amussen, Gender, family and the social order, 1560–1725, in Fletcher & Stevenson (1985) pp. 196–218. The themes raised here are discussed further in Amussen's, *An ordered society: gender and class in early modern England* (Oxford, 1988). I am grateful to K. Cowman for discussing modern gender theory with me.

3. For a contemporary introduction to women and the common law, see *The lawes resolution of womens rights: or, the lawes provision for women. A methodicall collection of such statutes and customes, with the cases, opinions and points of learning in the law, as doe properly concern women* (London, 1652).

4. For a list of these indictments see C. L'Estrange Ewen, *Witch hunting and witch trials: the indictments for witchcraft from the records of 1373 assizes held for the Home Circuit AD 1559–1736* (London, 1929), pp. 117–265.

5. Cf. materials for the Western Circuit printed in C. L'Estrange Ewen, *Witchcraft and demonianism: a concise account derived from sworn depositions and confessions obtained in the courts of England and Wales* (London, 1933), appendix L, pp. 439–46.

6. A. Macfarlane, *Witchcraft in Tudor and Stuart England: a regional and comparative study* (London, 1970), pp. 278–93.

7. *Ibid.*, pp. 117–18.

8. J. A. Sharpe, Witchcraft and women in seventeenth-century England: some northern evidence, *Continuity and Change*, **6**, 1991, pp. 179–99. For a somewhat different perspective on these issues, see C. Holmes, Women: witnesses and witches, *Past & Present*, **140**, 1993, pp. 45–78. Unfortunately Dr Holmes' article appeared too late to have its findings addressed in this essay.

9. Ewen, *Witchcraft and demonianism*, p. 63.

10. *The examination and confession of certain wytches at Chensford in the countie of Essex before the queens maiesties judges, the xxvi day of July anno 1566* (London, 1566).

11. *Court leet records, vol. 1, part 2, AD 1578–1602*, eds F. J. C. Hearnshaw & D. M. Hearnshaw, Southampton Record Society, I (Southampton, 1906), p. 187.

12. *A true and just recorde of the information, examination and confession of all the witches*

taken at S. Oses in the countie of Essex, whereof some were executed and others treated according to the determination of the law (London, 1582), sig D4.

13. W. Grange (ed.), *Daemonologia: a discourse on witchcraft, as it was acted in the family of Mr Edward Fairfax, of Fuyston, in the county of York, in the year 1621: along with the only two eclogues of the same author known to be in existence*, (Harrogate, 1882), p. 78; PRO, Northern Circuit Depositions, ASSI 45/3/2/129; ASSI 45/5/2/30; ASSI 45/4/1/131.

14. H. Goodcole, *The wonderfull discoverie of Elizabeth Sawyer a witch, late of Edmonton, her conviction and condemnation and death* (London, 1621), Sig B2v.–B3v.

15. *A true and exact relation of the severall informations, examinations and confessions of the late witches arraigned and executed in the county of Essex* (London, 1645), p. 26; Camb UL, Ely Assize Depositions Michaelmas 1647, EDR 12/20.

16. J. Boys, *The case of witchcraft at Coggeshall, Essex, in the year 1699* (London, 1909), pp. 21–2.

17. This is contrary to the opinion, which probably rests on an uncritical reading of the *Malleus Maleficarum* and other continental witchcraft treatises, that midwives were a group of women very much at risk to being accused of witchcraft: for a discussion of this point see D. Harley, Historians as demonologists: the myth of the midwife-witch, *Journal of the Society for the Social History of Medicine*, **3**, 1990, pp. 1–26.

18. Camb UL, EDR 12/3.

19. Suffolk RO, Aldeburgh Borough Records, Chamberlain's Account Books, EE1/12/2, ff. 248, 249v.

20. PRO, ASSI 45/5/5/1; 45/5/2/30.

21. Oxon RO, Quarter Sessions Records, Q3/1687 Mi/14.

22. For a case of this type see R. H. Helmholz, *Marriage litigation in medieval England* (Cambridge, 1974), p. 89. Yorkshire medieval cases are discussed and a number of references to relevant secondary materials made in F. Pedersen, Marriage litigation and the ecclesiastical courts in York in the fourteenth century, PhD thesis, University of Toronto, 1991, pp. 133–41. I am grateful to Dr Pedersen for providing me with information on this subject.

23. P. Hair, *Before the bawdy court: selections from the church court and other records relating to the correction of moral offences in England, Scotland and New England, 1300–1800* (London, 1972), p. 189.

24. This practice is discussed in *A calendar of assize records: introduction*, ed. J. S. Cockburn (London, 1985), pp. 121–3. See also J. C. Oldham, On pleading the belly: a history of the jury of matrons, *Criminal Justice History*, **6**, 1985, pp. 1–64.

25. These figures are based on an analysis of abstracts of assize cases given in Ewen, *Witch hunting and witch trials*, pp. 187–264. For analysis of the Northern Circuit Depositions, see Sharpe, Witchcraft and women.

26. These figures are derived from abstracts of indictments given in *A calendar of assize records: Hertfordshire indictments James I*, ed. J. S. Cockburn (London,

1975), pp. 70–223.

27. *Calendar of State Papers, Domestic, 1634–5*, p. 79.

28. Ewen, *Witchcraft and demonianism*, p. 125.

29. R. North, *The lives of the right hon Francis North, Baron Guildford; the hon Sir Dudley North; and the hon and rev Dr John North*, 3 vols (London, 1890), III, pp. 130–31 describes this case, where the judge was "a mild, passive man, who had neither dexterity nor spirit to oppose a popular rage".

30. *A full and impartial account of the discovery of sorcery and witchcraft practis'd by Jane Wenham of Walkerne in Hertfordshire, upon the bodies of Anne Thorne, Anne Street, &c* (London, 1712), p. 28.

31. *The tryal of Richard Hathaway upon an information for being a cheat and imposter for endeavouring to take away the life of Sarah Morduck for being a witch* (London, 1702), p. 20.

32. Ewen, *Witch hunting and witch trials*, p. 99, shows that of 513 persons accused of witchcraft at the Home Circuit assizes, 112 (or 22 per cent) were executed. Many others, of course, suffered lesser penalties.

33. The contemporary account of this case is printed in B. Rosen, *Witchcraft* (London, 1969), pp. 163–7.

34. A. Trapnel, *Anna Trapnel's report and plea or a narrative of her journey from London to Cornwal, the occasion of it, the Lord's encouragements to it, and sign of presence with her in it* (London, 1654), p. 24.

35. Ewen, *Witchcraft and demonianism*, p. 256. Landish was sentenced to death, PRO, Home Circuit Assizes Files, ASSI 35/86/1/84.

36. *The tryal, condemnation and execution of three witches, viz Temperance Floyd, Mary Floyd and Susanna Edwards, who were arraigned at Exeter on the 18th of August 1682* (London, 1682), p. 4.

37. *A prodigious and tragicall history of the tryall, confession and condemnation of six witches at Maidstone, in Kent, att the assizes held there in July, Fryday 30, this present year 1652* (London, 1652), p. 4.

38. Ewen, *Witchcraft and demonianism*, p. 197. Materials relating to this case are brought together in M. MacDonald, *Witchcraft and hysteria in Elizabethan London: Edward Jordan and the Mary Glover case* (London, 1990).

39. PRO, Star Chamber Records, STAC 8 4/10, f. 9.

40. Fairfax, *Daemonologia*, pp. 123–4.

41. This phenomenon is perhaps most familiar in the context of the trials at Salem, Massachusetts, in 1692. For a work which, although now somewhat dated, does focus on this issue, see M. L. Starkey, *The devil in Massachusetts: a modern enquiry into the Salem witch trials* (New York, 1950).

42. M. Moore, *Wonderfull news from the North: or, a true relation of the sad and grievous torments, inflicted upon the bodies of three children of Mr George Muschamp, late of the county of Northumberland* (London, 1650), pp. 15–6.

43. Goodcole, *Wonderfull discoverie of Elizabeth Sawyer*, sig D2v.

44. Ewen, *Witch hunting and witch trials*, p. 276.

45. Rosen, *Witchcraft*, pp. 166–7.
46. E. Bower, *Dr Lamb revived or witchcraft condemn'd in Anne Bodenham, a servant of his, who was arraigned and executed the Lent assizes last at Salisbury* (London, 1653), *passim*.
47. Chesh RO, Chester Consistory Court Papers, EDC 5(1662)63.
48. Sharpe, Witchcraft and women, pp. 192–5.

Chapter Six

Witchcraft and power in early modern England: the case of Margaret Moore

Malcolm Gaskill

A witch-hunt, instigated by Matthew Hopkins, the self-appointed Witchfinder-General, took place in East Anglia in the years 1645–7, and claimed the lives of around two hundred women and men.[1] This chapter examines the case of just one victim of the trials, in the light of some of the ideas which have emerged from historical studies of witchcraft in early modern England. Typically, these studies have sought to explain the rise and fall of prosecutions between about 1560 and 1680, among which the most popular explanation remains, in short, that the deterioration of social cohesion in communities raised fears of innocent villagers using witchcraft against those who denied them traditional charity. It will be suggested here that because witchcraft accusations arose from a wide variety of inter-personal conflicts, and because some accused witches believed in their own magical powers, in certain cases individuals might be seen to play out struggles in an imaginary supernatural arena. This chapter does not seek ecological causes for witchcraft accusations. Instead, it explores the possible meaning of a single supernatural occurrence in the broader context of popular beliefs and mentalities, with a view to understanding how ordinary people might perceive power – its limitations and its extension – in an extraordinary manner.

I

The model of the rise of English witchcraft prosecutions constructed over two decades ago by K. Thomas and A. Macfarlane, connects a small-scale dynamic of tension and accusation in local communities with the larger dynamic of long-term change in social relations in the country as a whole.

It is argued that in the second half of the sixteenth and first half of the seventeenth centuries, social and economic pressures caused English villagers to abandon their charitable obligations to the poor of the parish, thereby opening a gulf of misunderstanding and suspicion between neighbours at the lower end of the social order. Guilt produced by this abdication of responsibility thereafter manifested itself as a defensive fear of the magical revenge of those who had been denied charity. These dispossessed persons were usually elderly widows, often with a reputation for using cunning magic or *maleficium*. Accusations usually focused on specific misfortunes suffered after disagreement with a likely suspect – frequently involving the refusal of alms – which subsequently might be attributed to acts of witchcraft.[2]

Since then, historians have demonstrated that social and economic pressures could also lead to witchcraft accusations between competitors more intimately connected socially. Cynthia Herrup has suggested of witchcraft accusations in Sussex that "the accuser and accused were not exceptionally mismatched in terms of power", reflecting "ongoing competition rather than guilt or anger born of spurned hospitality".[3] Similarly, J. A. Sharpe has interpreted seventeenth-century Yorkshire witchcraft depositions in terms of tensions between women vying for prominence in female spheres of activity.[4] Many women (and men) accused of witchcraft elsewhere deviate from the stereotype of the poor, marginal figure, and instead appear to have been vocal and active members of the community whose very integration, rather than their isolation, brought them into conflict with their neighbours. Research into the background to pre-Civil War witchcraft prosecutions in Kent and Sussex (which superficially fit the Macfarlane–Thomas model) has revealed pre-existing conflicts based on local religious and political factionalism,[5] and in other instances, quarrels ending in allegations of *maleficium* stemmed from disputed ownership of land.[6] Similar arguments for the witch as a competitor for influence, space and material resources have also been advanced for Europe and the New World.[7]

However, both models outlined above, although correct to seek the causes of witchcraft accusations in social tensions, tend to neglect the participation of the witch in a shared culture of popular beliefs. In the 1920s a British anthropologist, M. Murray, argued that the witch-hunts of the sixteenth and seventeenth centuries represented the mass persecution of devotees of a widespread pagan fertility cult.[8] While this explanation is highly implausible, the compounded effect of functionalist refutations of her claims has been to strip witchcraft of any kind of reality as a belief in the mind of the accused, presenting it as a paranoid and oppressive dogma existing solely in the mind of the accuser.[9] Accordingly, all witches have been categorized as the passive and innocent victims of persecuting mentalities and impersonal economic tensions, and confessions of involvement with the black art have been presented as the products of inquisitorial duress or mental illness. After all, in anthropological terms, it is dysfunctional to accuse oneself of a capital crime.

Objections to this approach have formed the mainstay of criticism of Thomas & Macfarlane's work on witchcraft. It has been argued that magic cannot be understood outside complete systems of thought and belief, and that objective assessments of events made outside the mental and cultural context within which they took place have robbed them of their true meaning.[10] This meaning, H. Geertz has argued, stemmed "not so much from empirical testing but from the fact that a particular notion is set within a general pattern of cultural concepts".[11] Another critique levels the more direct charge that Thomas' work "was conducted within a specific framework of assumptions, and therefore could not produce any modification of the framework nor any test of the assumptions". In short, it is argued that the anthropological theories which underpinned *Religion and the decline of magic* must be seen as the product of modern mentalities, and, therefore, that the historical presentation of pre-industrial beliefs was essentially a "present-centred" exercise.[12]

Arguably, the study of witchcraft would benefit from a more self-consciously past-centred approach which seeks to insert the speech and action contained in recorded accusations back into the fluid structure of mentalities that shaped them. This raises a number of methodological difficulties, not least of which is the comparative sparseness of suitable evidence. Printed literary accounts are usually too sensational to be reliable, and most legal records are terse. One can say with certainty that the belief that diabolical power could be harnessed by humans to cause harm was widely held at all social levels, and that change in élite attitudes (given the currency of popular superstitions at least into the nineteenth century) caused the decline of formal witchcraft prosecutions. Applied to the basic details offered by a typical assize indictment, such knowledge merely confirms the established fact that people occasionally blamed naturally occurring misfortunes on the supernatural power of neighbours and sought redress at law. Detailed depositions provide greater insight in that they contain information about the relative standing of accused and accusers and often describe some of the circumstances preceding an accusation. However, in terms of mentalities, even depositions usually enable historians to do little more than illustrate recognized witch-beliefs in practice, confirming what is already known, without significantly penetrating the membrane that separates modern and early modern mental worlds.

Ideally, instead of accounts of supernatural interpretations of natural happenings, such as languishing illnesses, one requires firsthand descriptions of supernatural occurrences to which the modern reader cannot immediately ascribe a natural explanation. As R. Darnton has suggested, "by picking at the document where it is most opaque, we may be able to unravel an alien system of meaning".[13] Since accusers rarely offer more than an unproven equation between suspicion and misfortune, the opacity to which Darnton refers is mainly to be found in witches' confessions, for it is there that the witch might acknowledge and describe his or her own power, and indicate how and why it was acquired. Neither is it adequate always to ascribe such confessions to insanity – a dismissive present-centred reflex, precluding the need for further inquiry. Where possible, the claims made by witches should not be interpreted in terms of our own knowledge and experience, but treated instead as reflecting a facet of a thought-structure unique unto itself.[14] As one historian of German witchcraft prosecutions has argued, depositions need to be understood "as mental productions with an organization that is in itself significant".[15] In these terms, confessions of witchcraft constitute valuable and intriguing raw material for understanding an aspect of early modern mentalities that no longer occupies a place in the way the western world views its condition. In England, such admissions of guilt were not common outside of the 1645–7 trials, but in the few which do exist it is possible to see signs of a dynamic meeting between belief and behaviour.

So what did witchcraft represent in the early modern mind? Although it is difficult to separate élite and popular attitudes regarding magic, in the eyes of the authorities witchcraft was seen as an offence against religious and secular order, and both "white" and maleficent witchcraft were condemned as, at best, sacrilegious and superstitious, and, at worst, physically destructive.[16] More than any other sort of nonconformity, witchcraft could be held up by moralists to illustrate the ideal of religious and secular conformity because it displayed this ideal in its most inverted and corrupted form.[17] But in daily life witchcraft also posed a real and immediate threat to the health and property of individuals at all social levels. To ordinary people, given that many relied on magic in their daily lives, witchcraft could be both evil and beneficial; therefore, its deviant or criminal aspects were largely restricted to its destructive manifestations. Indeed, one could say that the only characteristic shared by cunning magic and maleficent witchcraft in the popular mind was the exercise, or the imagined exercise, of supernatural power by persons who were otherwise relatively powerless in terms of wealth and social status – particularly women. As J. A. Sharpe reminds us, witchcraft was "an explanation for misfortune, but also a means by which the powerless could wield power".[18]

In later sixteenth- and seventeenth-century England, opportunities to live according to individual preference were rare, and for most people the pattern of life was determined by adverse economic conditions over which they had little or no control: population increase; land hunger; inflation; dearth; and, as a result, competition for power, space and resources. Under such harsh conditions, it is easy to imagine that an atmosphere of fear and insecurity might form the backdrop to the daily life of many communities, and that charity and good neighbourliness existed as unrealized Christian ideals as much as they faithfully mirrored social relations in the period.[19] In many instances of conflict, often between close neighbours, and especially where disputants were too poor to engage in protracted litigation, impotence prevailed and a tense state of deadlock emerged. Equally, for many, life was a struggle not only with other people, but with the impersonal obstacles put up by the social and economic environment: poverty, disease and mortality. Women were particularly powerless, and therefore resorted to (or were believed to resort to) other means of overcoming hardship and opposition; the use of words to compensate for the lack of more direct female power, for example, has been suggested.[20]

In such straitened circumstances, personal frustration and despair encouraged the belief in some individuals that magical power might be harnessed as a means of extending the boundaries of terrestrial power. This is a familiar explanation of sorcery and cunning magic, where a consensus of belief usually existed between witch and client, but it is less commonly encountered in discussions of *maleficium* or diabolic communion because the witch trials have been inextricably linked to the history of persecuting societies – an approach which mutes any agency on the part of the witch. However, belief in an act of harmful magic was also *potentially* shared by accused and accuser alike. Viewed together, a physical world marked by hardship, and a mental world which permitted the possibility of witchcraft, provided fertile psychological ground either for delusion and desire in the witch, and/or paranoia and hostility on the part of the witch's victim.

Struggles with neighbours and nature alike could be elevated to an imaginary, supernatural plane, and ultimately resolved (on the part of a victim) in the material world of the criminal legal process. In this way, a dramatic paradigm was applied to real life, and depositions containing accusations and confessions might be seen, in modern terms, to overlay reality with fantasy as a conscious or subconscious means of influencing a court. Such documents constitute, then, a real and powerful "fiction in the archives".[21]

II

The lives of ordinary individuals in early modern England flicker for a moment before the eyes of historians fumbling in the darkness of the past, and then disappear as quickly as they appeared. The life of Margaret Moore is a case in point.[22] She lived in the first half of the seventeenth century in Sutton, a comparatively large village in the hundred of Witchford in the south-western corner of the Isle of Ely, Cambridgeshire. Then, as now, Sutton was dominated by a central street, at the eastern end of which stood the parish church, and behind which the village sloped away to the south, overlooking a large expanse of fenland towards the village of Haddenham. Until the eighteenth century this lowland was flooded, but elsewhere rich arable land was to be found, and Sutton was noted for its cherry orchards.[23] Moore had a husband, who may not have been present at the time she was accused of witchcraft, but was almost certainly still alive (she is consistently referred to as the wife of Robert Moore). At some point in her life she had four children, three of whom died in infancy – a fact which, it will be argued, is crucial to a proper understanding of the story. Various clues from the surviving documentation suggest that she was poor, although she was probably not among the poorest since she kept animals.[24] At present, this is virtually all that is known of her for certain prior to her apprehension as a witch in May 1647.[25]

Some time before this date, in the parish of Witchford just over three miles to the east of Sutton, three farmers suffered misfortunes which were attributed to the witchcraft of Margaret Moore. Thomas Maynes and John Foster both lost cattle, and Thomas Nix fell sick and died. According to Matthew Hopkins' associate, John Stearne, who mentions Moore specifically in his memoir of the witch-hunt, her murdered victim (presumably Nix) sold her a pig for 2s 2d but she paid him only the two shillings. Soon after coming to her door one day, either to collect the debt or reclaim the pig, he became ill and, thinking of his debtor Moore, summoned her, pleading that "he could not depart this life, untill hee had spoken with her". At first, she refused to go but finally was forced to attend by Nix's friends just prior to his death.[26] It is unusual that the approximate date of the bewitchings is not stated either in the depositions or in Stearne's account, and both narratives accordingly give the impression of a rapid transition from crime to apprehension, examination and trial. However, there are good reasons for believing that these events occurred as much as a decade earlier; e.g., the will of a Thomas Nyx, husbandman of Witchford, was proved at the consistory court at this time.[27] Witchcraft prosecutions occurring so long after the fact were by no means unusual, and may reflect the gradual accretion of suspicions and feelings of hostility against an individual over a period of time. By the time well nursed grudges spilled over into formal accusations, a long litany of alleged offences might be stored in the collective memory of the community.

If either Maynes or Fisher, or the family and friends of Thomas Nix, gave evidence against Moore, it does not survive. What is certain is that, some time after the alleged bewitchings, she was apprehended and examined informally by two gentlemen of Sutton, Benjamin Wyne and Perry Jetherell, before whom she confessed herself to be a witch and guilty of the charges laid against her. On 26 May 1647, Wyne and Jetherell then appeared with Moore before the magistrate at Haddenham, Lieutenant-Colonel Thomas Castell, where they deposed their evidence and were jointly bound to present a bill of indictment against Moore at the next assizes. Moore appeared before Castell on the same day, repeated her confession, expressing regret for what she had done, and was committed to Ely gaol pending trial.[28] Stearne concluded his summary of the case by saying that she wept at her trial, confessed her witchcraft a third time, and was condemned.[29]

From the Ely archives and Stearne's account, in 1646 and 1647 twenty persons from the Isle are known to have been prosecuted for maleficent witchcraft, of which two-thirds were women. Over half of this number lived in Sutton and its two neighbouring parishes, Stretham and Haddenham. It is certain that Hopkins and Stearne were active in Cambridgeshire at this time, and it is logical to suppose from this fact, and the content of the various surviving depositions, that they were involved with most, if not all, of these accusations.[30] In two cases Stearne appeared in person to give evidence.[31] In the last eleven days of May 1647, seven women and four men (four from Sutton; four from Stretham; three from Haddenham), most of whom confessed, were examined by Castell,[32] and at least nine of their number were committed to Ely gaol.[33] By the middle of September, there were twelve witches at Ely: seven men and five women.[34]

One is tempted to think that these patterns were formed by more than a witch panic, and that in Moore's case, specifically, relations between her family, the Sutton gentlemen, the magistrates of Haddenham and the Witchford farmers would be a significant factor.[35] Close examination of subsidy assessments, parish registers, wills and church court and manorial records would probably offer more information here, and politics – local and national – doubtless played an important rôle in forming the tensions which lay behind the events of May 1647. The Jetherell family, for example, were lessees of the manor of Sutton under the dean and chapter of the diocese of Ely, and from 1624 were involved in disputes with local people over rights of common in the fen. Drainage and enclosure provided a major source of discontent and disorder in the parish, leading to the withholding of fines, and the petitioning of Parliament by the poorer inhabitants on more than one occasion in the 1640s. In 1649 it was alleged that, four years earlier, seven petitioners were gaoled to prevent them going to fight the King's army,[36] and, indeed, fen drainage has been strongly linked to Civil War allegiance.[37] It has also been suggested that many of the witches accused by Hopkins were believed to be royalist informers (the capture of the King followed only days after Moore's apprehension). This theory could account for the disproportionate number of men accused, the outlandish nature of the confessions, and the relatively high social status of some of the accusers, but it cannot be adequately substantiated.[38]

The various details and possible connections assembled here are inconclusive, and serve only to provide background to the predicament in which Margaret Moore found herself in 1647, and to indicate the direction in which future studies of fenland witchcraft prosecutions in the seventeenth century might lie. For the present, our interest is solely with Margaret Moore, why she confessed to being a witch and what coded meanings might lay hidden in the account of what she was reported to have said.

The first witness, Benjamin Wyne, deposed that Moore had told him that she had surrendered her soul to the Devil "because shee would save the life of on[e] of hir Children which upon the Contract he would save & to doe for hir what she should Command". A familiar spirit named Annis was sent to her, which she allowed to suckle before sending it to bewitch Thomas Nix who died soon afterwards. Jetherell elaborated on this story, relating that Moore had confessed that one night, soon after the death of her three children, the following strange and poignant event had occurred:

> she herd a voyce Calling to hir after this Manner, Mother Mother to which the said Margeret answered sweet Children where are you what would you have with me & thay demanded of hir drincke w[hi]ch the said Margeret Answered that she had noe drincke then theire Came a voyce which the said Margeret Conceaved to be hir third Child & demanded of hir hir soule, otherwise she would take a-way the life of hir 4th Child which was the only Child she had left to which voyce the said Margeret made answer that rather then shee would lose hir last Child she would Consent unto the giving a-way of hir soule & then a spirit in the liknes of a naked Child appeared unto hir & suckt upon hir Body.[39]

Moore herself confessed before the magistrate that "she hard ye voyce of hir Children whoe had formerly died Calling unto hir in these words mother mother good sweet mother lett me In". She arose at once to open the door, and although she could see no one, the voice continued, "good mother give me some drincke", to which she answered that "she had noe drincke but water". She closed the door, returned to her bed, but the voice started again, closer to the bedside this time: "mother mother Give me yo[u]r soule & I will save the life of yo[u]r 4[th] Child w[hi]ch is now livinge w[i]th yow". Moore immediately agreed, sealed the covenant and then suckled her two spirits, Annis and Margaret, which she sent to Witchford to kill Thomas Nix, three of Thomas Maynes' bullocks and John Foster's cow. She ended by saying that she had perfomed many other acts of witchcraft, and that she was very sorry for all she had done.[40]

If Hopkins' and Stearne's motivations (and those of their clients) seem obscure, knowledge of their methods is perhaps more enlightening for explaining Moore's confession. Illegal torture, such as sleep deprivation followed by leading questioning (a favourite method of Hopkins and Stearne), cannot be ruled out in the case of Moore and the other Sutton witches.[41] One contemporary described these methods:

> Having Taken the suspected Witch, shee is placed in the middle of a room upon a stool, or Table, crosse legg'd, or in some other uneasie posture, to which if she submits not, she is bound with cords, there is she watcht & kept without meat or sleep for the space of 24 hours.[42]

Hopkins denied that this was a means of extracting confessions (adding that forced confessions were worthless for establishing guilt), and argued that "they being kept awake would be more the active to cal their Imps in open view the sooner to their helpe".[43] But Hopkins and Stearne contrived to justify this practice, in modern times extremes of fatigue have proved to be a highly effective means of extracting the most outlandish confessions from detainees without recourse to physical force.[44]

Conspiracy and malice against individuals cannot be ruled out as motivations for the accusations, especially when one considers that Moore's case was not isolated. On the same day that Moore was examined and committed, two other accused witches from Sutton, John Bonham and William Watson (Bonham's wife having been taken into custody five days earlier), also confessed and were sent to Ely for trial.[45] It is perhaps significant that the depositions for the three Sutton witches taken on this day consisted solely of the accused's confession and Wyne's brief and unsubstantiated information. The Bonhams were certainly unpopular in Sutton, and were prosecuted (unsuccessfully) at least twice for the suspected murder of their son – in 1636 and 1662; witchcraft was not mentioned in either prosecution.[46] Watson's and Bonham's confessions were relatively simple in content, and did not specify what the suspects had to gain from their diabolical pact. Both confessed that the Devil appeared to them as a large mouse and a mole respectively, and both fed their familiar on blood pricked from a finger, before it set off to inflict damage on local livestock. But the case of Margaret Moore is different. Accusations made against her may well have been malicious, but, as with the other cases, this is very difficult to demonstrate. Of greater interest than the sincerity of the accusers, is the style and content of Moore's confession, because it concerns imagined power, and therefore has implications for the way in which an ordinary person might view his or her place in the world.[47]

III

Even if Margaret Moore was the victim of torture, there are grounds for thinking that her story was not concocted by her tormentors, but constructed in her own mind from desire, emotion, experience and belief. Neither did the story necessarily originate at the time of her examination: long before that she could have believed that she had actually seen the spirits and given her soul to the Devil, thereby making her testimony a faithful account of an experience which, when challenged by her neighbours, she confessed out of a sense of remorse. In Continental trials, it was common for the suspect's adherence to a confession to last only as long as the torture under which it was extracted.[48] Moore, however, confessed three times before different audiences: to Wyne and Jetherell; to Castell; and to an assize court, suggesting the possibility of genuine belief in her own guilt. It is possible that accumulated vocalized suspicions, rumours and accusations of witchcraft suggested to her that she actually possessed the powers attributed to her by others. In criminological terms, "primary deviation" might have been succeeded by "secondary deviation" occurring when a suspect begins to accept his or her own allotted rôle as a social deviant.[49] In this circular fashion, Moore could have assumed the mantle of witch laid out for her by neighbours suspicious of her conversation and behaviour.

Regardless of the influence exerted by her neighbours, delusions of the kind described by her would have have been understandable considering the loss of three children and her natural concern for the life of the last surviving child.[50] A modern study of hallucinations experienced by the bereaved revealed that almost half the subjects studied experienced visions of the dead, while their mental state remained otherwise normal. Moreover, it is apparently common for such persons to believe in the objective reality of what they have witnessed, and to feel comforted by the experience.[51] Illusion and delusion deserve to be seen in the context of contemporary beliefs, since apparitions and fantasies, such as those experienced by Moore, were formed in an area between universal human anxieties and aspirations on the one hand, and specific cultural traits on the other.[52] Even if her experience can be attributed to psychological behaviour recurrent over the centuries, it remains an important event historically because of the specific form of the vision, and the manner in which she interpreted and described it.[53]

The same recommendation would apply if Moore's vision was, in fact, a dream. It was common in this period for the sources of dreams to be identified as carnal, divine or diabolic, and for their content to be interpreted in one of three ways: as an excursion of the soul into the spirit world; as a symbol; or as an apparition – a real encounter with a spirit.[55] Social anthropology provides an interesting parallel here: in his famous study of modern African witchcraft, Evans-Pritchard offered the following insight:

> It must be remembered that a bad dream is not a symbol of witchcraft but an actual experience of it. In waking life a man knows that he has been bewitched only by experiencing a subsequent misfortune or by oracular revelation, but in dreams he actually sees witches

and may even converse with them. We may say that Azande see witchcraft in a dream rather than that they dream of witchcraft.[56]

Many sixteenth- and seventeenth-century sources include references to persons who suffered nightmares attributed to the malign practices of witches.[57] But, as Moore's case might suggest, dreams of witchcraft could also invade the sleep of the witch, and therefore a functionalist assessment (such as that of Evans-Pritchard) could be extended to allow for a greater consensus of belief between accuser and accused. Some studies of early modern witchcraft have even described opponents playing out conflicts at the dream level, with both witch and victim dreaming their respective rôles.[58]

Boundaries separating the physical and the metaphysical, the natural and the supernatural, were drawn differently in the seventeenth-century mind,[59] and it has been argued that because the material world limits the possibilities open to the individual (in a way that the dream world does not), it is understandable that our ancestors were slow to dismiss the dream experience as an illusion. As one student of the subject has expressed it: "if the waking world has certain advantages of solidity and continuity, its social opportunities are terribly restricted".[60] If Moore's communion with the spirits of her children was indeed a dream – and it is no accident that this and similar visitations in other depositions occurred at night in the bed chamber – then considering her desperate condition, it may well have been an event of fundamental importance in her life, a perceived chance to enter an overlapping sphere between the worlds of life and death to alter the course of her fate.[61]

Seen in the context of prescientific mentalities in general, and her viewpoint in particular, Moore's witchcraft becomes just another form of power: defensive and offensive magic employed by a woman with limited command of the resources of the natural world for the benefit of her family. The power to inflict *maleficium* might even be seen as a skill towards which some men and women actually aspired.[62] Whatever misfortunes the farmers of Witchford might have seen fit to explain by witchcraft, arguably Moore was fighting her own battle with adversity, and her words can be interpreted as reflecting her desire to conquer it. Although in many ways it is true that this explanation simply takes refuge in traditional functionalism, it does at least return a greater measure of human agency to the equation, and the individual actions that constitute a witchcraft accusation can be seen to have been determined by personal belief and choice, rather than generalized patterns of behaviour shaped by impersonal forces. In other words, Moore could have been accused of witchcraft not simply because she looked and behaved according to a popular stereotype (the classic anthropological reduction), but because, for her own reasons, she herself believed that she was a witch.

There are obvious parallels between her case and the Faust myth: a transaction with the Devil in which the soul could be exchanged for material gain. This familiar fictional paradigm pervaded high literature, cheap print and folklore throughout medieval and early modern England,[63] but is less commonly encountered in real English witchcraft trials.[64] Faustian temptation played a part in the Lancashire trials of 1634, during which one suspect confessed that she was "in greate passion & anger & discontented & w[i]thall oppressed w[i]th some want", and the Devil appeared and offered her all she needed in return for her soul.[65] Overall though, the East Anglian examinations of the mid-1640s are unusual for the explicit presence of the Devil, and his offers of assistance to the poor, financial and otherwise.[66] Adam Sabie, for example, one of the suspects from Haddenham, confessed that a spirit had visited him in the form of a child and had comforted him with the words: "ffeare not Sabie for I am thy God" and then told him to go to Lady Sandys' house where he would be given £20 – a substantial sum to a poor fenman.[67] This pattern appears in the examination of suspects in other counties. In the Suffolk trials of 1645, one man was offered a deal by the Devil "he beinge at plowgh curseinge &c"; another was promised an annual income of £14 in return for his soul.[68]

These confessions, forced or voluntary, took the form that they did because it was (and remains) common for poor or otherwise oppressed people to fantasize about the reversal of their predicament – Margaret Moore's specific fantasy, as we have seen, concerned resisting the domination of death and poverty.[69] As one anthropologist has written: "Witchcraft is in many respects the classical resort of vulnerable subordinate groups who have little or no safe, open opportunity to challenge a form of domination that angers them".[70] In Moore's case though, as in many cases from the 1640s, the deployment of witchcraft by the poor and vulnerable person to resist domination serves constructive, personal ends at the expense of harm caused to others, not just causing harm for purposes of revenge. It is especially noticeable in Moore's confession (and in others similar to hers) that the story turns from a description of personal powerlessness to a situation where the witch is issuing commands, at the precise moment the diabolical compact is sealed. Furthermore, it must be significant that one of

Moore's familiar spirits shares her name, suggesting a more powerful alter ego, a supernatural version of herself, able to perform her will on earth in a way that she could not otherwise manage (the familiar of one of the other Sutton witches, John Bonham was named John).[71] In context, surrendering her soul for the sake of her child can be equated with a metaphysical extension of the principle of laying down life for love, and therefore represents an extension of power, whereby the soul is reified in an imaginary sphere as something with which she is able to bargain.

* * *

This study has not sought to explain the events which occurred at Sutton in 1647, still less to establish a new model of witchcraft prosecutions in early modern England as a whole. Rather, it has offered one interpretation among the many required to accommodate the wide variety of circumstances behind individual accusations – variety that more schematic interpretations can overlook. To this extent, neither argument nor example are intended to be in any way typical. On the other hand, an attempt has been made to readdress the more general problem of the functional value of witchcraft, by looking at a case where both accuser and accused offer their views on, first, the potency of magic and, secondly, the occasions on which such magic might have been used. Each of these areas of thought has an important implication for the long-term history of mentalities as a whole, and of witchcraft specifically. In the first place, participants in this drama demonstrate explicitly that they inhabit the same mental universe, a universe in which the boundary between the realms of the natural and supernatural was yet to be fixed. Secondly, it is possible to see that witchcraft accusations might be explained in terms of developing social and economic competition, without tying the dynamic to any particular aspect of this change. Together, these conclusions suggest that, until such time as developments in religious and scientific attitudes "disenchanted" the world, and mounting pressure of population against resources was relieved by more favourable economic conditions, overlap between the material and invisible worlds would continue to offer not only a means of explaining misfortune – as for Margaret Moore's accusers – but also a potential source of power with which the weak might seek to free themselves from the constraints of daily life and take control of their destinies.

Notes

1. There is no satisfactory account of this unique event. R. Deacon, *Matthew Hopkins: witch finder general* (London, 1976) has many failings, including an unawareness of the existence of the Ely records upon which this essay is based. M. Summers, *The discovery of witches. A study of Master Matthew Hopkins* (London, 1928), also skims over the Ely trials.

2. K. Thomas, *Religion and the decline of magic* (London, 1971; 1988 edn); A. Macfarlane, *Witchcraft in Tudor and Stuart England. A regional and comparative study* (London, 1970).

3. C. B. Herrup, *The common peace. Participation and the criminal law in seventeenth-century England* (Cambridge, 1987), p. 33.

4. J. A. Sharpe, Witchcraft and women in seventeenth-century England: some northern evidence, *Continuity and Change*, **6**, 1991, pp. 179–99. For a continental parallel, see L. Roper, Witchcraft and fantasy in early modern Germany, *History Workshop Journal*, **32**, 1991, pp. 19–43.

5. A. Gregory, Witchcraft, politics and "good neighbourhood" in early seventeenth-century Rye, *Past & Present*, **133**, 1991, pp. 31–66; M. Gaskill, Witchcraft in Tudor and Stuart Kent: stereotypes and the background to accusations, in *Witchcraft in early modern Europe: studies in culture and belief*, eds J. Barry, *et al.* (Cambridge, 1995).

6. For examples of witchcraft accusations connected to disputes over borders and land ownership in Yorkshire (1615), Sussex (1617), and Kent (1617), see J. A. Sharpe, *Witchcraft in seventeenth-century Yorkshire: accusations and counter measures*, Borthwick Papers, 81 (York, 1992), p. 9; Herrup, *Common peace*, p. 32; Kent RO, NR/JQ p1/30.

7. B. Ankarloo, Sweden: the mass burnings (1668–1676), in *Early modern European witchcraft. centres and peripheries*, eds B. Ankarloo & G. Henningsen (Oxford, 1990), pp. 310–12; G. R. Quaife, *Godly zeal and furious rage. The witch in early modern Europe* (London, 1987), p. 90; J. Favret-Saada, *Deadly words: witchcraft in the Bocage* (Cambridge, 1990), pp. 32, 104 and *passim*; D. Sabean, *Power in the blood. Popular culture and village discourse in early modern Germany* (Cambridge, 1984), pp. 56–8, 211; C. F. Karlsen, *The devil in the shape of a woman: witchcraft in colonial New England* (New York, 1987).

8. M. Murray, *The witch cult in western Europe* (Oxford, 1921).

9. Witch-hunts have even been portrayed as planned campaigns waged by a ruling class determined to enforce conformity. For a recent extreme recitation of this thesis, see J. Oplinger, *The politics of demonology. The European witchcraze and the mass production of deviance* (London & Toronto, 1990).

10. It should be remembered that, at the time of its publication, Murray's thesis was a refreshing antidote to the nineteenth-century "rationalist" view which utterly disregarded the belief aspect, preferring to see magic as nothing more than a symbol of ignorance and delusion. Cf. Thomas, *Religion and the decline of*

magic, p. 615.

11. E.g., H. Geertz, An anthropology of religion and magic, I, *Journal of Interdisciplinary History*, VI, 1975, pp. 71–89, esp. 72–7, quotation p. 84; T. G. Ashplant & A. Wilson, Present-centred history and the problem of historical knowledge, *Historical Journal*, **31**, 1988, pp. 257–60; C. Ginzburg, *Ecstasies. Deciphering the witches' sabbath* (London, 1990), pp. 3–6; C. Ginzburg, *The night battles. Witchcraft and agrarian cults in the sixteenth and seventeenth centuries* (Baltimore, 1983), see p. xiii for a partial resurrection of Murray. E. Le Roy Ladurie distinguishes between two historiographical models: the "archaic'" model of belief from below, and the "modern" model of witchcraft as a criminal practice defined by the state. Between the two, he argues, "an impoverishment is observable". *Jasmin's witch* (London, 1987), pp. 18–19.

12. Ashplant & Wilson, Present-centred history, pp. 253–74, quotation p. 260. See also E. P. Thompson, Anthropology and the discipline of historical context, *Midland History*, I (1972), pp. 41–55.

13. R. Darnton, *The great cat massacre and other episodes in French cultural history* (London, 1984), p. 13.

14. Useful on this this point are: L. Lévy-Bruhl, *The notebooks on primitive mentality* (London, 1975), p. 43; M. Foucault, *The order of things. An archaeology of the human sciences* (London, 1970), e.g., p. xv. On the other hand, past mentalities should not be artificially "defamiliarized". E. Muir, Introduction: observing trifles, in *Microhistory and the lost peoples of Europe*, eds E. Muir & G. Ruggiero (Baltimore, 1991), p. xiii.

15. Roper, Witchcraft and fantasy, pp. 21–2.

16. Some accounts are misleading on the question of the relationship between educated and popular witchcraft beliefs, for example, G. Scarre, *Witchcraft and magic in sixteenth- and seventeenth-century Europe*, (London, 1987), p. 48. The relationship is much more profitably explored in more dynamic terms, that is, beliefs demonstrated through actions. C. Holmes, Popular culture? Witches, magistrates and divines in early modern England, in *Understanding popular culture. Europe from the middle ages to the nineteenth century*, ed. S. L. Kaplan (Berlin, 1984), pp. 85–111. See also S. Clark, Protestant demonology: sin, superstition, and society (*c.* 1520–*c.* 1630), in Ankarloo & Henningsen (1990), p. 62.

17. See C. Larner, *Enemies of God: the witch-hunt in Scotland* (London, 1981); S. Clark, Inversion, misrule and and the meaning of witchcraft, *Past & Present*, **87** (1980), pp. 98–127.

18. Sharpe, *Witchcraft in seventeenth-century Yorkshire*, p. 8.

19. L. Stone, *The family, sex and marriage in England 1500–1800* (London, 1977), pp. 95, 98; Sabean, *Power in the blood*, pp. 31–2, 53–4; Gaskill, Witchcraft in Tudor and Stuart Kent, in J. Barry *et al.*, forthcoming.

20. See for example, C. Z. Wiener, Sex roles and crime in late Elizabethan Hertfordshire, *Journal of Social History*, **8**, 1975, pp. 46–9; D. E. Underdown, The taming of the scold: the enforcement of patriarchal authority in early modern

England, in *Order and disorder in early modern England*, eds A. Fletcher & J. Stevenson (Cambridge, 1985), pp. 116–36; J. A. Sharpe, *Defamation and sexual slander in early modern England: the church courts at York*, Borthwick Papers, 58 (York, 1980).

21. N. Z. Davis, *Fiction in the archives. Pardon tales and their tellers in sixteenth-century France* (Stanford, 1987).

22. The following profile, and subsequent discussion, is based on a deposition to be found in the assize files of the Ely Diocesan Records, E12 1647/14, in the Cambridge University Library [Camb UL]. An imperfect transcript is to be found in *East Anglian notes and queries*, XIII (1909), pp. 277–8.

23. *Victoria County History, Cambridgeshire* [*VCH*], IV, p. 159. An approximate estimate of the size of the parish in the first half of the seventeenth century can be made from a church seating plan, made in 1614 after a pew-dispute, which names 329 inhabitants: Camb UL, EDR, B/2/35, ff. 207–10v.

24. In 1673 a Robert Moore of Sutton made a will, in which he was styled "yeoman" and bequeathed several acres of copyhold land. There was, however, more than one man of this name in Sutton. See Cambs RO, Ely Consistory Wills, C32, ff. 219v.–20; P148/1/2 (21/4/1639, 22/1/1643).

25. The parish register of Sutton indicates that on 10 May 1641, Robert Moore married Margaret Holland. This name cannot be found elsewhere in the Sutton register, but there was a Holland family in nearby Stretham, to whom a daughter, Margaret, was born 17 July 1586. This is probably too early to be Moore, but it is interesting that the the verso of the 1647 deposition gives her parish as Stretham rather than Sutton. Cambs RO, P148/1/2 (Sutton, 1621–54); Transcript of Stretham parish register, p. 10. Camb UL, EDR, E12 1647/12.

26. J. Stearne, *A confirmation and discovery of witchcraft* (London, 1648), p. 21.

27. Cambs RO, Ely Consistory Court Wills, Thomas Nyx, (19 Feb. 1636/7). A suspect examined soon after Moore, Adam Sabie of Haddenham, specified that he was last visited by a spirit in 1636. Camb UL, EDR, E12 1647/17v. Also in 1636 a Sutton couple, later charged with witchcraft, were accused for the first time of the murder of their son (see p. 135). If events did take place then, it would mean that Moore's children came from an earlier marriage, given that she married Robert Moore in 1641.

28. According to one source, the trial took place at Ely on Wednesday 22 September 1647, where 17 cases were heard, 13 of which concerned witchcraft (eight women, five men). See *East Anglian notes and queries*, p. 277.

29. Stearne, *Confirmation and discovery of witchcraft*, p. 22.

30. There is no evidence that Stearne personally supervised any part of Moore's examination, but other depositions indicate that he was nearby at the time. Hopkins himself probably oversaw the Ely campaign from outside the county after the spring of 1646. Deacon, *Matthew Hopkins*, pp. 173–4; Summers, *Discovery of witches*, p. 45.

31. Robert Ellis of Stretham (30 May 1647), and Adam Sabie of Haddenham (1 June 1647). Camb UL, EDR, E12 1647/17-18.

32. Castell was assisted in the committals of 26 May by John Towers JP, who also lived at Haddenham.

33. A gaol calendar from September 1647 survives. In order of committal, the nine suspects were: Bridget Bonham, John Bonham, William Watson, Margaret Moore, Robert Ellis, Thomasine Reade, Elizabeth Foote, Adam Sabie and Joan Salter. (Between July and September another three suspected witches from Ely and Wisbech were committed), Camb UL, EDR, E12 1647/23. The other two Witchford suspects for whom depositions survive, but no entry in the gaol calendar, were Dorothy Ellis of Stretham and Joan Briggs of Haddenham, EDR, E12 1647/10, 15.

34. Camb UL, EDR, E12 1647/23.

35. The practice of witch-hunting in England, from above as it were, was rare, and here was probably only facilitated by the Civil War. The clergyman, John Gaule, who criticized Hopkins, wrote that witch-hunting was "a trade never taken up in England till this". However, Hopkins claimed that he never entered a village unless it was by invitation, and indeed, Gaule lamented that the people of the countryside admired "the infallible and wonderfull power of the Witchfinders". Macfarlane argues that, since they did not always appear as witnesses, witchfinding depended on widespread support, but Deacon denies that "persons other than Hopkins in any way encouraged or influenced this campaign against witches". J. Gaule, *Select cases of conscience touching witches and witchcrafts* (London, 1646), pp. 6, 93; M. Hopkins, *The discovery of witches* (London, 1647), p. 10; Thomas *Religion and the decline of magic*, pp. 544–5; Macfarlane, *Witchcraft*, ch. 9, esp. pp. 137–8, 140–41; Deacon, *Matthew Hopkins*, p. 87.

36. *VCH*, IV, pp. 159, 161; H. C. Darby, *The draining of the fens*, (Cambridge, second edn 1956), pp. 49–64; K. Lindley, *Fenland riots and the English revolution* (London, 1982), pp. 40, 60, 64, 142–3; C. Holmes, Drainers and fenmen: the problem of popular political consciousness in the seventeenth century, in Fletcher & Stevenson (1985), p. 194; Camb UL, Palmer Papers, B/70 (transcript of Chancery proceedings, 1622–3); House of Lords RO, Main Papers [1649]. Petition of divers poor inhabitants of the parish of Sutton. For a summary of the 1649 petition, see Historical Manuscripts Commission, *Seventh Report, Part I* (London, 1879), p. 75.

37. Lindley, *Fenland riots and the English revolution*, p. 142 and *passim*.

38. However, the evidence for this which does exist is tantalizing, see Deacon, *Matthew Hopkins*, pp. 14–15, 106–8, 164–5, 180–91, 196–7. Religion may also have been significant. Sutton was noted for its nonconformity and clerical absenteeism, and contained several Quaker households. *VCH*, IV, p. 159. For evidence of clerical shortcomings at Sutton in 1638, see also W. M. Palmer, *Episcopal visitation returns for Cambridgeshire . . . 1638–1665* (Cambridge,

1930), pp. 53–4. It is noteworthy that in one month in 1633 no less than 26 presentations for falling asleep during divine service were made. M. Cross, *The church and local society in the diocese of Ely, c. 1630–c. 1730*, PhD thesis, University of Cambridge, 1991, p. 63.

39. Camb UL, EDR, E12 1647/14. None of the three children were found in the parish register under the name of Moore, suggesting either Civil War under-registration, that they died before they could be christened or that they were christened elsewhere.

40. Camb UL, EDR, E12 1647/14v.

41. On confessions extracted by Hopkins and others, see Thomas, *Religion and the decline of magic*, pp. 617–20. Macfarlane asserts that one should not discount the effectiveness of "indirect pressures" for eliciting confession: subtle persuasion, intimidation, threats and promises, directed at the suspect by neighbours, clergy and magistrates. Macfarlane, *Witchcraft*, p. 20.

42. Gaule, *Select cases of conscience*, p. 78.

43. Hopkins, *Discovery of witches*, pp. 5, 7.

44. See, for example, A. Koestler, *Darkness at noon* (London, 1940).

45. Both Bonham and Watson appeared among the list of poor petitioners in the 1620s, cf. Camb UL, Palmer Papers, B/70.

46. Camb UL, EDR, E9/1/20 (1636); E45 Quarter Sessions Files, 1662 (unnumbered); E42 Fragments (unnumbered). Evidently, the Bonhams were acquitted of witchcraft in 1647.

47. Roper makes the point that, in spite of the stereotyped form of confessions, witches added their own personal inflections, and constructed their own narratives; Witchcraft and fantasy, pp. 24–6. For a historian who is more pessimistic – where judicial sources are concerned – of the ability to "unsnarl ordinary beliefs from the manipulative processes in which they were embedded", see R. C. Sawyer, "Strangely Handled In All Her Lyms": witchcraft and healing in Jacobean England, *Journal of Social History*, **22** (1989), pp. 462–3.

48. B. P. Levack, *The witch-hunt in early modern Europe* (London, 1987), pp. 13, 16.

49. E. Lemert, *Human deviance. Social problems and social control* (New Jersey, 1972), ch. 3. See also R. Muchembled, *Les derniers bûchers* (Paris, 1981), cited by Ladurie, who writes of the confessional witch: "At first, she is unaware of the character attributed to her. She does not notice that she is maleficent. Then, gradually, she yields to this circumstance". *Jasmin's witch*, p. 18.

50. The emotionally charged issue of the lives of children could provide the key to other accusations in 1647; one of the Haddenham witches confessed that although she agreed to signing a pact with the Devil, she refused to surrender the life of her child. Camb UL, EDR, E12 1647/11v. (T. Read, Haddenham, 29 May 1647). In the early seventeenth century a high proportion of the cases of "disturbing grief" encountered by the physician Richard Napier were bereaved mothers; see M. MacDonald, *Mystical bedlam. Madness, anxiety, and healing in seventeenth-century England* (Cambridge, 1981), p. 82.

51. W. D. Rees, The hallucinations of widowhood, *British Medical Journal*, **4**, 1971, pp. 37–41; E. Parish, *Hallucinations and illusions. A study of the fallacies of perception* (London, 1897), p. 36; W. F. Matchett, Repeated hallucinatory experiences as a part of the mourning process among Hopi Indian women, *Psychiatry*, **35**, 1971, pp. 185–94. See also J. Wertheimer, Some hypotheses about the genesis of visual hallucinations in dementia, in *Delusions and hallucinations in old age*, eds C. Katona & R. Levy (London, 1992), pp. 201–208, esp. p. 207, where it is stated that visions of the bereaved manifest "the hallucinatory realization of the desire to rediscover the departed, and fantasized ambiguity of the absent presence".

52. E. R. Dodds, *The Greeks and the irrational* (Berkeley, 1951), pp. 103–4, 116–17.

53. On the difficulty of separating universal and specific components of mentalities, see G. E. R. Lloyd, *Demystifying mentalities* (Cambridge, 1990), pp. 135–6.

54. For a seventeenth-century ballad where, in different circumstances, starving children calling for food and drink haunt the dreams of the woman responsible for their death, see *The midwife's maid's lamentation, in Newgate* (London, 1693), in *The Pepys ballads*, 8 vols, ed. H. E. Rollins (Cambridge, MA, 1929–32), **VII**, pp. 14–16.

55. Thomas, *Religion and the decline of magic*, pp. 151–3, 176, 286, 768–9; A. Macfarlane, *The family life of Ralph Josselin, a seventeenth-century clergyman* (Cambridge, 1970), p. 183*n*; H. J. Rose, *Primitive culture in Greece* (London, 1925), pp. 151–2. The ancient Greeks did not speak of "having" dreams, but of "seeing" them. Dodds, *Greeks and the irrational*, p. 105. Visions in early modern England were also described as waking dreams: in the 1680s Francis North explained the confessions by witches in these terms. R. North, *The lives of the Norths*, ed. A. Jessopp, 3 vols (London, 1890), **III**, p. 152. On the symbolic meaning of dreams, see Macfarlane, *Family life of Ralph Josselin*, ch. 12; P. Burke, L'histoire sociale des rêves, *Annales Economies, Societés, Civilisations*, **2** (1973), pp. 329–42.

56. E. E. Evans-Pritchard, *Witchcraft, oracles and magic among the Azande*, abridged edn (Oxford, 1976), p. 230.

57. For some sixteenth-century examples of this, see C. L'Estrange Ewen, *Witchcraft and demonianism* (London, 1933), pp. 70, 75–6.

58. Ginzburg, *Night battles*; Ladurie, *Jasmin's witch*, pp. 50, 60. See also G. Henningsen, *The witches' advocate: Basque witchcraft and the Spanish Inquisition (1609–1619)* (Nevada, 1980), which describes the dream aspect of sorcery and counter-sorcery in the Basque country in the early seventeenth century. On witchcraft fantasies, dreams and confessions, see Levack, *Witch-hunt*, pp. 16–18.

59. Macfarlane writes of "reciprocity": associations of thought and event which "worked across the artificial boundaries demarcating the social, physical and spiritual worlds". *Family life of Ralph Josselin*, p. 195.

60. Dodds, *Greeks and the irrational*, p. 102.

61. D. H. Lawrence once wrote: "When anything threatens us from the world of death, then a dream may become so vivid that it arouses the actual soul. And when a dream is so intense that it arouses the soul – then we must attend to it". *Fantasia of the unconscious* (London, 1923; Penguin edn, 1971), p. 165.

62. In 1632 an Essex woman was presented before the archdeacon's court for wishing herself to be a witch so as to be revenged on a neighbour with whom she had previously fought in the street. Macfarlane, *Witchcraft*, p. 286.

63. For a seventeenth-century broadside ballad which describes the power fantasy of a poor man and his subsequent temptation by the Devil, see *The Roxburghe Ballads*, 8 vols eds W. Chappell & J. W. Ebsworth (London & Hertford, 1871–95), II, pp. 222–8. See also *A true relation of the most inhumane and bloody murther* (London, 1609). In 1655 Essex clergyman Ralph Josselin noted that an acquaintance had claimed to have signed a diabolical pact to satisfy his craving for money. A. Macfarlane (ed.), *The diary of Ralph Josselin 1661–1683* (Oxford, 1976), p. 347. A similar tale was related by Lawrence Southerne in *Fearefull newes from Coventry, or, a true relation and lamentable story of one Thomas Holt . . . who through covetousnesse and immoderate love of money, sold himselfe to the devill* (London, 1642).

64. On this theme generally, see Thomas, *Religion and the decline of magic*, pp. 564–5. In one late sixteenth-century trial, a witch was reputed to have refused to renounce her allegience to the Devil, because he had served her well for the past 30 years. H. More, *An antidote against atheisme* (London, 1653), p. 111.

65. BL, Add. MS 36,674, f. 196.

66. For a fuller discussion of the place of the Devil in these trials, see J. A. Sharpe, The devil in East Anglia: the Matthew Hopkins trials reconsidered, in J. Barry *et al.*

67. Camb UL, EDR, E12 1647/17v.

68. BL, Add. MS 27,402, ff. 108v., 120. For other examples and a discussion of poverty as a motivation for witchcraft, see Thomas, *Religion and the decline of magic*, pp. 620–24.

69. The 1649 petition suggests that this was a time of high mortality, unemployment, and poverty in Sutton, and called for redress for its inhabitants "soe they may not all perish by famine in time of plentie as many allreddie doe". House of Lords RO, Main Papers [1649]. Petition of divers poor inhabitants of . . . Sutton.

70. J. C. Scott, *Domination and the arts of resistance. Hidden transcripts* (Yale, 1990), pp. 36–44.

71. In the 1660s a poor Lancashire woman confessed to having been a witch since her mother died 30 years earlier. The mother had nothing to bequeath, and so left her daughters a pair of familiars. T. Heywood (ed.), *The Moore Rental*, Chetham Society, Old Series, II (1847), pp. 59–60.

Chapter Seven

Negotiating for blood money: war widows and the courts in seventeenth-century England

Geoffrey L. Hudson

"Death makes me poore"[1]

English war widows received state pensions in the mid-seventeenth century. This was not to happen again for over 200 years.[2] Stipends were granted to thousands of war widows by the central government between the mid-1640s and 1660, and by county justices in sessions for approximately 30 years from the late 1640s. Historians have ignored this aspect of the history of English women, men and the state. Thus a recent mention of the existence of petitions to quarter sessions during the mid-1600s that "tell harrowing stories of men crippled" in military conflict ignores the numerous petitions from war widows that tell a different story.[3] This chapter endeavours to remedy such oversights by focusing on the tactics used by war widows to secure county pensions.

It will also add an important dimension to our understanding of gender relations outside the domestic sphere in the mid-seventeenth century. Keith Thomas, Patricia Higgins, Antonia Fraser and others have explored the expansion of women's fields of activity during and after the civil wars,[4] and we know that as well as being prominent in the new religious sects, women were active in the physical conflict. They served as couriers, soldiers and spies; formed committees to raise troops; worked on fortifications; and nursed. Women also petitioned parliament for peace in the early 1640s and later, as levellers, for the release of prisoners. In addition, wives of royalists dealt with the new regime's officialdom when they had to petition the Committee for Compounding.[5]

In an article on women and war in Ireland during the 1640s, Mary O'Dowd has tried to correct the impression of optimism left by earlier historians and argued that it is "misleading to suggest that the war was overall a positive experience for women allowing them participation in public affairs". Instead, "there is overwhelming evidence to suggest that for the majority of women, the war was a miserable and often harrowing experience . . . regardless of their class or economic background".[6] O'Dowd maintains that the experience of women with the land settlement legislation was far from satisfactory. Those women who "lacked access to the appropriate male networks" were "powerless in practice" and did not have "their claims and rights to property confirmed".[7] My examination of the relief of war widows in England, rather than Ireland, suggests a very different experience.

In practice both the provision for war widows, and women's response to it, represent a shift in the gender based discrimination with regard to the poor. The award of state benefits for war widows put these women into a special category of the impoverished previously occupied only by men. Maimed ex-servicemen and now, for the first time, war widows merited relief for their contribution to the state, whereas the rest of the poor merely needed assistance. State provision for women as war widows was indeed a recognition of their participation in the political nation during horrific civil war.

This is not to deny that the army/state that tried to rule England from the late 1640s until the Restoration adopted such provision for hard-nosed military and political purposes. Men and women *were* being manipulated to accept civil war and the new regime. Rather, it is to argue that such an explanation alone is too simple. Algernon Sidney – the republican and intellectual enemy of Robert Filmer's ideas on patriarchy and the divine right of kings – neatly summarized the combination of reasons why he and his fellows thought war widows should be given state pensions. In a letter of recommendation for the widow of one of his men to the Kent bench he maintained that "I doubt not [that a pension grant] will appeare to be not only an acte of *Justice* & mercy, but an encouragement to others to adventure their lives for the State in hope of the like reliefe for theirs".[8] Not all those who supported the provision of state pensions for war widows offered the same purely secular arguments as Sidney. In February 1652/3 Richard Deane, the regicide and close associate of Cromwell, wrote to Sir Henry Vane, an Admiralty Commissioner, to recommend an order of parliament for navy war widows (pensions to be paid on a monthly basis by the treasurer of the navy). He began his letter by commenting that "I know your affection to the poore widdowes of the seamen now slaine as to procureing them comfortable maintenance" but went on to suggest that other business might very well prevent prompt action. This would be unacceptable, Deane argued. In the past the state's sailors had, by their deaths, been "instrumentally serviceable in obteyning our liberty & securing our Lives" and, moreover, in the last "engagement the Lord put a spirit of Courage into your men & that the victory is purchased with the blood of those who were precious in the eies of the Lord". The implication: to deny the war widows was to deny God.[9]

Sidney was not an extreme proponent of women gaining state pensions as war widows. This belief soon came to exist at the heart of the new regime – as Cromwell came to secure power. In a letter to five recently widowed Cheshire women in mid-1651 a Captain Hugh Bertles asked that they petition the Cheshire authorities for pensions (and encouraged them to inform other war widows to do likewise). He maintained that

> the Lord General Cromwell hath taken into consideracion the sad condiscion of all such as have lost their husbands in the service in Scotland . . . and hath sent unto the deputie Lieutenants that there shall be allowed out of the treasurie such meanes as hath bene allowed to others which are in the same condission.[10]

Cromwell's concern with the relief of war widows is further illustrated by his personal interventions on behalf of individuals. One such example is the case of Hannah Smith. Smith's husband had not died in actual conflict, which made her application to the Commission for Sick and Wounded in the mid-1650s problematic. Cromwell subscribed her petition with the comment that "it is all one as if the petitioner's husband had been killed by a shot from the enemy, as to have his brains beaten out with the anchor". He continued: "I think that in *equity* the relict of the person so killed . . . should be considered of as the widow of one slain in the fight".[11]

II

Women's words and actions show that a knowledge of entitlement existed among war widows. Katherine Legg of Taunton petitioned the Somerset bench in the 1650s. She argued that despite having received a £3 gratuity she had as yet "neuer receaued any recompence" for the loss of her husband in the state's service. She wanted a pension.[12] Others were equally forthright. Margaret Pemberton in her petition for a stipend complained that she "hath not as yet receaued any releefe for the losse of her husbands life". In mid–1651 a Cheshire war widow applied for the reinstatement of her pension demanding "that shee may not loose her dear husband & pension too".

Some widows applied both on the basis of the death of their husbands in the military and on their own service. In her petition to the Cheshire bench Margaret Knowlesley maintained that

> your petitioner hath been true and faithfull for the Comon Wealthes good not onely against the Enimye att the Seige att Namptwich and ventured her life in her iorney to Wervin [St. Oswald, Chester] to prevent the betrayinge of that by the Kings partye and alsoe att Litchefeild and Stafford and other places.[13]

In another example an Alice Stannard – a royalist – petitioned the Privy Council in 1670 for help in obtaining a pension in Hampshire maintaining that she "was a great sufferer for her Loyalty, being imprisoned for the space of twelue Moneths & lay in Irons all that time, & afterwards was arraigned & tryed for her Life".[14]

In Cheshire a significant minority of war widows – 11 of 67 (16.5 per cent) – with surviving petitions who requested county funds prior to the Restoration, cited the law and/or the precedent created by other pension-holding war widows in their arguments for relief. These women indeed demonstrated a notion of entitlement. One commented that other war widows had been granted pensions "which your petitioner wants [i.e. lacks] though equally necessitated with them". A number of Cheshire war widows contrasted their favourable legal right to relief with the unwelcome alternative of common charity. In doing so they demonstrated their belief that a war widow pension was not charity. Alice Webster declared that she would likely "bee cast upon the charity of the people" unless she was granted a pension according to the "Intencon & pleasure of Parliament declared for releife of distressed widdowes & orphans". Others also commented on the undesirable nature of charity. One maintained that "wee now live in the worst of tymes Charity being growne soe extreame cold", while another commented that to lose her pension would make her "an obiect of charity & consequently of distress & misery".[15] These opinions may have been influenced by the problem of partisanship. This problem was hinted at by the Lancashire neighbour of a serviceman's wife in his letter of support to her application to the bench for assistance. He declared that she could not get parish relief although "trulie this womans [cause] is palpable & cries out for speedie Releife at least her twoo yongest children", and pleaded that "if you can doo any thing help them/for them poore that favor the armie haue few helpers".[16] Widows of royalists also experienced the problem of partisanship before the Restoration. Grace Batishill petitioned the Devon bench for a stipend in 1662. As her husband had been hanged for his service to Charles I she had never received any public funds, only charity. She argued, therefore, that she had been treated "contrary to law, equitie and good sconcyence" [sic].[17]

That many women felt entitled to pensions as war widows is clear. There is also evidence that a sense of entitlement to state assistance existed among women applying for their husband's arrears of pay, county sequestration funds and the king's Bounty created after the Restoration. Writing from London to the Cheshire County Committee in 1648 (where she was petitioning parliament for her husband's arrears) one war widow commented that

> though I have binn in hoops every day to be disspact yet such is the hardnes of the harts of men that nothing is brought to perfection as yet[,] but as soone as it shall please god to put an end to this miserable bondage and that i may have this monny which I have so deerely bought I intend . . . to return againe. Wherfore gentel men [I] in treate you that you will consider my distresed condistion and the gret lose that I had with you and the great charg [of children] upon my hand and nothing to support them but what was bought with the blood of my deere husban[18]

Two and a half decades later this argument was repeated by an applicant to the Bounty. The petitioner declared that state relief was owed her for her "husbands life", being "the price of Blood . . . spilt in war".[19]

III

Before outlining war widows' tactics it is necessary to discuss briefly law and practice. The common soldiers and their representatives, the agitators, pressured parliament in 1647 to pass ordinances to provide relief for war widows and orphans as well as maimed ex-servicemen.[20] These laws resurrected the 1593 county pension scheme for maimed soldiers that had been in abeyance in most counties since 1642. The legislation also provided for large increases in the parochial taxation that funded the scheme, and expanded the criteria for eligibility. Under the new scheme it was necessary for a woman to prove that her deceased husband had fought for parliament, and that she was in poverty because of the death of her husband.[21] The 1662 Act, in its provisions for widows, was almost identical to the legislation of 1647. The major difference was that applicants had to prove their husbands' loyal service to the king in order to be entitled to relief.[22] When in 1679 the 1662 legislation lapsed, so too did women's entitlement to relief from the county scheme. However, despite the law, some widows managed to remain on the county pension lists after 1679. In Shropshire, for example, Jean White received a stipend prior to mid-1666 that was paid until Easter 1700 (although her pension was reduced from 50s to 30s per annum in 1679).[23]

The central government's fund for the victims of war, operating until 1660, provided pensions for men and women. By 1659 there were over 2500 maimed soldier and 4000 widow and orphan pensioners.[24] The county scheme, however, stipulated that war widows and their children were only entitled to claim monies that were surplus after maimed soldiers had been paid their stipends. Parishes were required to hold war widows in special regard. In practice, war widows were paid pensions in relatively large numbers in many jurisdictions prior to 1660. The Restoration brought a dramatic change. Outside of London women were rarely granted stipends and had to settle for gratuities. In at least two counties this change occurred soon after the Restoration. Warwickshire and Shropshire eliminated all women from their county pension lists in Michaelmas 1660 and July 1661 respectively. In most other localities the change seems to have followed the 1662 Act that was quoted in extenso in many order books (unlike the identical provisions of the 1647 ordinances) thus making the inferior legal position of war widows explicit. In 1663, for example, Norfolk ordered that soldiers granted pensions between Easter 1642 and Easter 1660, and all war widows were to be barred from stipends in the future.[25] This change seems to reflect the attitudes of the royalists to women and the armed forces – both were to be returned to firm control (the army to the king, and the war widows to their parish officers).[26]

Royalist theoreticians made an analogy between the family and state which supported an authoritarian-absolutist notion of monarchy. In this analogy the relationship between husband and wife was as indissoluble and strictly hierarchical as that between king and subjects – no resistance to the man's authority being permitted. In a Ford lecture entitled "The man in the moon: levelling, gender, and popular politics, 1646–1660" (21 February 1992, Oxford University), David Underdown outlined the popular royalist attack on the new regime in the late 1640s. An important part of the royalist critique was a charge that the influence of women was excessive and that, therefore, the government was weak and illegitimate. Royalists seem to have been reluctant to break with the tradition (established in the period 1593–1642) of granting war widows parish relief. They were unwilling to accord women the same status as maimed soldiers and grant them state military pensions. It is quite possible that the often aggressive tactics adopted by widows in the period 1647–60 (discussed below) convinced many royalists that in practice women should not be granted equal status with men in this area of political life. The change after the Restoration also mirrored the difference between the two sides in the period 1642–6. Whereas parliament promised in October 1642 to care for all its widows (and attempted to fulfil its commitment) the king only proclaimed his intention to care for his disabled ex-servicemen and failed conspicuously to announce any plans to care for royalist widows.[27]

Table 7.1 provides information extracted from a number of treasurers' accounts. I have given the typical range in the numbers of widows who managed to obtain pensions from local authorities. What I would like to highlight is that, proportionally, war widows received an equitable share of the monies spent by a given county. The reasons for the difference between local authorities are not readily apparent. It could reflect varying levels of participation by women during the civil wars. It may be no coincidence, for example, that Nottinghamshire paid many women pensions when pro-parliament women were active during the conflict. They patrolled Nottingham in groups of 50 for at least two weeks after an enemy retreat

Table 7.1   Treasurers' accounts.[28]

North Cheshire (3 of 7 Hundreds) April 1651	Worcester Co. 1653–5	Notts Co. Jan. 1654/5	Wilts 1660 (pre-Rest.)	City of London 1671/2
Number of widow pensioners				
32	5	24	6	89
(47% of total no. of pensioners)	(12%)	(63%)	(19%)	(62%)
Amount expended on widows' pensions				
£49 11s	£12 12s	£47	£29 6s 8d	£203 10s
(47% of expenditure)	(13%)	(64%)	(24%)	(62%)
Average pension level for widows				
£1 11s per year	£2 10s 5d	£1 19s 2d	£4 17s 9d	£2 5s 9d

during the wars in order to discover royalist arsonists.[29]

War widows made their applications to quarter sessions on the basis that husbands had died either while in service or later because of wounds. Poverty, the inability to maintain herself sufficiently, and children to support were all cited. If a husband had been hanged by the enemy or butchered in a massacre this was emphasized.

One major difference between mens' and womens' petitions was that women very rarely mentioned their occupation but instead were more likely to mention their children, and how many and whether they were small (one county defined small as aged under seven).[30] War widowhood meant that a woman became a widow earlier than usual. She was more likely to be left with more and younger children.[31] Table 7.2 gives an overview of the citation of children by Cheshire applicants for county military funds.

Table 7.2 Children and Cheshire ex-servicemen and war widows, 1647–60 (from petition evidence).[32]

	War widows	Ex-servicemen
No mention of children in petition	13	58
One child	14 (7 widows declared their children to be small)	1 (0 cited as small)
Two or more children	42 (25 cited children as small)	29 (12 cited as small)

Of the Cheshire women cited in Table 7.2, 51 specified the exact number of children they had. These war widows claimed to have 128 children among them (mean average of 2.5 per woman). Of these children 95 (74 per cent) were declared to be small. Justices discriminated among applicants on the basis of need, and the number of children – the size of the woman's charge in contemporary language – was an important factor in her favour.[33] Printed letters of recommendation provided by the central government treasurers, for example, did not have a space for indicating whether an ex-serviceman had a family but did provide a place to indicate how many children – orphans – a war widow had.[34] Applicants with more than one child were either more or as likely to be successful than those with one child (and were certainly more successful than those who did not declare if they had any children). The rich Cheshire records tend to confirm one of Barbara Todd's conclusions in her thesis on widowhood: those having two or more children were regarded as needing relief as they were forced by circumstances to be full-time mothers.[35] Todd also argued that "regular relief provided poor widows with an effective alternative to matrimony". Whatever the case regarding parish relief, in the implementation of the war widow pension scheme there is almost no evidence that widows were taken off the pension lists for remarriage. Of course, county justices were not as likely as parish officers to know if a given widow had married again. Thus, although the Yorkshire north riding justices announced in 1659 that widows who remarried would lose their pensions, the JPs could not easily enforce this extra-statutory measure.[36]

Since the petitions from war widows seldom mention their occupation or that of their deceased husbands, it is not possible to make the same analysis of social status that can be achieved for maimed soldiers. Records of a few war widows who applied for relief reveal that some had been relatively well off before the conflict. Ann Platt, for example, was the widow of a royalist officer. She maintained that her husband, a captain,

> was slaine in his late Majesties service at Newbury in the head of a Troop of his owne raising, for the doing of which hee sold your petitioners Jewells and all his personall estate which would now have bin a subsistence to her promising her to settle an estate of 600[li] a yeare upon her (which hee was heire to,) when things were composed. But being prevented of making that setlement by his said untimely death, your petitioner has bin ever since exposed to great hardships for a living.

Her story was certified as true by others and she was granted a city of London pension after the Restoration.[37] There is nothing to indicate, however, that the social composition of war widows was markedly different from that of the ex-servicemen who applied for pensions; few were from élite backgrounds. We know the status of 159 of the 677 male applicants to the Devon bench from 1660–90 (23.5 per cent). The breakdown for the men was as follows: gentry/yeomen, 6 (3.8 per cent); trades/crafts, 68 (42.8 per cent); mariners, 20 (12.5 per cent); husbandmen, 44 (27.7 per cent); professional soldiers, 3 (1.9 per cent); unskilled labourers, 18 (11.3 per cent). The figures for Dorset are similar.[38]

War widows had to find ways to survive apart from applying for a county pension. The variety of subsistence strategies utilized by these women is indicated by the petitions from 33 war widows who applied for relief to the Cheshire bench from 1647 to 1666. These women provided a total of 43 explanations for how they maintained themselves prior to their petition. The stories told most often were of help from neighbours, friends and family, as well as their own labour (Table 7.3). Examples of the former include neighbours lodging a widow, a grandfather caring for a widow's son, and the financial support of a recently deceased mother.[39] Work included "hand labor in knitting one paire of mens stockings a weeke" and the sale of ale.[40]

Table 7.3   Tales of subsistence (Cheshire war widows, 1647–66).[41]

20	supported by family, friends and/or neighbours
14	worked
5	sold belongings/consumed estate
2	parish relief recently terminated
1	central government pension since ceased
1	obtained credit

Several war widows applied to build cottages on the waste, thereby taking advantage of the Cheshire justices relatively liberal implementation of the 1589 statute governing such matters after the civil wars.[42]

Many others obtained parish pensions. Quarter sessions materials from Cheshire and the other counties reveal that war widows applied for assistance to the bench in their quest for parochial relief, or were referred to parish authorities for pensions by county justices. Paul Slack has shown that there was a large increase in the numbers of pensioners in several jurisdictions in the late 1640s and early 1650s. It is very likely that many of these new parish pensioners would have been some of the thousands of women recently widowed by the civil wars (especially since men rarely accounted for more than one third of parish dole recipients).[43] Some places were more affected than others. In Cheshire the Nantwich parish officers and 40 other substantial inhabitants petitioned the bench at Easter 1648 complaining of the large numbers of poor people receiving relief. In particular they commented that

> by reasons of the late warres and duringe [the] seige and Garrisson there divers stranger and souldiers have married wives there and begotten children and have since left that Towne or byn slayne in the warres and have left theyre wives and children to the Charge of the parish.

Similarly, when the parish officers responsible for Lower Wapping in the parish of Stepney petitioned the Middlesex bench in August 1676 for financial assistance they cited the effects of "the seuerall late Warrs" which "have and still doe unavoidably cause many widdowes and orphans to become chargeable to the said hamlett and parish."[44]

For some war widows, however, partisanship and other problems caused refusal of parish pensions as well as county stipends. Elizabeth Harrison applied for a county pension in 1661. In her petition she declared that she was refused local relief prior to the Restoration because her husband had fought for the king. With young children to care for she had been forced to sell her clothes and other personal possessions and "went abegging . . . for releife in the Cuntrey".[45] Others who had been unable to procure relief were forced to take even more desperate measures. A widow Appleton, of Black Jack Lane in Wapping, was driven by her poverty to take her two small daughters to Whitehall, the seat of government, in late 1653 and abandon them there. Her husband, a trumpeter, had been killed two years earlier in service. The council of state saw fit to relieve the orphans initially. Eventually the parish was ordered to maintain them.[46]

The war widow's petition, like that of the maimed soldier, was almost always written by someone else. Drawers of petitions whom I have identified include parish clerks and military commanders.[47] It is likely that many petitions were composed by scriveners, sessions' clerks, vicars, schoolmasters and servants of supportive gentry (as in the case of ex-servicemen). Such documents must be treated very carefully. They were written in a formulaic manner to say what the justices wanted to hear. And they were written for the purpose of obtaining an important material reward. As with the sixteenth century pardon petitions examined by Natalie Zemon Davis, war widows' petitions were a form of fiction. That said, it is also necessary to avoid total cynicism – just as with Davis' pardon seekers there is overwhelming evidence that war widows had to appear in court to petition.[48] In Cheshire, for example, written petitions were subscribed "absent" and not considered if the woman failed to present herself at quarter sessions. They would be expected to confirm their story in their own words. Women also needed on occasions to garner support from others. The petitions thus had to stand up to some scrutiny and must have been based on the women's own stories.

It would also be a mistake to view these widows as passive recipients of male patronage. They were purchasing their petitions and there is evidence of their activity in soliciting letters of recommendation. When Margaret

Pervin applied for a pension increase at the Trinity sessions of the Cheshire bench she presented a supporting letter from her parish written in response to "the ernest request" of the widow.[49]

IV

One tactic commonly employed by war widows was persistence or, as contemporaries more accurately called it, importunity – burdensome, troublesome pertinacity in solicitation. This took several forms. Generally, women were prepared to press their demands. In Cheshire 27 of the 92 (29 per cent) war widows who are recorded as having applied for county funds between 1647 and 1660 returned to sessions on at least one occasion to petition again.[50] More specifically, war widows demonstrated their importunity by their tendency to return to sessions, sometimes several times, after having been granted a gratuity, in order to ask for additional one-off payments or a pension. In Devon prior to 1660, 40 per cent of the 65 recorded parliamentary war widows returned to court; and, of these, three-quarters (29) came back on at least one more occasion and were successful in obtaining relief. Importunity was hard work. A Cheshire widow, Margaret Pratchet, petitioned the bench in the mid-1650s for a pension, or the arrears due for her efforts in caring for wounded ex-servicemen in her home. She commented she had "taken great paynes and spente much money about gettinge her arreers, haueinge beene 7 tymes at [the] Chester [sessions], twice at Knuttesford, and once at Middlewich and all on foote about this business".[51]

In many counties there are examples of women returning to sessions to apply for relief after previously accepting one-off payments on the understanding that they would not trouble the court for money in the future. A large number of war widows in West Kent returned to sessions regularly from 1663 to 1672 to solicit gratuities. In 1670 the justices ordered that the gratuities were not to be repeated. Despite this order 11 of the 15 told not to return did so (and nine of these managed to obtain two more one-offs each). The record for success in defying such orders goes to Katherine Truron of Tavistock, Devon. After the Restoration she received five gratuities. She agreed not to return to court each and every time.[52]

Importunity as a tactic was meant to improve a woman's chances in competition with other war widows and maimed men for limited resources. In this competition war widows used other tactics as well. They were careful to watch for, and act upon, pension vacancies. A pension usually became available upon the death of a pension holder. The obituaries were (figuratively speaking) scanned intently. Applying for a pension from the City of London in May of 1673, Alice Lunn asked to be admitted in the place of Jane Chambers, another pensioner, "who lately dyed at your petitioner['s] howse poore & not able to pay her rent . . ." In the same year Katherine Wild, "being credibly informed that Ellinor Ellis who was lately one of the pentoners of this City is now dead", applied to replace her. Both of these London women were successful.[53] Many women had a distinct advantage. If a woman's deceased husband had been a maimed-soldier pensioner, she was probably the first to know about and apply for the newly available pension.[54] In the 1650s Devon widows of maimed-soldier pensioners were reported not to have bothered even to apply for the stipends of their dearly departed. Instead they continued to collect their husbands' pensions from the treasurer after their husbands' death without having obtained orders from the court.[55]

There is also evidence that war widows were willing to inform on other pensioners. The informer was a fixture of the legal system of seventeenth century England and the military pension scheme was not exempt. In Cheshire in the mid-1650s, for example, Elinor Bostock provided information against a pensioner named John Hickock. She claimed he was an enlisted soldier in the garrison of Chester, of able body, and worth £200. The information was investigated and found credible. As a reward half of Hickock's pension was transferred to the war widow.[56]

One reason war widows reapplied for relief after having accepted composition payments was that they could rely on magisterial amnesia. The membership of the bench changed from session to session, especially in counties with sittings in different towns, and almost completely after the Restoration, and a great deal of business was conducted in a short space of time. Magisterial amnesia allowed war widows to lie successfully for material advantage. Widows lied about which side their husband had fought on. I have discovered several instances of parliamentary widows trying either to restore or acquire pensions after the Restoration (and one case of a royalist widow soliciting county funds during the republic).[57] Four war widows applied to Cheshire together for reinstatement to their pensions on the basis that "some" of their husbands had served during Elizabeth's reign, and that they had been granted stipends subsequently as war widows. In fact the "some" was *one* Elizabeth Lindope whose husband (William) had been pensioned in the late 1630s. Elizabeth received a pension during the 1650s. Her three sons fought for parliament.[58]

In order to acquire relief, several war widows went above the heads of the county bench to seek the support of the treasurers for maimed soldiers and war widows in London, Cromwell and, after the Restoration, the privy council.[59] At times the women, in doing so, sought to overturn decisions made by the county bench. Mary Burden of Wiltshire used this tactic. Her story also serves to reveal further the importunity and mendacity that some war widows employed.

Burden produced two letters of recommendation from Oliver Cromwell during her persistent attempts to acquire a pension in the 1650s. Her husband had died of wounds received shortly after arriving for service in Ireland. Although an officer he had had to borrow to equip himself for service. Mary Burden was left in debt, with six children and, as she claimed, no means of support. On her first appearance in court in Michaelmas 1652 she produced a certificate from Cromwell attesting to her husband's death in service and recommending her for a pension. She was instead granted a gratuity. Six months later she returned claiming to be in fear of arrest for her husband's debt. Again she was granted only a one-off payment. Some time during the next year she was indeed imprisoned for debt and only permitted to come to court in the spring of 1654 to petition. At the Easter 1654 sessions she adopted a tactic which she would continue to use for the next two years. She claimed that in her first appearance she had been granted a pension, and sought reinstatement of it. This was not true and she must have known it. It is quite possible that it was a lie needed to satisfy her creditors that she had a potential source of income.

During the year from Easter 1654 she petitioned the court every quarter bar one, receiving one-off payments and promising each time never to return. During the summer of 1655 she journeyed to London and solicited a second letter from Cromwell – now the Lord Protector – recommending her for a pension. On the basis of this document she acquired yet another one-off in October of that year and, finally, in Easter of 1656, she was granted a pension. During that sessions she also claimed that her original pension had been withdrawn because the clerk of the peace had lost the first letter from Cromwell. This claim was immaterial. Six months later, despite having agreed on acceptance of her pension not to request more money, she was back in court doing just that. She petitioned for a pension increase. The JPs referred her to a justice who was allowed to grant her a one-off in addition to her stipend if he found she was in sufficient need. Despite all her efforts, Burden's pension was withdrawn after 18 months – in October 1657 – during a review of pensioners. The last mention of her is in a petition for reinstatement to her pension in early 1659. It was refused despite her assertion that she was still in debt because of her husband's service. Instead she was granted yet another gratuity.[60]

Some war widows who were granted parish pensions went above the heads of their parish officers to the bench when dissatisfied. Elizabeth Newton of Cheshire, for example, told the JPs that her overseer had "contemptuously neglected" to pay her a pension as ordered by two JPs. The court asked the relevant two justices to see that the woman was paid her stipend and ordered the overseer to attend the next sessions to answer for his negligence.[61]

A number of women were flexible in their demands for relief before the justices. Flexibility was a tactic designed to increase the likelihood of some form of material reward. A given widow would request that the justices grant her a pension "or otherwise to provide for her as you in your wisdomes shall thinke fitt". Other widows provided specific alternatives to a stipend which the bench was legally entitled to grant. Joane Stockton, for example, applied to the Cheshire bench in the mid-1650s and asked for either a stipend or an order granting her permission to erect a cottage on the waste.[62]

V

So far I have outlined the tactics used by individual war widows in pursuit of limited resources. There are, however, several cases of war widows combining to apply for funds and changes in practice. It was quite common for war widows to apply together to the sessions if they came from the same parish or town. An interesting example is that of Joan Evans, Elizabeth Ball and Alice Worth, all of Plymouth. Together they applied for relief to the Devon bench in October 1649. They did so after having first applied to the town for assistance. Refused, they petitioned the judges of assize, complaining that despite losing their husbands in the siege, having three or four children each, and having contributed their goods for the maintenance of the soldiery, "all the comfort we can receive from the authority heare is they would it did lye in theire power to helpe us." The judges of assize referred them to the county bench which was to order for their relief according to "the statute and Ordinances of parliament." Having been awarded gratuities the widows returned to future sessions and had acquired nine one-off payments among them by early 1654.[63]

Combining was prevalent. In Cheshire 19 of the 92 (21 per cent) war widows who are recorded as applying for county funds prior to the Restoration at one time or another petitioned in a group. Nine of these 19 petitioned two or more times in combination with others. There are also examples of war widows combining with maimed soldiers. Of the 17 group petitions in Cheshire that survive from the late 1640s and 1650s, five were from both war widows and maimed soldiers (a further three being from war widows only).[64] As well as petitioning for pensions together,[65] war widows and ex-servicemen on three occasions complained to the bench that their treasurers had failed to pay their pensions properly,[66] and in another case ten maimed soldiers and four war widows petitioned to keep an efficient deputy treasurer in his job. They argued that he "hath taken a great deal of care and paynes to procure us our pay according to order . . ." There are also two group petitions for back-pay in Cheshire. One of these was from six ex-servicemen and the widows of three other men hired by the parish of Knutsford for service at Worcester.[67]

At the national level parliament was treated to numerous petitions from war widows and maimed soldiers in the later 1650s and in 1660 when the central fund was in difficulty. Indeed, even as the convention parliament was debating how to scrap the fund in December 1660 there were reported to be over 100 war widows and ex-servicemen "which continually attend the House Door" with a petition. Eventually it was read and laid aside.[68]

All the tactics used by war widows had been and were used by maimed soldiers. The women soon became adept at working the system that had been developed by ex-servicemen since 1593. Sometimes the learning process is explicit. Elizabeth Didlow, for example, told the court that she was applying for a pension increase because soldiers had informed her that others had received comparable rises.[69] A comparison of the Essex war widows and maimed soldiers indicates that the women had learnt well and were relatively successful in their use of tactics such as importunity. Men and women were fairly equal in successfully soliciting pension increases, returning to sessions and securing a pension after initial denial, and seeking further relief after being ordered not to do so.[70]

An examination of the 31 surviving petitions and letters of recommendation of the parliamentary Essex war widows and ex-servicemen reveals that while a slim majority of the men had the support either of former military commanders, justices or central government authorities, only a quarter of the women had such support. Despite this difference the women were not completely disadvantaged or unsuccessful. Of the 110 men and women recorded as applying for or receiving relief, 33 (30 per cent) were women. Of those recorded as receiving pensions, 20 (35 per cent) were war widows. This is despite the fact that, strictly speaking, the law only allowed them to receive monies surplus after the men had been pensioned.[71] The difference between the genders is not as marked in Cheshire. In that county, although men seem to have had better support from more potentially influential patrons, the difference was minimal. The surviving petition evidence reveals that 41 per cent of ex-servicemen (36 of 88) and 37.5 per cent of war widows (25 of 67) applying for county funds had the support of JPs, military commanders, deputy lieutenants, judges of the court of great sessions, or central government authorities. Excluding applications for which the result is unknown, 67 per cent of ex-servicemen and 71 per cent of war widows were granted county or parochial funds.[72]

VI

One historian has commented that in studying the history of women "victimization is only one part of the story . . . which is really about survival".[73] Mary O'Dowd has argued that in practice Irish war widows and wives were powerless and failed to have their new legal rights confirmed. English war widows seeking pensions seem to have done rather better until the Restoration. Women did succeed in obtaining relief from funds intended primarily to pay pensions to men, that is to maimed soldiers. Indeed, in some areas, war widows formed the majority of the pensioners. Proportionally women were granted as much money as the men. War widows successfully adopted tactics used by the men and in their actions and words demonstrated a keen awareness of entitlement to pensions. They exercised and confirmed their new rights. For these women the Restoration in practice was a revolution indeed. They were turned back.

Notes

1. Jane Damport, on hearing of the death of her soldier husband. T. Dekker, *The shoemakers' holiday*, act 3, scene 4, line 149. In this chapter all quoted abbreviations have been silently expanded, but the spelling of the original has been preserved.
2. M. Trustram incorrectly dates the first widows' pensions to early in this century in, *Women of the regiment: marriage and the Victorian army* (Cambridge, 1984), p. 92.
3. J. A. Sharpe, *Early modern England: a social history 1550–1760* (London, 1987),

p. 22. Dr Sharpe has promised to correct this omission in the second edition.

4. K. Thomas, Women and the civil war sects, in *Crisis in Europe 1560–1660*, ed. T. Aston (London, 1965), pp. 317–40; P. Higgins, Women in the English civil war, MA thesis, University of Manchester, 1965; P. Higgins, The reactions of women, with special reference to women petitioners, in *Politics, religion and the English civil war*, ed. B. Manning (Manchester, 1973), pp. 177–222; A. Fraser, *The weaker vessel: woman's lot in seventeenth-century England* (London, 1985), part two; E. A. McArthur, Women petitioners and the long parliament, *English Historical Review*, 24, 1909, pp. 698–709 (criticized by Higgins in her thesis for inaccurate chronology of events); for a brief overview see A. Laurence, Women's work and the English civil war, *History Today*, 42, 1992, pp. 20–25.

5. B. Nemes is writing an important thesis on this subject, Women and the defence of property, 1640–60. PhD thesis, University of Cambridge.

6. M. O'Dowd, Women and war in Ireland in the 1640s, in *Women in early modern Ireland*, eds M. MacCurtain & M. O'Dowd (Edinburgh, 1991), pp. 91–111: 98–9.

7. O'Dowd, Women and war in Ireland, p. 108. For another pessimistic view see P. Crawford, Historians, women and the civil war sects, 1640–1660s, *Parergon*, New series 6, 1988, pp. 19–32. Laurence is also pessimistic in her article: "it is possible to argue that in the long term the English Civil War limited, rather than expanded, the opportunities open to them [women]" (p. 25). Unfortunately Laurence does not present any argument. I trust she argues the case in her new book, *Women in England 1500–1760, a social history* (London, 1994).

8. Kent RO, Q/SB1/45, my emphasis. The petition from the war widow also survives (Q/SB1/24). For Algernon Sidney's activities in Kent see A. Everitt, *The community of Kent and the great rebellion, 1640–60* (Leicester, 1966), pp. 272, 281, 309–11. Sidney's later views on war and the state concur with those expressed in this letter written on behalf of a war widow. See A. Sidney, *Discourses concerning government* (Indianapolis, Liberty Classics, 1990), sections 22–23. For more on Sidney see J. Scott, *Algernon Sidney and the English Republic, 1623–1677* (Cambridge, 1988), especially pp. 102–105.

9. PRO, State Papers, 46/114, f. 123. For more on Deane see B. Capp, *Cromwell's Navy: The Fleet and the English Revolution, 1648–1660* (Oxford, 1989).

10. Chesh RO, quarter sessions files (QJF) 79/3, f. 161 (Michaelmas 1651, letter dated 12 July 1651).

11. *Calendar of state papers domestic, 1656–7* (London, 1883) p. 154, (10 Nov. 1656); my emphasis.

12. Somerset RO, Q/Spet/1/128, n. d.

13. Pemberton, Chesh RO: QJF 84/4, f. 113 (Epiphany 1656/7); 79/2, f. 142 (Trinity 1651). Knowsley, QJF 85/4, f. 124–5 (Epiphany 1657/8).

14. PRO, PC 2/61, f. 234 (29 July 1670).

15. Chesh RO, QJF 1647–60; 84/2, f. 260 (Trinity 1656). Webster; 78/4, ff. 52–3 (Epiphany 1650/1); 83/2, f. 185 (Trinity 1655); 79/2, f. 142 (Trinity 1651).

16. Lancs RO, QSP/24, f. 24 (Michaelmas 1649).

17. Devon RO, Q/S, 128/102/1.

18. PRO, State Papers, 28/224, f. 91.

19. PRO, ADM, 106/3023.

20. See M. A. Kishlansky, *The rise of the New Model Army* (Cambridge, 1979), p. 201; A. Woolrych, *Soldiers and statesmen* (Oxford, 1987), p. 97; B. Whitelock, *Memorials of the English affairs*, 2 (Oxford, 1853), pp. 123, 125, 144–5, 147, 203, 213, 215–6, 251, 258, 279–80; BL, E388(18), *Divers papers from the army-Answer of army to Marshall General Skippons speech to the Army on 15 May*, p. 5; BL, E389(3), *The kingdomes weekly intelligencer* (18–25 May 1647) pp. 534–5, 539; *The case of the army truly stated* . . . (18 Oct. 1647), in *The leveller tracts 1647–1653*, eds W. Haller and G. Davies (Gloucester, MA, Peter Smith, 1964, 1st pub. 1944), pp. 64–87; BL, E412(6), *Two letters from the agents of the five regiments of horse* . . . (28 October 1647) p. 5; BL, E475(13), *The humble representation of the desires of the officers and souldiers in the regiment of horse, for* . . . *Northumberland* (December 1648) p. 3.

21. *Acts and ordinances of the Interregnum, 1642–1660*, I, eds C. H. Firth & R. S. Rait (London, 1911), pp. 938–40 (28 May 1647), 997–8 (10 Aug. 1647), 1055 (24 Dec. 1647); II, 556–9 (30 Sept. 1651).

22. *Statutes of the realm* (London, 1810–28), 14 Car. II. c. 9.

23. Salop RO, Quarter Sessions 177.

24. *Journal of the House of Commons*, VII, p. 627 (7 April 1659); C. H. Firth, *Cromwell's army* (London, 1902), pp. 262, 267–9.

25. *Warwick county records*, IV, eds S. C. Ratcliff & H. C. Johnson (Warwick, 1938), p. 130; Salop RO, Draft QS Order Book, n.f. Trinity 1661; Norfolk RO, C/S2/2, n. f. Michaelmas 1663. An example of a lengthy extract in an order book: Devon RO, Q/S, 1/10, n.f. Trinity 1662.

26. For the army see R. Hutton, *The Restoration* (Oxford, 1985), pp. 138–9. For women see S. D. Amussen, Gender, family and the social order, 1560–1725, in *Order and disorder in early modern England*, eds A. Fletcher & J. Stevenson (Cambridge, 1985), pp. 196–217: 198–9; M. Shanley, Marriage contract and social contract in seventeenth century England, *Western Political Quarterly*, 32(1), 1979, pp. 79–91.

27. Firth & Rait, *Ordinances*, I, pp. 36–7 (24 Oct. 1642), 102–103 (6 March 1642/3), 328–30 (31 Oct. 1643); *Stuart royal proclamations*, II, ed. J. F. Larkin (Oxford, 1983), nos. 413 (3 May 1643), 414 (7 May 1643), 432 (7 July 1643).

28. Chesh RO, QJF 79/1, f. 1; Hereford & Worcester RO, 110.90.23; *Nottinghamshire county records*, ed. H. H. Copnall (Nottingham, 1915), p. 94; Wilts RO, QS A1/110, Hilary 1660/1, f. 121; London Corporation RO, 35B, military and naval maimed soldiers and sailors annual list of pensioners 1671/2–1678/9. In the West Riding of Yorkshire between 1648 and 1657, 310 individuals were pensioned of whom 93 (30 per cent) were war widows. West Yorks RO, QS 10/2 & 10/3. The following treasurers' accounts reported no war widow pension-

ers: West Riding Yorkshire at Easter 1661, Surrey at Hilary 1662/3, Oxford City at Michaelmas 1663, Middlesex at Michaelmas 1669, and Gloucestershire at Hilary 1673/4. West Yorks RO, QS/10/4, ff. 22–3; *Surrey quarter sessions records*, VII, eds H. Jenkinson & D.L. Powell (Surrey, 1935), p. 70; Oxford City Library, 0.5.11; Greater London RO, MJ/SBB/263, ff. 38–45; Gloucs RO, QSO, Order Book 1, 1672–1681, n.f. Hilary 1672/3. West Sussex at Michaelmas 1662 had two widow pensioners, there was one war widow pensioner in Staffordshire at Michaelmas 1661 and West Hampshire had two widows receiving stipends at Easter 1663. East Sussex RO, QO/EW4, ff. 45–6; Staffs RO, Q/SO/7, n.f. Easter 1661 (sic); Hants RO, 44M69/029.

29. L. Hutchinson, *Memoirs of the life of colonel Hutchinson, with the fragment of an autobiography of Mrs. Hutchinson*, ed. J. Sutherland (London, 1973), p. 100. Higgins, (Women in the English civil war, p. 39) cited this information from an earlier edition of Hutchinson.

30. West Yorks RO, QS, 10/2, ff. 146 & 262; Pamela Sharpe found that 8 years was a common age for paupers to be apprenticed in her 1991 examination of: Poor children as apprentices in Colyton 1598–1830, *Continuity and Change*, 6(2), 1991, pp. 253–70: 255.

31. For consideration of children and war widows in an earlier period see J. T. Rosenthal, Other victims: peeresses as war widows, 1450–1500, *History*, 72(235), 1987, pp. 213–30: 228–9.

32. Chesh RO, Quarter Sessions files and order book (QJF & QJB 1/6), 1647–60 (includes two individuals for whom petitions do not survive but for whom the orders in the book are sufficiently detailed).

33. In West Yorkshire during the late 1640s a number of widows were paid pensions "till the youngest child be 7 years old", thus explicitly linking their right to a pension to their need to support children who were too young to be apprenticed. West Yorks RO, QS10/2, ff. 146, 262. In all other counties examined, however, the link was implicit and no attempt was made to withdraw pensions from widows when their children grew older.

34. See Essex RO, Q/SBa/2/82 for an example of a printed letter of recommendation for a war widow, and Q/SBa/2/78 for a letter for an ex-serviceman. These letters were produced in connection with the ordinance of 30 September 1651 (Firth & Rait, *Ordinances*, II, pp. 556–9) for the ex-servicemen and war widows of the recent campaigns in Scotland and Ireland.

35. B. Todd, Widowhood in a market town: Abingdon, 1540–1720, DPhil thesis, University of Oxford, 1983, p. 243. There is evidence that five of the 13 widows (38 per cent) applying to the Cheshire bench from 1647 to 1660 without mentioning if they had children received county or parish funds. Of the 14 women who declared that they had one child, 11 (79 per cent) were granted relief; 42 women maintained that they had two or more children, and of these 32 (76 per cent) were successful. If the applications for which results are unknown are excluded the figures are: no mention of children (five of seven, 71

per cent); one child (11 of 14, 79 per cent); two or more children (32 of 37, 86 per cent). Chesh RO, QJF & QJB 1/6, 1647–60. In Essex, where the petition evidence is less complete than Cheshire, it is still clear that the citation of children was important. In the 13 cases in which war widows declared in their petitions that they had two or more children, seven women were granted pensions, one was referred to her parish for relief, and five received gratuities. All received something – which was not the case for other war widows applying for monies in that county. Essex RO, quarter sessions papers (Q/SBa/2) and order book (Q/SO/1) to Easter 1660.

36. B. Todd, The remarrying widow: a stereotype reconsidered, in *Women in English society, 1500–1800*, ed. M. Prior (London, 1985), pp. 54–92: 79; *Quarter sessions records*, VI, ed. J. C. Atkinson (London, 1888), p. 23.

37. London Corporation RO, Petitions and Orders, misc. mss. 163. 8, petition of Ann Platt.

38. Devon RO, Q/S 128; Q/S 1/9–1/13; BL add. mss. 34012 (Major Generals' 1655 list of royalist suspects, many of whom applied for pensions after the Restoration). For Dorset, see D. Underdown, *Revel, riot, and rebellion: popular politics and culture in England, 1603–1660* (Oxford, 1985), p. 295.

39. Chesh RO, QJF 80/1, f. 145 (Easter 1652); QJF 79/2, f. 162 (Trinity 1651); QJF 81/3, f. 106 (Michaelmas 1653) & 81/4, f. 103 (Epiphany 1653/4).

40. Stockings: Chesh RO, QJF 83/2, f. 185 (Trinity 1655); Ale: QJF 84/2, f. 260 (Trinity 1656) & QJF 94/1, f. 129 (Easter 1666). For consideration of the work available to widows in this period, see A. L. Erickson, Introduction to A. Clark, *Working life of women in the seventeenth century* (London, 1992); M. Prior, Women and the urban economy: Oxford 1500–1800, in *Women in English society 1500–1800*, ed. M. Prior (London, 1985), pp. 93–117; S. Wright, "Churmaids, huswyfes and hucksters": the employment of women in Tudor and Stuart Salisbury, in *Women and work in pre-industrial England*, eds L. Charles & L. Duffin (London, 1985), pp. 100–121; K. D. M. Snell, *Annals of the labouring poor* (Cambridge, 1985), ch. 6; I. K. Ben-Amos, Women apprentices in the trades and crafts of early modern Bristol, *Continuity and Change*, 6(2), 1991, pp. 227–52.

41. Chesh RO, QJF & QJB 1/6, 1647–66.

42. J. S. Morrill, *Cheshire 1630–1660: county government and society during the English revolution* (Oxford, 1974), pp. 247–9. Examples include: Elinor Bostock, Chesh RO, QJF 79/3, f. 143 (Michaelmas 1651), 80/2, f. 159 (Trinity 1652), 85/1, ff. 117–18 (Easter 1657); Anne French, QJB 1/6, f. 92v. (Michaelmas 1645) & QJF 73/3, f. 93 (Michaelmas 1645); Margaret Massy, QJB 1/6, f. 268v. (Michaelmas 1650); Ellen Kenard, QJF 78/1, f. 50 (Easter 1650), 80/1, 145 (Easter 1652); Joane Stockton, 81/4, f. 103 (Epiphany 1653/4). Kenard petitioned to erect a cottage in two different parishes claiming to have been born and brought up in each place. The two petitions provide ample information to confirm that it is the same woman.

43. P. A. Slack, *Poverty & policy in Tudor & Stuart England* (London, 1988), pp. 175–181. For a good example of a war widow on parish relief in this period see T. Wales, Poverty, poor relief and the life cycle: some evidence from seventeenth-century Norfolk, in *Land, kinship and life cycle*, ed. R. Smith (Cambridge, 1984), pp. 351–404: 380–1.

44. Chesh RO, QJB 1/6, f. 166v.: Stepney, Greater London RO, MJ/SBB/336.

45. Chesh RO, QJF 89/2, f. 211 (Trinity 1661).

46. Greater London RO, MJ/SBB/126, f. 39 (12 Dec. 1653).

47. Military commander: Chesh RO, QJF 79/3, f. 102 (Michaelmas 1651); Parish clerk: 88/3, f. 54 (Michaelmas 1660) & 88/4, f. 43 (Epiphany 1660/1).

48. N. Z. Davis, *Fiction in the archives: pardon tales and their tellers in sixteenth-century France* (Oxford, 1988), pp. 20–1.

49. Chesh RO, QJF 79/2, f. 139 (Trinity 1651).

50. Chesh RO, QJF & QJB 1/6, 1647–60. This figure is probably an underestimate of the widows' persistence as the Cheshire order books are missing for much of the 1650s.

51. Devon RO, quarter sessions order books (Q/S 1/8 & 1/9), 1647–1660. Chesh RO, QJF 82/4, f. 145 (Epiphany 1654/5).

52. Kent RO Q/SO/W2 & W3, n. f. Easter 1663 to Easter 1672. See also Sarah Boniface, Q/SO/E1 ff. 24 (Hilary 1656/7) & 30 (Hilary 1657/8). Katherine Truron: Devon RO, Q/S, 1/10, n. f. Hilary 1662/3, Michaelmas 1670; 1/11, n. f. Michaelmas 1671, Trinity 1674; 1/12, n. f. Hilary 1684/5. In Devon RO, see also Elizabeth Betty, Q/S 1/9, n. f. Easter 1659, Trinity 1659, Hilary 1659/60; Elizabeth Causey, 1/9, n. f. Michaelmas 1653, Trinity 1658; Anne Pomeroy, 1/10, n. f. Trinity 1665, Michaelmas 1670, Michaelmas 1671, list of widows on back cover, 1/128/99/1 (1665); Ann Weekes, 1/10, n. f. Easter 1663, Easter 1666, list of widows on back cover. In Essex RO see Elizabeth Bridge, Q/SO/I, ff. 92v. (Hilary 1654/5), 103v. (Trinity 1655); Jane Hodgskins, ff. 162r. (Hilary 1657/8), 169v. (Easter 1658). In Wilts RO see Alice Carroway, A1/160/1, n. f. (Trinity 1650), n. f. (Trinity 1651), A1 110, (Trinity 1659), f. 156; Mary Burden of Wiltshire (see below in chapter).

53. London Corporation RO, misc. mss. 163. 8 (petitions of Alice Lunn and Katherine Wild); 35B, military and naval maimed soldiers and sailors annual list of pensioners 1671/2–1678/9.

54. For example, London Corporation RO, misc. mss. 163. 8 (petitions of Susanna Gouge & Martha Mott). Mary Burnham: Essex RO Q/SBa/2/82 (Easter 1653). Chesh RO Elizabeth Lindope, QJF 78/4, f. 32 (Epiphany 1650/1); Joane Oulton, 82/2, f. 183 (Trinity 1654); Elizabeth Rowlinson, 79/4, f. 115 (Epiphany 1651/2); Margaret Brayne, 83/1, f. 147 (Easter 1655). See also Ellinor Harris: Wilts RO , A1 110, Easter 1657, f. 162.

55. Devon RO, Q/S, 1/9, n.f. Trinity 1657.

56. Chesh RO, QJF 85/1, ff. 117–18 (Easter 1657).

57. Ann Plum (a blind war widow): Essex RO, Q/SO/1, ff. 30v. (Michaelmas

1652) & 98r. (Easter 1655); Q/SBa/2/82 (Easter 1653); Q/SO/2, f. 96r. (Hilary 1674/5). Margaret Perrin: Chesh RO, QJF 79/2, ff. 139–40 (Trinity 1651); 88/3, f. 54 (Michaelmas 1660); 88/4, f. 43 (Epiphany 1660/1). In Chesh RO see also Ann Morgan QJF 88/3, f. 33 (Michaelmas 1660); 92/1, f. 118 (Easter 1664); 99/1, f. 167 (Easter 1671): Joane Hoole and Judeth Hampton, 88/3, f. 54 (Michaelmas 1660) & 88/4, 43 (Epiphany 1660/61). The royalist war widow (Ellen Jennings) can be identified as such by the subscription on the bottom of her 1652 petition to the Cheshire bench. The subscription contains the names of four of her deceased husband's fellow servicemen testifying to his military record. Two of these former comrades later acquired pensions as royalist maimed soldiers after the Restoration. Chesh RO, QJF 80/2, f. 162 (Trinity 1652). These royalist pensioners were Richard Fleet and Richard Jarvis. For Jarvis see: Chesh RO, QJF 96/1, f. 141 (Easter 1668); 105/4, f. 146 (Epiphany 1677/8); and the Nantwich hundred treasurers' accounts for the period 25 March 1668/9–1678/9 (Chesh RO, QJF 97/2, f. 59; 98/2, f. 65; 99/2, f. 130; 100/3, f. 145; 101/2, f. 42; 102/2, f. 112; 104/2, f. 113; 105/2, f. 132; 106/2, f. 128; 107/2, f. 112). Fleet's relief history can be found in the Nantwich treasurers' accounts for 25 March 1670/1–1676/7 and Chesh RO, QJF 105/4, f. 148 (Epiphany 1677/8).

58. Group: Chesh RO, JRF, 88/4, f. 43 (Hilary, 1660/61); Lindope, 67/4, f. 22 (Epiphany 1638/9), QJB 1/5, f. 499v. (Epiphany 1638/9), 1/6, f. 145r. (Easter 1647), QJF 78/4, f. 32 (Epiphany 1650/1), 79/2, f. 152 (Trinity 1651).

59. Privy Council examples: Jane Lane (City of London), PRO, PC2/57, f. 224 & 2/58, f. 118; Ann Hollowell (Middlesex), PC2/61, f. 164; Alice Stannard (Hampshire) PC2/61, f. 234.

60. Wilts RO, A1 110, Easter 1653, f. 244; Easter 1654, n. f. ; Michaelmas 1654, f. 189; Easter 1655, f. 252; Easter 1656, f. 181; Michaelmas 1656, f. 61; Easter 1659, f. 207; 160/1, n. f. (Michaelmas 1652), (Easter 1653); 160/2, n. f. (Michaelmas 1654), ff. 32, 38 (Easter 1655), 41 (Michaelmas 1655), 58 (Easter 1656), 69 (Michaelmas 1656), 105 (Michaelmas 1657), 150 (Easter 1659).

61. Chesh RO, QJF 76/4, f. 51 (Epiphany 1648/9). Other examples: Anne Parker, QJF 79/3, f. 160 (Michaelmas 1651), 80/1, f. 109 (Easter 1652), 82/2, f. 170 (Trinity 1654); Elizabeth Rogerson, 80/1, f. 109 (Easter 1652); Alice Webster, 78/4, ff. 52–3 (Epiphany 1650/1), 79/3, f. 161 (Michaelmas 1651), 80/1, f. 108 (Easter 1652).

62. Chesh RO, QJF 80/2, f. 163 (Trinity 1652): Stockton, 81/4, f. 103 (Epiphany 1653/4).

63. R. N. Worth, The siege of Plymouth: a chapter of Plymouth history re-written, *Annual report and transactions of the Plymouth institution and Devon and Cornwall natural history society*, **5**, 1876, p. 308; Devon RO, Q/S 1/8, n. f. Michaelmas 1649 & Easter 1651; 1/9, n. f. Easter 1653 & Easter 1654.

64. Chesh RO, QJF 74/1, f. 52 (Easter 1646); 76/1, f. 22 (Easter 1648); 77/4, 27 (Epiphany 1649/50); 79/1, f. 111 (Easter 1651); 79/2, f. 145 (Trinity 1651);

79/3, ff. 89, 126, 136, 137, 139, 151 & 160–3 (Michaelmas 1651); 80/1, f. 109 (Easter 1652); 80/2, f. 134 (Trinity 1652); 85/1, f. 128 (Easter 1657); 86/3, f. 137 (Michaelmas 1658). See endnote 58 for a post-1660 group petition.

65. Chesh RO, QJF 77/4, f. 27 (Epiphany 1649/50).

66. Chesh RO, QJF 79/2, f. 145 (Trinity 1651); 85/1, f. 128 (Easter 1657); 86/3, f. 137 (Michaelmas 1658).

67. Chesh RO, QJF 80/2, f. 134 (Trinity 1652). Groups: QJF, 79/3, f. 127 (Michaelmas 1651); 79/4, f. 110 (Epiphany 1651/2), Knutsford petition. Another example of war widows petitioning with maimed ex-servicemen occurred in Lancashire. In 1651 four war widows put their marks on a petition with four maimed soldiers on behalf of all military pensioners in the county requesting the reinstatement of stipends formerly paid out of sequestration funds. *Historic manuscripts commission, 13th Report. Manuscripts of his grace the duke of Portland*, (London, 1891), p. 568. Pensions and gratuities were paid out of sequestration funds in Lancashire and many other counties prior to the implementation of the 1647 ordinances. For several such orders in Cheshire see PRO, State Papers, 28/224 & 225 (4 parts).

68. *Journal of the House of Commons*, VIII, p. 236 (29 December 1660); See also: VII pp. 627 (7 April 1659), 655 (16 May 1659), 771 (1 Sept. 1659); Vol. 8, pp. 46 (26 May 1660), 204 (11 Dec. 1660).

69. Chesh RO, QFJ 79/3, f. 121 (Michaelmas 1651).

70. Essex RO, Q/SBa/2 & Q/SO/I, 1647–60. Six of 57 maimed soldier, and two of 20 war widow pensioners are recorded as gaining pension increases. Eight of 57 maimed soldiers and four of 20 war widows returned to sessions and secured a pension after initial denial. Six of 15 maimed soldiers and two of four war widows, told not to return to sessions for more money instead came back to court to seek further relief.

71. Essex RO, Q/SBa/2 & Q/SO/I, 1647–60. The petition evidence consists of 19 applications from ex-servicemen and 11 from war widows.

72. Taken from petition evidence found in Chesh RO, QJF, 1647–60. In cases where the petitioner had the support of a variety of patrons he or she was placed in the category assigned the higher number in the following scheme: (1) no supporters, (2) servicemen only, (3) inhabitants of parish or township of residence, (4) JPs, (5) military commander(s), (6) deputy lieutenants, (7) judges of great sessions, (8) central government authorities (e.g. Cromwell). 47 of 70 maimed soldiers and 42 of 59 widows had petition evidence for which results are known. These figures reinforce the evidence provided by the 1651 Cheshire treasurer account quoted in Table 7.1: war widows were granted roughly half the sums available in the county.

73. M. E. Perry, *Gender and disorder in early modern Seville* (New Jersey, 1990), p. 178. See also N. Z. Davis and A. Farge, Women as historical actors, in *A history of women in the West Vol. III, Renaissance and Enlightenment paradoxes*, eds Davis & Farge (Cambridge, MA, 1993), pp. 1–7, especially p. 4.

Chapter Eight

Women, custom and equity in the court of requests

Tim Stretton

Today we look back far in time. To a town or village green. The turf is old. Animals have grazed there for hundreds of years. Nowadays they are pleasant stretches of grass where people sit and talk. Sometimes they play cricket or kick a ball about. But in mediaeval times it was the place where the young men mustered with their bows and arrows. They shot at the butts. There might be stocks there where offenders were put for their petty misdemeanours. In the month of May they set up a maypole and danced around it. We have no record of when it all began, but the poet tells us:

> On the green they watched their sons
> Playing till too dark to see,
> As their fathers watched them once,
> As my father once watched me.

The villagers have an undoubted right to play games on their green. But whence comes their right? Not in deeds or in statutes. Only in custom from time immemorial.

Lord Denning, Court of Appeal (1975).[1]

The subject of custom has rarely been as popular among historians of early modern England as it is today. Custom, that is, in the sense of social practice: the festivals, feast days, charivaris, traditional songs and other communal activities that now extend to include such a range of human action, that the convenient hold-all label "popular culture" can no longer adequately contain it. Customary law, the law of the manor which so interested R. H. Tawney, and which is attracting renewed interest among eighteenth-century historians like E. P. Thompson, attracts considerably less attention nowadays from social historians of the sixteenth and seventeenth centuries.[2] This neglect is due in part to the unforgiving nature of the sources. As F. W. Maitland observed a hundred years ago, court rolls "are taciturn, they do not easily yield up their testimony".[3] However, it also reflects the tendency of many social and legal historians to consider customary law as being in decline by the sixteenth century, and, like Lord Denning, to regard it as being immemorial – to see customary law as backward looking and inflexible, a rigid maintainer of continuities that was becoming increasingly out of place in an age of legal centralization and growing change.[4]

The influence of custom was certainly waning in the sixteenth century, yet for many communities the law of the manor remained important well into the eighteenth century and sometimes beyond.[5] Local customs could survive unaltered for centuries, as the example of Denning's village green attests. However, the fact that customs *could* remain unchanged does not mean that they *did* remain unchanged. As E. P. Thompson notes, "so far from having the steady permanence suggested by the word 'tradition', custom was a field of change and of contest, an arena in which opposing interests made conflicting claims".[6] In a similar context R. W. Hoyle has stressed that the northern custom of tenant right was not "a static entity", but "a flexible relationship between lords and tenants actively being moulded by the forces applied to it".[7] The contests which interest historians such as Hoyle and Thompson are the vertical contests between tenants and lords, between Thompson's "patricians and plebs". Women were of course parties to these contests, as tenants and as ladies of the manor, but more often they involved themselves in horizontal contests with fellow tenants. My intention in this chapter is to examine these horizontal contests in a study of the custom of widow's estate, or freebench, in the county of Somerset, using the records of the central equity court of Requests.[8] The aim is to focus not on the longevity of custom, but on its flexibility, and to explore some of the implications of that flexibility for women.

Alice Clark, writing in 1919 and Doris Stenton, writing 40 years later, both stressed the superiority of custom over the common law in the field of women's rights. Clark suggested that "the changes which during the seventeenth century were abrogating customs in favour of common law" had the effect of eliminating women "from what was equivalent to a share in the custody and interpretation of law", powers that, "henceforward remained exclusively in the hands of men".[9] Stenton went so far as to say that rights under custom were such that among the native peasant stock of late-medieval Lincolnshire, "the ancient tradition of the rough equality between men and women had not yet been entirely forgotten".[10] Clark pointed out that women who held customary interests had to serve on "homages", the juries of tenants which made "presentments" or recommendations to the officials presiding in customary courts, and this representation gave them a say in the policing of custom, which was removed as the common law, or "national custom", rose to prominence. Stenton provided instances of married women appearing in court both as their husbands' agents and in their own right – behaviour which was technically impossible under the common law. More recently, Amy Erickson has warned against confining discussions of women and law to the common law and thereby ignoring the influence on women's lives of alternative bodies of law such as custom.[11] There is clearly a need for continued exploration of customary law as it affected women, and not merely the use women made of this particular code of law, but the changing nature of that code during the long and slow decline in its influence.

The archive of a central court is not the most obvious place to look for information about local customary law, yet a surprising number of men and women from manors all over England appealed to the judges, or "Masters", of Requests to hear their customary causes, either because they felt unhappy with the decisions they had received in the manor court, or because they were convinced that the bias of the lord, lady or steward of their manor, or the power and influence of their opponent, meant they would never gain a fair hearing there. The Masters who dealt with these matters were amateurs, in the sense that they could not pretend knowledge of the customs of all the manors of England, and consequently they needed to gather together detailed information before they could safely pass judgment on deeply local conflicts.

This information survives in the form of interrogatories, depositions, copies of documents and commission reports. Along with case materials and the written decisions and orders of the court, it provides a rich body of source material. The records are not a substitute for court rolls. They contain few reliable facts, only squabbling litigants' word for facts. And the cases which reached the court were, by definition, exceptional and obviously not representative of what actually happened on manors day by day. But by virtue of being exceptional they show custom under pressure, and these records provide a unique source for investigating how customary law worked, how lords, ladies, stewards and tenants regarded custom and how they sought to prove unwritten customs in a Westminster court.

The custom of widow's estate was one of the commonest customs from Somerset to be litigated in Requests. Information from the concise and often frustrating unpublished calendars suggests that about 290 of the 750 Somerset Requests actions that survive for Elizabeth's reign (about 39 per cent) involved at least one woman litigant.[12] Of these 290, I estimate that just under half involved disputes over copyhold, and a quarter, perhaps 70 or 80, involved widow's estate.[13] In principle the custom of widow's estate was a simple right. It allowed the widow of any copyholding tenant who had died in possession of a copyhold estate to enter and enjoy that estate, or part of it, for as long as she remained chaste and unmarried and paid the rents and performed the services due. In practice, the custom could be the subject of bitter disagreement and conflict, as the following example illustrates.

Joan Ellis brought a suit in Requests in 1558 claiming her widow's estate in a customary messuage in Baltonsborough. She described how after her husband died the steward and his men "with vyolens dyd dryve oute of the said howse your said subjecte & vii of her childer".[14] In asking for redress she argued that the custom of widow's estate in Baltonsborough was universal, giving a life interest to the widow of any copyholder who died in possession of a copyhold estate.[15] The defendants answered that the custom did not extend to every widow: it had exceptions. They alleged that previous estates in remainder granted to other tenants took precedence over widow's estate, if they had been granted before the date of the widow's marriage. In this case, they said, the local abbot had granted the reversion of the property to one of the defendants, Margaret Poole, before Joan married her husband, and therefore she could not sustain a claim under custom.[16]

The Masters established a commission to gather evidence and Joan called tenants from Baltonsborough and surrounding manors to answer interrogatories prepared on her behalf. All agreed that in principle every widow had a right to her husband's lands under custom. An 80-year-old deponent from Glastonbury said that Joan should have her widow's estate, "if old custumes shuld take place", and a husbandman who had lived in Baltonsborough for only six years said that although he was a newcomer, from what he had heard she should have her widow's estate.[17] But they had different impressions, or were simply unsure, about the details of customary law and of Joan's particular circumstances. Few of the witnesses could remember whether Joan had married her husband before or after the granting of the reversion to Margaret. Some were unsure about which customs applied to which manors. One man said that he thought that the manors of Baltonsborough and Badcom shared customs, and in Badcom widow's received their estates. Most deponents did not hazard opinions, but gave examples of widows whose rights had been recognized in the past. William Pypett told his examiners how "the wydowes of them that have died tenants have had ther widowes astate in their husbands tenements that they have died possessed of", and he gave examples of two widows who had paid heriots to enter their widow's estate ahead of remainder holders, both of whom later agreed to give up possession in return for a money pension.

A lone husbandman from the manor deposed on behalf of the defendants. He told his examiners that the disputed lands had been granted to Margaret Poole in remainder before Joan had married her husband. He had been present at court when the homage had been at variance and unable to decide whether or not to vote Joan an estate. He said they had referred the matter to the lord of the manor, who in turn referred it to the assizes at Chard, but in the meantime Margaret Poole was admitted tenant. He alleged that the widows the deponents claimed had enjoyed widow's estates in preference to the holders of estates in remainder, had all subsequently been evicted from their lands, and the pensions that some of them had received had been voluntary, and not linked to customary widow's rights, for none of the widows had paid heriots after their husbands died.

The defendants lost this case. As Joan narrated in a later case, the Masters decided this action in her favour on the basis of deposition evidence and the testimony of "religious persons now in the monastery of westminster" who had formerly been monks in Glastonbury, despite the fact that, in Joan's words, "there be divers wytnesses which have deposed that widowes shoulde not have theyr wydowes estate in the saide manor of Baltonsboroughe".[18] They ordered that Joan should have possession of the premises during her widowhood according to custom, until and unless the defendants could produce additional evidence to satisfy the court that Joan did not have good title.[19] The defendants duly produced new evidence, not the word of a husbandman this time, but the opinions of knights, squires and gentlemen who came from Glastonbury, and from manors up to 12 miles away from Baltonsborough. These men presented evidence of a more "legal" nature than the opinions and anecdotes from memory favoured by husbandmen of the manor, and their views add weight to C. E. Searle's argument, concerning the eighteenth century, that the definition of local custom "was highly variable in relation to class position".[20] The local surveyor said that he possessed court rolls and books of record that proved that reversions took precedence over widow's estates by custom. A gentleman said that he was the servant of the surveyor of the Barony of Glastonbury and he had seen and kept the court rolls which proved the same.[21]

No other documents or a decision survive from this later case, suggesting that the new bill was dismissed without further process, that the defendants chose not to pursue their appeal, or that this information has been lost. Nevertheless, the surviving records are revealing and raise interesting points about the mechanics of custom, as it operated on the manor and as it was dealt with in Requests, and about the intricate details that litigants alleged attached to the custom of widow's estate. First of all, they show the depth of uncertainty that could surround something as apparently certain as ancient custom. The confusion of Joan's deponents about the finer details of widow's estate, and the suggestion that the homage had been at variance and had suggested the matter be referred to assizes, both point to the fragility of custom in people's minds. Much of this fragility is, of course, artificial, caused by the distortion of the legal process; disagreement over matters of fact is an integral part of any adversarial legal system. But deep disagreement over matters of law was rare in Requests actions, and the fact that the parties openly claimed incompatible customs, disagreeing over the form of custom as well as its applicability, suggests that custom was sufficiently unclear to be included in the gamesmanship of the court room.

Customary law was uncertain because it was intensely local; the rules settled for one tenement might or might not apply to a neighbouring tenement. It was uncertain because it was essentially unwritten. Of course in practice stewards wrote down "unwritten" customs in custumals and recorded customary transactions in court rolls but, as Thompson has noted, customs as they were recorded in custumals could be very different from the "denser reality of social practice".[22] Most of all customary law was uncertain because it was changeable. However timeless customs appeared to onlookers, customary law was fluid and the form of customs might shift from generation to generation, or even from year to year. In a case from 1571, where the issue was whether reversions could be granted without the consent of the current tenant, deponents on both sides agreed that according to ancient custom, reversions could *not* be granted without consent. But they also acknowledged that at least a dozen reversions *had* been granted without consent within the preceding 30 years. Supporters of the custom were adamant that it was still in force, but as many of them spoke in terms of "the custom until 20 or 30 years ago", it seems that they had not been so adamant on previous occasions.[23] This was how custom worked: tenants fiercely asserting that custom in general was inviolable, but voting on the homage for, or turning a blind eye to, subtle shifts of custom in individual cases, according to their personal attitudes and current community norms.

The second, related, point that comes out of the Ellis case is the importance the Masters placed on oral testimony, and the tension that seems to have existed in their minds between the force of oral testimony and the authority of written evidence. Eric Kerridge has argued that when faced with matters of custom, Requests Masters based their judgments solely on written proof. He supports Alexander Savine, who wrote that "The court of Requests looks for truth, not in the *Rechtsbewusstsein* [legal consciousness] of the local population, but in the dust of the manorial records".[24] It is true the Masters took heed of manorial records wherever they were available. In a customary dispute from Oxfordshire in 1562 they dismissed a claim because the custom alleged by the complainants was not listed in the steward's book.[25] But it is also clear that they remained reluctant to pass judgment on the basis of documentary proof alone.[26]

In most cases, rather than rely on dusty manorial records, they chose to establish a commission, empowering commissioners to interview witnesses and arbitrate a local solution, or to supply depositions and a commissioners' report to assist them in making a decision. The Masters appointed commissioners for a number of reasons. To begin with, the integrity of documents could rarely be assured in any Requests case, and allegations of forgery were rife.[27] Even where documents were genuine they might not apply to the individuals or to the interests in question, and the Masters were aware of the dangers of relying on uncorroborated documentary evidence, just as they were concerned that their use of equitable intervention to right local wrongs should not cause any further injustice. But again, the Masters' frequent demands for local examinations of parties also stemmed from their recognition of the flexibility of customary law and the fact that customs were rarely fixed or immovable. They realized that for a custom to be valid, it had to have existed "time out of the memory of man", and so considered it only right to consult the memories of local men and women. Their understanding of time immemorial was subtly different from Lord Denning's. Under modern law, immemorial custom means in uninterrupted existence since before 3 September 1189 (a date set by the Statute of Westminster as a limiting date for writs of right). In a case from 1872, for example, a stall holder asserted his right to set up a market stall under an ancient custom linked to "statute session" hiring fairs. His opponents defeated his claim by demonstrating that these statute sessions had originally been authorized by the Statute of Labourers, passed in the reign of Edward III, and that therefore the custom had not been in existence in 1189.[28]

In the sixteenth century, when recordkeeping, the consultation of records, printed law reports and modern ideas about legal precedent were just beginning to make inroads into a still largely oral society, "time out of the memory of man" was a far less definite concept and held different meanings for different people. For Edward Coke and other Westminster jurists it meant outside the collective recollections, based on documentary records, of society in general. But for most people it meant outside the reliable memories of particular individuals. As Theodore Plucknett pointed out in his *Concise history of common law*, "in an age when custom was an active living factor in the development of society there was much less insistence upon actual or fictitious antiquity".[29] The Masters of Requests were themselves Westminster jurists and they saw eye to eye with Coke on the general principal of immemorial custom, but as judges in a working equity court they remained sensitive to the meaning given to immemorial custom by the landlords and, more importantly, the tenants, who lived by it.[30]

To prove that the custom of widow's estate had existed "time out of mind or memory of man" in Baltonsborough, Joan Ellis called the oldest residents of the manor to depose on her behalf. The 22 tenants who gave evidence for her all said that they were over 40 years old, and eight claimed to be 70 or older. All of them asserted that widows had "always" received widow's estate on their manor, but none gave examples from outside their own personal experience or memory. Memory of the memory of others could extend the period of recall by a few decades. A 60-year-old yeoman deposing in another case described the details of widow's estate on his manor, "the contynuance of which custom he knoweth to have ben observed by the space of [50] yeres and more and hathe herde by credyble reporte that the custom was suche afore the tyme of his knoledge".[31]

"Credyble reportes" aside, "time out of the memory" effectively meant not much longer than the 60 or 70 years of living memory. Sometimes it meant a shorter time. The complainant in this last case called as a deponent the foreman of the homage that had voted to exclude her from her lands. He was foreman because at 37 he was the oldest customary tenant on the homage, and he explained how he and his fellow tenants had made a presentment against the plaintiff because her copy included three lives, whereas the custom only permitted copyholds for two lives. The homage had believed this to be the custom, "not knowing of matter to the contrary", however, he had since discovered that his own tenement had previously been granted for three lives, "to one Horlock, who quietly enjoyed". He now knew that another tenement had also been so granted, and that the steward agreed that such grants were good. A 65-year-old deponent described how the foreman had told him, "that he was a younge man and knewe not what he did and was very sory for his so doinge and . . . that he thinketh in his consyence that the Complainant hathe not made any forfeicture of her saide grounde". Westminster might have been having its memory unfettered through effective recordkeeping, but to tenants of Somerset manors recent precedents were as important as ancient precedents, and while the age of customs was prized, the age of evidence was not. A widow from Taunton made a claim under the "anciente custome" of widow's estate in which she challenged her opponent's evidence, a certificate of custom, alleging that it had been prepared by a clerk who had referred to "ancient" court rolls.[32] The implication is that ancient court rolls and custumals made suspect evidence because they might be out of date.

The importance of the long heritage of any custom in people's minds must not be underestimated, but most people's everyday dependence on the short timescale of living memory, despite the growing influence of written authority, needs to be realized. Keith Thomas, for example, has pointed out the consternation felt by Oxfordshire villagers when an epidemic ravaged the elderly population so that, as Thomas Willis reported, "there scarce remained alive any for upholding the customs and privileges of the parish". The Masters recognized the importance of living memory and went out of their way to ascertain local opinion, for they understood that while a written record might establish antiquity, it often said nothing about whether a custom had been, and remained, common practice. Customary law was not so indelibly inscribed in the past that it could not change, and despite the increasingly successful attempts of common lawyers like Edward Coke to bring it closer under the wing of the common law, in areas where it survived it remained surprisingly responsive to local pressures, needs and attitudes.

When customs changed, the change could be sudden and involve the conscious decision of a community. An early seventeenth-century commentator on Chancery described how lords and tenants could alter customs on their manor by indenture, providing that all affected parties consented to the change. He described a case in Chancery that involved such an indenture, and explained how the Lord Keeper had shown a willingness to recognize and enforce the new customs, "because els all the Coppieholders of that Mannor or of any other Mannor of England which have altered their Customes in like Case by consent shalbe prevented & altered & nothinge wilbe certaine".[34] More often change was gradual, and all but imperceptible to witnesses. Christopher Dyer mentions in his study of Whitstones how witnesses in an inheritance dispute in 1538 agreed that, "they never knew any man's daughter was adjudged to any customary tenement . . . and that . . . [never] they had any such custom there used". This was, as Dyer notes, "in flat contradiction of the court rolls which show daughters inheriting as late as 1462".[35]

With regard to the widows of Elizabethan Somerset, the fact that customary law was not rigidly fixed helps to explain why so apparently simple a custom as widow's estate could become the subject of intense litigation in manor courts and in Requests. For while widow's estate itself was one of the most constant of customs, the customary tenure it most commonly attached to in the sixteenth century, copyholds for lives, changed markedly over time. Copyhold, holding by copy of court roll, developed out of feudal villeinage some time in the fourteenth or fifteenth centuries.[36] Originally, copyholds were granted for one life. If a male copyholder died leaving a widow, her claim to widow's estate, (assuming the custom applied), could not interfere with the claim of another interest holder, because no other interest holder existed. Over time copyholds became heritable, and when a copyholder died custom dictated that reverting interests be regranted to his or her heir. This innovation gave security to families, but it did so by creating future interests, and with them the possibility of conflicting claims. Future interests became severable from the family with the advent of copyholds for lives, which allowed a copyholder to write the names of future holders into his or her copy.

This form of tenure was the subject of almost half of Somerset Requests actions, but when Coke wrote his treatise on copyholds he decided to omit it. As Richard Fisher explained in his work on custom in 1794,

> in his excellent little Treatise, called "The Compleat Copyholder," in laying down general positions, [Coke] treats only of pure and genuine Copyholds; whereas at this time of day, there is a sort of bastard species, (if the expression may be allowed) of Copyhold Tenures; namely, Copyholds for lives.[37]

As has been shown, copyholds for lives flourished when Coke wrote.

Future interests were the bane of the common law, and perhaps by neglecting them he hoped that they would simply go away. But despite this snub, they continued to develop. By the late eighteenth century a whole range of new forms had sprung up, including copyholds for three lives in which the persons named in the copy never enjoyed possession, but acted merely as trustees for an unnamed tenant in possession. Charles Watkins tried to make sense of the shifting history of copyhold in his 1797 treatise, in which he explained,

> He [the author] has endeavoured to extract something at least like consistency from the crude mass of matter which the books afford. He has even endeavoured to reconcile the jarring and discordant cases on several points which he had to consider; but this, he must confess, sometimes appeared to be rather out of the reach of the powers usually allotted to humanity; and which he, consequently, could only lament.[38]

The course of change from copyholds for one life to copyholds as increasingly marketable interests and copyholders as trustees was, of course, slow and unpredictable. In Whitstones, Christopher Dyer found that dealings in interests in land were fluid and reversions common in the late fourteenth-century and for much of the fifteenth century, but after 1500 copyholds tended once again to pass within families, as they had done in the past prior to 1349.[39] However, the more fluid the land market and the greater the number of remainders, reversions and other future interests, the more likely a widow seeking widow's estate might face competition. The Requests records are full of "jarring and discordant cases" that expose the clash of interests between widows and future-interest holders, as well as the changeable nature of copyholds for lives. In a case from 1573, the complainant Agnes Grove was adamant that the right of widow's estate accrued to the widow of *any* copyholder named in a copy for three lives. Her opponent countered that *only* the widow of a purchaser could claim an estate.[40] In a case from 1586 a defendant claimed her widow's estate as widow of the purchaser of a copy for three lives. Her opponent argued that only the widow of the longest living of the three persons named in the copy had any rights to widow's estate.[41] Other litigants from other manors raised different issues. Could holders of copies for lives surrender their interests at any time, to the prejudice of the others named in their copies? Could a husband surrender an interest without the consent of his wife? And so on, and so on.

Two strong themes emerge from the mayhem of the cases. The first is the important point that copyholds for lives offered a superior alternative to widow's estate.[42] A wife named in a copy had an interest for life if she survived her husband, not just an interest for the duration of a chaste widowhood. In fact, it is likely that the majority of widows on Somerset manors where copyholds were granted for lives held interests by virtue of being named in a copy. However, the need to be named could work against certain women, and *second* wives of copyholders in particular were often at a disadvantage. A tenant might have made provision for his first wife by naming her in a copy. But if he married again he was less likely to make a similar arrangement for his second wife, because to do so he would have to surrender his copy and pay a fine to take a new one. The Requests records are consequently full of cases involving widows who were second wives, struggling to claim widow's estate, often against opponents who argued that custom did not allow a widow to claim her husbands interest if his copy contained the name of a previous wife.

This leads on to the second theme current in the sort of disputes which reached Requests: namely the importance of the relationships between litigants. As I have tried to demonstrate, changes in copyholding custom and practice could exert pressure on widows claiming widow's estate, by increasing the number of rival claimants widows unlucky enough not to be named in a copy could expect to face. However, the existence of a future interest did not in itself challenge a widow's rights. Widow's estate almost always delayed the interest of another interest holder, if only an inheriting son or daughter. The possibility that a woman might outlive her husband and claim her widow's estate was to be expected. Conflict arose when the possibility that a widow might claim widow's estate was *not* expected, in other words when it disturbed the expectations of the next holder, as happened in the Ellis case.

A variety of circumstances could interfere with the expectations of holders of future interests, but the commonest trait shared by widows claiming or defending widow's estate in Requests was that their husbands had been married before. Second wives, through no real fault of their own, could disturb community or family perceptions of the accepted ordering of life. For example, children named in copies might, and often did, resent the unexpected interruption to their plans of a step-mother claiming her widow's estate.[43] To fellow tenants on the homage, a widow who had worked on a customary holding for decades beside her husband might have appeared a worthier recipient of widow's estate than a young second wife widowed after only a year. In this sense custom could be normative, offering greater protection for common behaviour than for uncommon or less common behaviour.

Second or subsequent wives regularly faced opposition from rival claimants amongst the tenantry, but in conflicts between tenants and their landlords some second wives participated in the exploitation of the custom of widow's estate for profit. J. H. Bettey has found a series of cases from seventeenth-century Dorset in which ageing tenants married young brides to deprive lords and stewards of entry fines and the possession of customary interests. Men who were the last named in copies, or who had failed to have their children's names entered in copies, married young women after making them agree to divert a proportion of the profits from their widow's estate to named individuals. In the 1620s a dying man married a young widow after making her sign an agreement that after his death she would permit his eldest son to farm the lands and share the profits with the other children. She was to get £5 a year, houseroom and fuel. Women in a position to bargain could make a profit from such deals, but others, girls as young as 12 years old, might gain little from these arrangements except for a premature widowhood. Bettey suggests that "frauds" like these may have been common, and they were certainly long lasting. William Stevenson complained as late as 1812 of "customary tenants marrying in the last stage of decrepit old age to very young girls". The only Somerset case he looked at demonstrates that this practice could be influential in encouraging landlords to try to extinguish copyholds and replace them with leaseholds. As a result of a survey conducted in 1674 a sickly tenant in his eighties was offered £150 if he would surrender his copyhold. He refused and married a young servant maid. The steward then advised the lord, "I say have not anything to do with them except they will turne their Coppys into Leasehold".[44]

If custom was flexible and occasionally unpredictable, so too was the Master's response in customary actions. They negotiated the problems of discovering the facts in the cases before them as best they could, encouraged local solutions wherever possible, and sought to ascertain, from the evidence of documents and witness testimony, which party in each action had the better claim. They went out of their way to avoid interfering with custom itself.[45] In these cases their concern was with the unfairness or mistakes of people, not with the possible unfairness of custom. If they decided a claimant had a valid interest they were willing to use the authority of equity to override the authority of local lords, ladies and stewards. But

sometimes they went further, making equitable decisions in favour of litigants who appeared to have no legally sustainable claim. In 1562 a complainant alleged that a widow could have no interest by copy in the lands
she possessed, because the lands were not copyhold. Upon examination
and hearing, the court agreed that they were not copyhold, and that the
widow, therefore, had no rights in them at all. However, they ordered,
with the consent of the parties, that she should surrender the copy by
which she had claimed,

> And that thereupon the said complainant in consideracion of the
> greate Age and povertie of the saide Defendant shall by Dede
> Indented demise the premisses . . . to the saide Defendant for terme
> of fowertie yeres then nexte ensueinge (if she live so longe . . .).[46]

The defendant had to pay rent for this land, "assessed by the saide
Counsaill of the saide courte", and to maintain the house at her expense,
but the grant is noteworthy none the less. In another case from the same
year a widow failed to prove her right to widow's estate in lands occupied
by the defendant. Having respect "that the said complainant ys a woman of
grete age and verie poore" the Masters ordered that the defendant should
continue in occupation, but that he should pay "yerelie unto the said complainant [£30] during her naturall lief".[47] As Hoyle remarked, noting an
earlier example of largess shown by the Masters, "the tempering of strict
law with such humanity appears to have been typical of early modern
judicial practice". The Masters' compromise solutions brought a degree of
equity to the manor, but as Tawney pointed out, their overriding of manor
court decisions unavoidably undermined the integrity of customary law,
and perhaps hastened its decline.[49]

Over the course of Elizabeth's reign the Masters meddled less and less
with the decisions of manor courts and made fewer, what to modern eyes
appear to be arbitrary, charitable orders. The increasing willingness of the
central common law courts to allow actions of trespass concerning copyhold land, meant that the Masters were faced with fewer customary
actions, and they dismissed an increasing number without hearing, as
"matters best fit to be heard at the common law".[50] Nevertheless, they
maintained an influence in many cases by directing the shape that common
law proceedings took and by reserving final judgment on any remaining
matters of equity.[51]

Widows like Joan Ellis who turned to Requests when rivals threatened
their interests found the court responsive to their claims. The Masters

investigated their rights with diligence, and occasionally made equitable orders imbued with a considerable spirit of charity, showing sympathy to the poor, the aged, the intimidated and the voiceless. Widows who claimed customary estates were not a special case, they simply happened to fall into these categories more often than most. At first sight these findings confirm the views of Alice Clark and Doris Stenton. Widows of copyholders were usually well protected by custom. Those named in copies enjoyed their late husbands' interests for life. Those not named in copies usually enjoyed an interest under widow's estate in all (or in some areas in a proportion) of their husbands' lands for the duration of their widowhood. This compares well with common law dower, which could be difficult to claim, and which offered widows a life interest in only a third of their husbands' property.[52] It also compares well with jointures, (agreed shares of property negotiated at the time of marriage), in the sense that although they could assure women reasonable rights in property should they become widows, jointures had to be arranged – a process which could be complicated and costly.[53] Widow's estate, by contrast, applied automatically. However, the view of custom from Requests is not uniformly positive, and it is difficult looking at Elizabethan Somerset to share Clark's optimism about women's participation in the customary process. The sampled cases contain no references to women serving in person on homages, and convention forced most female copyholders to send deputies in their stead.[54] Furthermore, the depositions from 50 sampled cases show that 9 out of 211 deponents who testified before commissioners were female.[55] The custody of custom was apparently seen as a male preserve and the majority of litigants in Requests preferred to call men as witnesses to describe the experiences of widows, rather than calling the widows themselves.

Another important point is that custom offered women few rights apart from widow's estate. Daughters, for example, did not inherit equally with sons, and if a woman with a customary interest married, her husband gained control of that interest for the duration of the couple's marriage.[56] It is true he could not surrender or sell the interest without her consent (confirmed to the lord or steward in private to assure that it was given voluntarily), but the cases demonstrate the pressure unscrupulous husbands could put on their wives.[57] If some women did well under custom, clearly many others did not. Courts like Requests and Chancery offered a safety net, and access to these central equity courts, as well as to common law courts like Queen's Bench and Common Pleas, was surprisingly wide. If a woman lacked the funds necessary to litigate in these courts, she could petition to gain entry *in forma pauperis* and have an attorney and other legal counsel supplied and her fees waived. Nevertheless, the ancillary costs of litigation, such as travel and accommodation, combined with women's ignorance of their legal opportunities, meant that the silent majority were not in a position to defend their customary interests in central courts such as Requests.

What the Requests' records demonstrate is that as well as comparing women's rights under custom with women's rights under the common law, equity and ecclesiastical law, it is important to realize that women's rights under custom were not static. They differed from manor to manor, they could shift and change on the same manor over time and, given the normative effect of custom, they could even differ markedly, in terms of the strength of support they offered, from individual to individual. Custom certainly offered advantages to many women, because it was local, and because it was less formal than the common law and its process generally less expensive. However, the flexibility of custom meant that, as a system of law, it would have been as capable of absorbing, as it was of withstanding, the prejudice against women that is so often associated with the common law. It would therefore be naive to assume that any erosion of women's rights attributable to the growth in importance of the common law would not have occurred over a similar period under custom.[58]

It is clear from the Requests' archive that custom continued to affect the lives of many people in Somerset and elsewhere in England in the sixteenth century, and social historians can learn much from records of customary disputes. The force of custom as a concept is also strongly apparent. All parties in customary actions repeated the same formulaic phrases, "according to the custom of the manor", "time whereof the memory of man was not to the contrary" and "time out of memory of man" over and over, in their attempts to harness the almost spiritual authority of custom to their cause. However, the strength of custom in people's minds stood in marked contrast to the malleability of customary law in practice, as Thompson, Hoyle, Searle and others have demonstrated with respect to long-running customary tussles between lords and tenants.[60] The slip between the illusion of the immutability of custom and its flexibility in daily use gave custom, as a system of law, its enduring strength. While common lawyers worried about "jarring and discordant cases", under customary law such cases were simply forgotten.[60]

Customs survived only when they were regularly asserted and etched into the memories of each generation. This was obviously more likely to happen when customs reflected or expressed local feeling, when they tapped into or constituted part of a community's "moral economy". Put very simply, customs survived in localities when enough people wanted them to survive. Most members of communities agreed in principle that widows deserved support and, despite the fact that widow's estate faced competition, and in some places was denied, in the main it survived wherever the tenure of copyhold survived, carrying on into the eighteenth century and beyond. Where customs lacked this kind of deep local support or were rarely asserted they could quickly lapse. And customs that favoured women who were not widows, by giving them property or independence, were probably less likely than other customs to receive such support.

When considering the resilience of long lived customs it is important to recall the apparent amnesia of Christopher Dyer's Whitstone tenants, who in 1538 were unaware that daughters had regularly inherited on their manor until less than 70 years before. If this process of collective forgetting, as well as collective remembering, can be more precisely analyzed, it may hold the key to how other ideas and beliefs change and pass within communities. In particular, how restrictive, patriarchal attitudes to women pass from generation to generation, and how they adapt to other changes in society.

Notes

1. New Windsor Corporation v. Mellor (C.A.), [1975] Ch. 380, p. 386.
2. Exceptions include M. Spufford, *Contrasting communities: English villagers in the sixteenth and seventeenth centuries* (Cambridge, 1979); A. Erickson, *The property ownership and financial decisions of ordinary women in early modern England*, PhD thesis, University of Cambridge, 1990; J. H. Bettey, Manorial custom and widows' estate, *Archives*, **XX**, 1992, pp. 208–216; C. W. Brooks, *Pettyfoggers and vipers of the commonwealth* (Cambridge, 1986), pp. 73–4, 197–203; T. H. Aston & C. H. E. Philpin, *The Brenner debate: agrarian class structure and economic developments in pre-industrial Europe* (Cambridge, 1987).
3. F. W. Maitland, *Select pleas in manorial and other seignorial courts*, vol. 1, Selden Society, **II** (London, 1889), p. xi.
4. This is a manifestation of the tendency to assume the dominance of the "immemorial" Ancient Constitution in English legal thought. See C. W. Brooks, The place of Magna Carta and the Ancient Constitution in sixteenth-century English legal thought, in *The roots of liberty: Magna Carta, Ancient Constitution, and the Anglo-American tradition of rule of law*, ed. E. Sandoz (Columbia: University of Missouri Press, 1993), pp. 57–9.
5. Brooks, *Pettyfoggers and vipers of the commonwealth*, p. 36. As E. P. Thompson

argues, it is a mistake to judge the influence of custom by counting the number of acres of customary land. You must count the number of tenants; E. P. Thompson, The grid of inheritance: a comment, in *Family and inheritance: rural society in Western Europe, 1200–1800*, eds J. Goody *et al.* (Cambridge, 1976), pp. 328–9; Bettey's recent study of 49 manorial surveys in seventeenth-century Dorset, for example, reveals that 6 per cent of interests holders were freeholders, 5 per cent were leaseholders and 89 per cent were copyholders; Bettey, Manorial custom and widows' estate, p. 208.

6. E. P. Thompson, *Customs in common*, (London, 1991), p. 6.

7. R. W. Hoyle, An ancient and laudable custom: the definition and development of tenant right in north-western England in the sixteenth century, *Past & Present*, **116**, 1987, pp. 24–55, p. 24; and see C. E. Searle, Custom, class conflict and agrarian capitalism: the Cumbrian customary economy in the eighteenth century, *Past & Present*, **110**, 1986, pp. 106–133, p. 113.

8. For information about the history and procedures of the Court of Requests, see G. R. Elton, *The Tudor constitution: documents and commentary*, (Cambridge, 1968), pp. 184–95; T. Stretton, *Women and litigation in the Elizabethan Court of Requests*, PhD thesis, University of Cambridge, 1993, ch. 3.

9. A. Clark, *Working life of women in the seventeenth century*, ed. Amy Erikson (London, 1982), p. 237.

10. D. Stenton, *The English woman in history* (London, 1957), p. 79.

11. Erickson, *Property ownership and financial decisions*, pp. 58–60.

12. Overall, women appear to have participated in about 32 per cent of Requests actions during Elizabeth's reign; Stretton, *Women and litigation*, p. 47.

13. Estimates based on entries for cases identified as originating in Somerset found in *Public Record Office lists & indexes no. 21*, List of proceedings in the Court of Requests preserved in the Public Record Office (New York: Kraus Reprint Corporation, 1963) and in MS. Requests calendars housed in the PRO. The calendars do not always distinguish whether customary disputes involved widow's estate, so this estimate is consequently speculative.

14. Johane Eles v. Humphrey Poole *et al.*, PRO, Req 2/165/64, Bill.

15. PRO, Req 2/165/64, B; Req 2/23/94, B.

16. PRO, Req 2/165/64, Answer.

17. For all that follows see PRO, Req 2/165/64, Depositions, deponents William Hutchens and Edward Hebbar, William George, William Pypett, and John Rushe.

18. PRO, Req 2/23/94, B.

19. PRO, Req 2/23/94, B; Req 2/22/13, copy of order.

20. Searle, Custom, class conflict and agrarian capitalism, p. 120.

21. PRO, Req 2/165/64, D, deponents Ralph Hopton & Richard Powys.

22. Thompson, The grid of inheritance, p. 337.

23. Thomas & Johanne Crace v. William Stokes, PRO, Req 2/188/62, D, deponents John Bydsham, William Myllard, John Kene & John Lewes.

24. E. Kerridge, *Agrarian problems in the sixteenth century and after* (London, 1969), p. 67.

25. Richard & Agnes Jones v. John Colder, PRO, Req 1/11, pp. 201–204.

26. On the relative importance of oral and written authority, see D. R. Woolf, Speech, text, and time: the sense of hearing and the sense of the past in Renaissance England, *Albion*, **18**, 1986, pp. 159–93.

27. Richard Compton recorded details in his law reports of an entire custumal that had been forged; R. Crompton, *Star Chamber cases* (London, 1630), pp. 37–40.

28. Simpson v. Wells (1872) L. R. 7 Q. B. 214, as described in C. K. Allen, *Law in the making*, seventh edn (Oxford, 1964), pp. 134–5.

29. T. Plucknett, *A concise history of common law*, fourth edn, (London, 1948), pp. 290–91.

30. It is revealing that when Requests came under attack from common lawyers in the 1590s the court's apologist Julius Caesar attempted to defend the court's legitimacy by proving its existence since time immemorial (through the Masters' associations with the King's Council); see L. M. Hill (ed.), *The ancient state authoritie, and proceedings of the Court of Requests by Sir Julius Caesar* (Cambridge, 1975), pp. ix–xviii.

31. For all that follows see Mary Palmer v. Christopher Rolles, PRO, Req 2/33/108, D, deponents John Willis, William Byshoppe and William Wykes.

32. Alice John v. George Hill & Margaret Togwell, PRO, Req 2/226/48, B & Replication.

33. K. Thomas, Age and authority in early modern England, *Proceedings of the British Academy*, **62** (1976), pp. 205–248, p. 234.

34. Camb UL, Gg. 2. 31 fol. 476v.

35. C. Dyer, Changes in the size of peasant holdings in some West Midland villages 1400–1540, in *Land, kinship and lifecycle*, ed. R. M. Smith (Cambridge, 1984), pp. 291–2.

36. Plucknett, *A concise history of common law*, pp. 293–4.

37. R. B. Fisher, *A practical treatise on copyhold tenure, with the methods of holding courts leet, court baron and other courts* (London, 1794), p. iv.

38. C. Watkins, *Treatise on copyholds* (London, 1797), p. vii.

39. Dyer, Changes in the size of peasant holdings, pp. 285–6.

40. Agnes Grove v. John Thynne et al., PRO, Req 2/210/118, B & A; 2/35/50, B & A.

41. William Allambrigge v. Anne Allambrigge, PRO, Req 2/168/19, B & A.

42. Stenton, *The English woman in history*, p. 103.

43. See, for example, John Willet v. Johane Willet, PRO, Req 2/283/55; Margaret Upham v. Richard Upham, Req 2/281/15; Alice Gibbes v. Ambrose Butler, Req 2/209/18.

44. Bettey, Manorial custom and widow's estate, pp. 210–14.

45. The Chancery bench took a similar view; W. J. Jones, *The Elizabethan court of*

Chancery (Oxford, 1967), p. 264.

46. William Manner v. Joane Gregory, PRO, Req 1/11, p. 155.

47. Elizabeth Prowse v. John Powe, PRO, Req 1/11, pp. 220–21.

48. R. W. Hoyle, Tenure and the land market in early modern England: or a late contribution to the Brenner debate, *The Economic History Review*, second series, **XLIII**, 1990, pp. 1–20: p. 3.

49. R. H. Tawney, *The agrarian problem in the sixteenth century* (London, 1912), p. 296.

50. Kerridge, *Agrarian problems in the sixteenth century and after*, p. 72; William Hammond v. Thomas Dockwra, PRO, Req 1/21, p. 186.

51. See, for example PRO, Req 1/17, p. 312; 1/15, p. 105; Ann Anncell v. Michael Anncell, Req 1/21, p. 55; Alice Langton v. Thomas Fletcher, Req 1/19, p. 243.

52. On the difficulty of claiming dower, see N. F. Cantor, correspondence, *Times Literary Supplement*, 25 January 1991, p. 15.

53. For information about jointures and marriage settlements, see Erickson, The property ownership and financial decisions of ordinary women in early modern England, *passim*.

54. On female attendance on homages see C. Stopes, *British freewomen: their historical privilege*, third edn (London, 1907), pp. 81–5, 94–6.

55. Sample of 50 cases involving women litigants from Elizabeth's reign, taken from the class PRO Req 2.

56. An exception is the inheritance custom of third shares which took primacy over primogeniture in York and London, and which saw that a third of an intestate's estate was divided equally between his or her children, whether male or female; Erickson, The property ownership and financial decisions of ordinary women, pp. 51–2.

57. And see T. E., *The lawes resolutions of womens rights* (London, 1632), pp. 179–80.

58. The question of whether women's legal position "improved" or "declined" over this period is still hotly debated. Given the complexity of "the law" and the difference in experiences of women according to their status, location, access to different courts and so forth, it is possible to argue that attempting to generalize in this way is unhelpful; Stretton, *Women and litigation*, pp. 265–8; and see S. Staves, *Married women's separate property in England, 1660–1833* (Cambridge, MA, 1990), p. 229.

59. Thompson, *Customs in common*; Thompson, A grid of inheritance; Hoyle, An ancient and laudable custom; Searle, Custom, class conflict and agrarian capitalism.

60. J. Goody, *The logic of writing and the organization of society* (Cambridge, 1986), p. 137.

Glossary

alienate   to sell or give away land or goods, thus separating them from an estate.

assizes   regular courts of the king's judges held in certain major towns in every county of England. Judges travelled round a "circuit", presiding over criminal trials at the assizes and acting in a supervisory capacity over the magistrates serving in the county quarter sessions.

billa vera   a *true Bill*. The term used to describe either an indictment or a presentment which had been found by a grand jury as having sufficient supporting evidence for a case to proceed to trial.

burglary   breaking into a house by night with intent to commit a felony. "Housebreaking" was the same offence committed in the daytime.

canon law   church law enforced through the consistory courts.

consistory court   diocesan or bishop's court, concerned with religious, moral and matrimonial causes in canon law.

court of requests   a central court of equity in civil matters, especially disputes over customary rights. Originally, "to give justice to men too poor and uninfluential to secure their ends in the ordinary courts".

custom   a local and popular form of law, based upon the ancient accumulation of rights, which developed through the manorial courts (local estate courts). They generally related to such issues as land use, tenure, conditions of service, inheritance and collective responsibilities.

deposition and examination   evidence taken from plaintiffs, witnesses and defendants.

dower   a wife's right in a life tenancy of her husband's lands after his death, but only to one third of the lands which he owned at death (i.e. in which *he* was seised, not that which they owned jointly).

equity   process of judgement based upon principles of natural justice, which developed in the Chancery from the late fourteenth century.

felony   originally, a crime perpetrated with evil intent. Felonies carried the death penalty.

feme covert   a married woman. Largely a legal fiction whereby a wife's independent existence was suspended during marriage.

feme sole   a single woman. Thus a married woman acting independently would be described as a *feme sole*.

grand jury   composed of "discreet, able and sufficient men of the shire". On their judgement an indictment or presentment was either dismissed as *ignoramus* or proceeded as *billa vera* to be tried. They also presented defaults and abuses known to them.

indictment   the legal process and the document bringing a public accusation against an individual. Presentments by a justice of the peace or the grand jury had the force of an indictment.

information   could take the form of a deposition or examination, or a petition to the bench at quarter sessions or assizes.

ignoramus   the endorsement made by the grand jury that there was no case to answer.

jointure   the holding of a property to the joint use of a husband and wife for life or in tail, as a provision for the wife in the event of her widowhood. By extension this meant a sole estate limited to the wife, being "a competent livelihood of freehold for the wife of lands and tenements, to take effect upon the death of the husband for the life of the wife at least".

justice of the peace   a magistrate. A member of the county élite, commissioned by the Crown to keep the peace, he presided over the judicial and administrative business of the county.

larceny   theft, the felonious taking and carrying away of the personal goods of another. Grand larceny involved goods valued at 12*d* or more; petty larceny involved goods valued at less than 12*d*, and was not a capital offence.

mitigation   abatement or relaxation of the severity or full force of the law.

petty sessions   met more frequently than quarter sessions to hear lesser actions.

petty jury   the jury which tried each case to a verdict.

presentment   a statement on oath which initiated an action, usually in matters of public concern regulated by statute and by law, such as keeping the peace, poor law and highway maintenance.

quarter sessions   a county based judicial court and executive body, the key agency of local government. It met quarterly and was presided over by justices of the peace.

recognizance   a bond to perform a specified condition on pain of a fine. It was used to secure attendance at court, to bind individuals to keep the peace or to be of good behaviour, and to enforce personal contacts.

remain/remainder   such goods remain *away* from the stem family.

revert/reversion   goods or land revert *back* to the stem family.

widow's bench   a custom in some places (e.g. London), which gave the widow the right to remain in her husband's house for 40 days after his death.

Bibliography

Abbott, M., *Family ties. English families 1540–1920*, (London, 1993).

Allen, C. K., *Law in the making*, seventh edn (Oxford, 1964).

Amussen, S. D., Gender, family and the social order, 1560–1725, in *Order and disorder in early modern England*, eds A. J. Fletcher & J. Stevenson (Cambridge, 1985), pp.196–218.

Amussen, S. D., *An ordered society: gender and class in early modern England* (Oxford, 1988).

Anderson, A. & Gordon, R., Witchcraft and the status of women – the case of England, *British Journal of Sociology*, **29**, 1978, pp. 171–84.

Ankarloo, B. & Henningsen, G. (eds), *Early modern European witchcraft: centres and peripheries* (Oxford, 1990).

Ankarloo, B., Sweden: the mass burnings (1668–1676), in *Early modern European witchcraft*, eds B. Ankarloo & G. Henningsen (Oxford, 1990), pp.310–12.

Archer, I., *The pursuit of stability: social relations in Elizabethan London* (Cambridge, 1991).

Ashplant, T. G. & Wilson, A., Present-centred history and the problem of historical knowledge, *Historical Journal*, **31**, 1988, pp. 253–74.

Ashton, T. H. & Philpin, C. H. E. (eds), *The Brenner debate: agrarian class structure and economic devlopment in pre-industrial Europe* (Cambridge, 1985).

Aston, T. (ed.), *Crisis in Europe* (London, 1965).

Aylmer, G. E., The meaning and definition of 'property' in seventeenth-century England, *Past & Present*, **86**, 1980, pp. 87–97, Note, *ibid*. **89**, 1980, p. 143.

Baker, J. H., *An introduction to legal history*, third edn (London, 1990)

Baker, J. H. (ed.), *Legal records and the historian*. Royal Historical Society (London, 1978).

Barry, J. *et al.* (eds), *Witchcraft in early modern Europe: studies in culture and belief* (Cambridge, 1995).

Barstow, A. L., On studying witchcraft as women's history: a historiography of the

European witch persecutions, *Journal of Feminist Studies in Religion*, **4**, 1988, pp. 7–19.

Bashar, N., Rape in England between 1550 and 1700, in *The sexual dynamics of history*, ed. London Feminist History Group (London, 1983), pp. 28–42.

✶ Beattie, J. M., The criminality of women in eighteenth-century England, *Journal of Social History*, **8**, 1974–5, pp. 80–116.

✶ Beattie, J. M., The pattern of crime in England, 1660–1800, *Past & Present*, **62**, 1974, pp. 47–95.

Beattie, J. M., *Crime and the courts in England, 1660–1800* (Oxford, 1986).

Ben-Amos, I. K., Women apprentices in the trades and crafts of early modern Bristol, *Continuity and Change*, **6**, 1991, pp. 227–52.

Bennett, J. M., Feminism and history, *Gender and History*, **1**, 1989, pp. 251–72.

Berg, M., What difference did women's work make to the industrial revolution? *History Workshop Journal*, **35**, 1993, pp. 22–44.

Bettey, J. H., The revolts over the enclosure of the royal forest at Gillingham 1626–1630, *Proceedings of the Dorset Natural History and Archaeological Society*, **XCVII** (1976).

Bettey, J. H., Manorial custom and widows' estate, *Archives*, **XX**, 1992, pp. 208–216.

Bonfield, L. et al. (eds), *The world we have gained: histories of population and social structure. Essays presented to Peter Laslett on his seventieth birthday* (Oxford, 1986).

Bowler, C. A., Carted whores and white shrouded apologies: slander in the county courts of seventeenth-century Virginia, *The Virginia Magazine of History and Biography*, **85**, 1977, pp. 411–26.

Boyer, P. & Nissenbaum, S., *Salem possessed, the social origins of witchcraft* (Cambridge, MA, 1974).

Boys, J., The case of witchcraft at Coggeshall, Essex, in the year 1699 (London, 1909).

Brewer, J. & Styles, J. (eds), *An ungovernable people* (London, 1983).

Briggs, R., Witchcraft and popular mentality in Lorraine, 1580–1630, in *Occult and scientific mentalities in the Renaissance,* ed. B. Vickers (Cambridge, 1984), pp. 337–49.

Briggs, R., Women as victims? Witches, judges and the community in early modern France, *French History*, **5**, 1991, pp. 438–50.

Brooks, C. W., *Pettyfoggers and vipers of the commonwealth* (Cambridge, 1986).

Brooks, C. W., The place of Magna Carta and the Ancient Constitution in sixteenth-century English legal thought, in *The roots of liberty: Magna Carta, Ancient Constitution, and the Anglo-American tradition of rule of law,* ed. E. Sandoz (Columbia, 1993).

Brushfield, T. N., On obsolete punishments, with particular reference to those of Cheshire. Part I: the brank, or scold's bridle; Part II: the cucking stool and allied punishments, *Journal of the Architectural, Archaeological, and Historic Society . . . of Chester . . . December 1855 to December 1862*, **II**, 1864, pp. 31–48.

de Bruyn, L., *Woman and the devil in sixteenth-century literature* (Tisbury, 1979).

Buck, A., Buying clothes in Bedfordshire: customers and tradesmen, 1700–1800, *Textile History*, **22**, 1991, pp. 211–38.

Burke, P., L'histoire sociale des rêves, *Annales E. S. C.*, **2**, 1973, pp. 329–42.

Burke, P., The art of insult in early modern Italy, *Culture and History*, **2**, 1987, pp. 68–79.

Burke, P. (ed.), *New perspectives on historical writing* (Oxford, 1991).

Burke, P., The language of orders in early modern Europe, in *Social orders and social classes,* ed. M. L. Bush (London, 1992), pp. 1–14.

Bush, M. L. (ed.), *Social orders and social classes in Europe since 1500* (London, 1992).

Butler, J., *Gender trouble: feminism and the subversion of identity* (New York, 1990).

Capp, B., *Cromwell's Navy: The Fleet and the English Revolution, 1648–1660* (Oxford, 1989).

Capp, B., *Astrology and the popular press: English almanacs 1500–1800* (London and Boston, 1979).

Carrington, F. A., On certain ancient Wiltshire customs, *Wiltshire Archaeological and Natural History Magazine*, **I**, 1854, pp.68–79.

Charles, L. & Duffin L. (eds), *Women and work in pre-industrial England* (London, 1985).

Charles, L., Introduction to *Women and work in pre-industrial England*, eds L. Charles & L. Duffin (London, 1985), pp. 1–23.

Chesler, P., *Women and madness* (New York, 1972).

Clark, A., *Working life of women in the seventeenth century*, new edn (London, 1992)

Clark, A., Whores and gossips: sexual reputation in London, 1770–1825, in *Current issues in women's history*, eds A. Angerman *et al.* (London, 1989), pp. 231–48.

Clark, J. D. C., *English society, 1688–1832, ideology, social structure and political practice during the ancien regime* (Cambridge, 1985).

Clark, S., Inversion, misrule and and the meaning of witchcraft, *Past & Present*, **87**, 1980, pp. 98–127.

Clark, S., Protestant demonology: sin, superstition, and society (*c.* 1520–*c.*1630), in *Early modern European witchcraft*, eds B. Ankarloo & G. Henningsen, pp. 45–81.

Clarke, P., *The English alehouse a social history, 1200–1830* (London, 1983).

Cockburn, J. S., The nature and incidence of crime in England, 1559–1625, in *Crime in England, 1500–1800*, ed. J. S. Cockburn (London, 1977), pp. 49–71.

Cockburn, J. S., Early modern assize records as historical evidence, *Journal of the Society of Archivists*, **5**, 1975, pp. 215–31.

Cockburn, J. S., Trial by book? Fact and theory in the criminal process, 1558–1625, in *Legal records and the historian*, ed. J. H. Baker, Royal Historical Society (London, 1978), pp. 60–79.

Cockburn, J. S., *Introduction to the Assize Calendars* (London, 1985).

Collyer, R. & Horsfall Turner, J., *Ilkley: ancient and modern* (Leeds, 1885).

Crawford, P., Historians, women and the civil war sects, 1640–1660s, *Parergon*, new series, **6**, 1988, pp. 19–32.

Crawford, P., Review of Ian Archer's *The pursuit of stability: social relations in Elizabethan London*, in *Continuity and Change*, **8**, 1993, pp. 129–31.

Crawford, P., The construction and experience of maternity in seventeenth-century England, *Women as mothers in pre-industrial England*, ed. Valerie Fildes (London, 1990), pp. 3–38.

Crawford, P., Public duty, conscience and women in early modern England, in *Public duty, private conscience in seventeenth-century England. Essays presented to G. E. Aylmer*, eds J. Morrill *et al.* (Oxford, 1993), pp. 57–76.

Crawford, W. H., Women in the domestic linen industry, in *Women in early modern Ireland*, eds M. MacCurtain & M. O'Dowd (Edinburgh, 1991), pp. 255–64.

Cross, M. The church and local society in the diocese of Ely, *c.*1630–*c.*1730, PhD thesis, University of Cambridge, 1991.

Cullen, N., Women and the preparation of food in eighteenth-century Ireland, in *Women in early modern Ireland*, eds M. MacCurtain & M. O'Dowd (Edinburgh, 1991), pp. 265–75.

Curtis, T. C., Quarter Sessions appearances and their background: a seventeenth-century regional study, in *Crime in England 1550–1800*, ed. J. S. Cockburn (London, 1977), pp. 135–54.

Darby, H. C., *The draining of the Fens*, second edn (Cambridge, 1956).

Darnton, R., *The great cat massacre and other episodes in French cultural history* (London, 1984).

Davie, N., Chalk and cheese? "Fielden" and "forest" communities in early modern England, *Journal of Historical Sociology*, **IV**, 1991, pp. 1–31.

Davies, K. M., Continuity and change in literary advice on marriage, in *Marriage and society: studies in the social history of marriage*, ed. R. B. Outhwaite (London, 1981), pp. 58–80.

Davidoff, L., & Hall, C., *Family fortunes. Men and women of the English middle class, 1780–1850* (London, 1987).

Davis, N. Z. & Farge, A., Women as historical actors, in *A history of women in the west, vol. III. Renaissance and enlightenment paradoxes*, eds N. Z. Davis & A. Farge (Cambridge, MA, 1993), pp. 1–7.

Davis, N. Z., *Fiction in the archives. Pardon tales and their tellers in sixteenth-century France* (Cambridge and Stanford, 1987).

Deacon, R., *Matthew Hopkins: witch finder general* (London, 1976).

Dodds, E. R., *The Greeks and the irrational* (Berkeley, 1951).

Douglas, M. (ed.), *Witchcraft confessions and accusations* (London, 1970).

Dyer, C., Changes in the size of peasant holdings in some West Midland villages 1400–1540, in *Land, kinship and lifecycle*, ed. R. M. Smith (Cambridge, 1984), pp. 277–94.

Earle, P., *The making of the English middle class* (London, 1989).

Earle, P., The female labour market in London in the seventeenth and early eighteenth centuries, *The Economic History Review*, second series, **XLII**, 1989, pp. 328–53.

Elton, G. R., *The Tudor revolution in government* (Cambridge, 1953).

Elton, G. R., *England under the Tudors* (London, 1955).

Elton, G. R., *The Tudor constitution: documents and commentary*, (Cambridge, 1968).

Eley, G. & Hunt, W. (eds), *Reviving the English Revolution* (London, 1988).

Emmison, F. G., *Elizabethan life: disorder* (Chelmsford, 1970).

Emmison, F. G., *Elizabethan life: home, work and land* (Chelmsford and Plymouth, Mass., 1976).

Emmison, F. G., *Elizabethan life: morals and the church courts* (Chelmsford, 1973).

Erickson, A. L., The property ownership and financial decisions of ordinary women in early modern England, PhD thesis, University of Cambridge, 1990.

Erickson, A.L., Common law versus common practice: the use of marriage settlements in early modern England, *The Economic History Review*, second series, **XLIII**, 1990, pp. 21–39.

Erickson, A. L., Introduction to *Alice Clark, working life of women in the seventeenth century*, new edn (London, 1992), pp. vii–lv.

Erickson, A. L., *Women and property in early modern England* (London, 1993).

Evans-Pritchard, E. E., *Witchcraft, oracles and magic among the Azande* (abridged edn Oxford, 1976).

Everitt, A., *The community of Kent and the great rebellion, 1640–60* (Leicester, 1966).

L'Estrange Ewen, C., *Witchcraft in the Star Chamber* (n.p., 1938).

Favret-Saada, J., *Deadly words: witchcraft in the Bocage* (Cambridge, 1990).

Fletcher, A. J. & Stevenson, J., *Order and disorder in early modern England*, (Cambridge, 1985).

Foucault, M., *The order of things. An archaeology of the human sciences* (London, 1970).

Fraser, A., *The weaker vessel: women's lot in seventeenth-century England* (London, 1984).

Gaskill, M., Witchcraft in Tudor and Stuart Kent: stereotypes and the background to accusations, in *Witchcraft in early modern Europe*, eds J. Barry *et al.* (forthcoming).

Geertz, H., An anthropology of religion and magic, I, *Journal of Interdisciplinary History*, **VI**, 1975, pp. 71–89.

Geis, G., Lord Hale, witches and rape, *British Journal of Law and Society*, **5**(1), 1978, pp. 26–44.

Gibson, J., *Hanged for witchcraft: Elizabeth Lowys and her successors* (Canberra, 1988).

Gillespie, R., Women and crime in seventeenth-century Ireland, in *Women in early modern Ireland*, eds M. MacCurtain & M. O'Dowd (Edinburgh, 1991), pp. 43–52.

Ginsburg, G., Rags to riches: the second hand clothes trade, 1700–1978, *Costume*, **14**, 1980, pp. 121–35.

Ginzburg, C., *The night battles. Witchcraft and agrarian cults in the sixteenth and seventeenth centuries* (Baltimore, 1983).

Ginzburg, C., *Ecstasies. Deciphering the witches' sabbath* (London, 1990).

Goody, J., *The logic of writing and the organization of society* (Cambridge, 1986).

Gowing, L., Women, sex and honour: the London church courts, 1572–1640, PhD thesis, University of London, 1993.

Gowing, L., Gender and the language of insult in early modern London, *History Workshop Journal*, 35 (1993), pp. 1–21.

Gregory, A., Slander accusations and social control in late sixteenth and early seventeenth century England, with particular reference to Rye (Sussex), DPhil thesis, University of Sussex, 1984.

Gregory, A., Witchcraft, politics and 'Good Neighbourhood' in early seventeenth-century Rye, *Past & Present*, **133**, 1991, pp. 31–66.

Hair, P. E. H., *Before the bawdy court: selections from the church court and other records relating to the correction of moral offences in England, Scotland and New England, 1300–1800* (London, 1972).

Hall, H., Some Elizabethan penances in the diocese of Ely, *Transactions of the Royal Historical Society*, third series, **I**, 1907, pp. 263–77.

Hanawalt, B. A., *Crime and conflict in English communities 1300–1348* (Cambridge, MA, 1979).

Hanawalt, B. A., The female felon in fourteenth-century England, *Viator*, **5**, 1974, pp. 253–68.

Harley, D., Historians as demonologists: the myth of the midwife-witch, *Social History of Medicine*, **3**, 1990, pp. 1–26.

Harte, N. B., State control of dress and social change in pre-industrial England, in *Trade, government and economy in pre-industrial England. Essays presented to F. J. Fisher*, eds D. C. Coleman & A. H. John (London, 1976), pp. 132–65.

Hay, D., War, dearth and theft in the eighteenth century: the record of the English courts, *Past & Present*, **95**, 1982, pp. 117–59.

Helmholz, R. H., *Marriage litigation in medieval England* (Cambridge, 1974).

Henningsen, G., *The witches' advocate: Basque witchcraft and the Spanish Inquisition (1609–1619)* (Nevada, 1980).

Herrup, C. B., *The common peace. Participation and the criminal law in seventeenth-century England* (Cambridge, 1987).

Higgins, P., Women in the English civil war, MA thesis, University of Manchester, 1965.

Higgins, P., The reactions of women, with special reference to women petitioners, in *Politics, religion and the English civil war*, ed. B. Manning (Manchester, 1973), pp. 177–222.

Higgins, R., Popular beliefs about witches: the evidence from East London, 1645–1660, *East London Record*, **4**, 1981, pp. 36–41.

Hill, C. *The English revolution : an essay* (London, 1955, reprinted 1977).

Hill, C., *The world turned upside down: radical ideas during the English revolution* (London, 1972).

Hill, C., A one class society? in *Change and continuity in seventeenth-century England*, ed. C. Hill (London, 1974, reprinted 1991).

Hill, L. M., *The ancient state authoritie, and proceedings of the Court of Requests by Sir*

Julius Caesar (Cambridge, 1975)

Hoffer, P. C. & N. E. Hull, *Murdering mothers: infanticide in England and New England 1558–1803* (New York, 1981).

Hogrefe, P., Legal rights of Tudor women and the circumvention by men and women, *Sixteenth Century Journal*, **3**, 1972, pp. 97–105.

Holdsworth, W. K., Adultery or witchcraft – a new note on an old case in Connecticut, *New England Quarterly*, **48**, 1975, pp. 394–409.

Holmes, C., Popular culture? Witches, magistrates and divines in early modern England, in *Understanding popular culture. Europe from the middle ages to the nineteenth century*, ed. S. L. Kaplan (Berlin, 1984), pp. 85–111.

Holmes, C., Drainers and fenmen: the problem of popular political consciousness in the seventeenth century, in *Order and disorder in early modern England*, eds A. J. Fletcher & J. Stevenson (Cambridge, 1985), pp. 166–95.

Holmes, C., Women: witnesses and witches, *Past & Present*, **140**, 1993) pp. 45–78.

Horsley, R. A., Who were the witches? The social roles of the accused in the European witch trials, *Journal of Interdisciplinary History*, **IX**, 1979, pp. 689–715.

Horsley, J. A. & Horsley, R. A., On the trial of the "witches": wise women, midwives, and the European witch hunts, in *Women in German Yearbook*, 3, eds M. Burkhard & E. Waldstein (Lanham, MD., 1986), pp. 1–28.

Houlbrooke, R. A., *Church courts and the people during the English Reformation, 1520–1570*, (Oxford, 1979).

Houlbrooke, R. A., *The English family 1450–1700* (London, 1984).

Hoyle, R. W., An ancient and laudable custom: the definition and development of tenant right in north-western England in the sixteenth century, *Past & Present*, **116**, 1987, pp. 24–55.

Hoyle, R. W., Tenure and the land market in early modern England: or a late contribution to the Brenner debate, *The Economic History Review*, second series, **XLIII**, 1990, pp. 1–20.

Hudson, P. & Berg, M., Rehabilitating the industrial revolution, *The Economic History Review*, second series, **XLV**, 1992, pp. 35–8.

Hutton, R., *The Restoration* (Oxford, 1985).

Ingram, M. J., Communities and courts: law and disorder in early seventeenth-century Wiltshire, in *Crime in England, 1550–1800*, ed. J. S. Cockburn (London, 1977), pp. 122–4.

Ingram, M. J., The reform of popular culture? Sex and marriage in early modern England, in *Popular culture in seventeenth-century England*, ed. B. Reay (London, 1985), pp. 129–65.

Ingram, M. J., Ridings, rough music and mocking rhymes in early modern England, in *Popular culture in seventeenth-century England*, ed. B. Reay (London, 1985), pp. 166–97.

Ingram, M. J., *Church courts, sex and marriage in England, 1570–1640* (Cambridge, 1987).

Jones, W. J., *The Elizabethan court of Chancery* (Oxford, 1967).

Karlsen, C. F., *The devil in the shape of a woman: witchcraft in colonial New England* (New York, 1987).

Karras, R. M., The regulation of brothels in later medieval England, in *Sisters and workers in the middle ages*, eds J. M. Bennett *et al.* (Chicago, 1989), pp. 97–127.

Kerridge, E., *The agrarian problems in the sixteenth century and after* (London, 1969).

King, W. J., Untapped resources for social historians: court leet records, *Journal of Social History*, **15**, 1981–82, pp. 699–704.

King, P., Decision makers and decision-making in the English criminal law, 1750–1800, *The Historical Journal*, **27**, 1984, pp. 25–58.

Kishlansky, M. A., *The rise of the New Model Army* (Cambridge, 1979).

Kittredge, G. L., *Witchcraft in old and New England* (Cambridge, MA, 1929).

Koestler, A., *Darkness at noon* (London, 1940).

Ladurie, E. Le Roy, *Jasmin's witch* (London, 1987).

Landau, N., Going local: the social history of Stuart and Hanoverian England, *Journal of British Studies*, **24**, 1985, pp. 273–81.

Larner, C., Crimen exceptum? The crime of witchcraft in Europe, in *Crime and the law, the social history of crime in western Europe since 1500*, eds V. A. C. Gatrell *et al.* (London, 1980), pp. 49–75.

Larner, C., *Enemies of God: the witch-hunt in Scotland* (London, 1981).

Larner, C., *Witchcraft and religion: the politics of popular belief* (Oxford, 1984).

Laurence, A., Women's work and the English civil war, *History Today*, **42**, 1992, pp. 20–25.

Laurence, A., *A social history of women in England 1500–1760*, forthcoming.

Lawrence, D. H., *Fantasia of the unconscious* (London, 1923).

Lemert, E., *Human deviance. Social problems and social control* (New Jersey, 1972).

Lemire, B., Consumerism in pre-industrial and early industrial England: the trade in secondhand clothes, *Journal of British Studies*, **17**, 1988, pp. 1–24.

Lemire, B., Peddling fashion: salesmen, pawnbrokers, taylors, thieves and the second-hand clothes trade in England, *c.*1700–1800, *Textile History*, **22**, 1991, pp. 67–82.

Levack, B. P., *The witch-hunt in early modern Europe* (London, 1987).

Levi, G., On microhistory, in Burke, *New perspectives on historical writing*, pp. 93–113.

Lindley, K., *Fenland riots and the English revolution* (London, 1982).

McArthur, E. A., Women petitioners and the long parliament, *English Historical Review*, **24**, 1909, pp. 698–709.

MacCurtain, M. & M. O'Dowd (eds), *Women in early modern Ireland* (Edinburgh, 1991).

MacDonald, M., *Mystical bedlam. Madness, anxiety, and healing in seventeenth-century England* (Cambridge, 1981).

MacDonald, M., *Witchcraft and hysteria in Elizabethan London: Edward Jordan and the Mary Glover case* (London, 1990).

Macfarlane, A., *Witchcraft in Tudor and Stuart England. A regional and comparative study*

(London, 1970).

Macfarlane, A., *The family life of Ralph Josselin, a seventeenth-century clergyman* (Cambridge, 1970).

Macfarlane, A., A Tudor anthropologist: George Gifford's 'Discourse and Dialogue', in *The damned art. Essays in the literature of witchcraft*, ed. S. Anglo (London, 1977), pp. 140–55.

McIntosh, M. K., Local change and community control in England, 1465–1500, *Huntington Library Quarterly*, **49**, 1986, pp. 219–42.

McLachlan, H. V. & Swales, J. K., Stereotypes and Scottish witchcraft, *Contemporary Review*, **234**, 1979, pp. 88–94.

McLachlan, H. V. & Swales, J. K., Lord Hale, witches and rape: a comment, *British Journal of Law and Society*, **5**(2), 1978, pp. 251–61.

McLynn, F., *Crime in eighteenth-century England* (Oxford, 1991).

McMullan, J. L., *The canting crew. London's criminal underworld 1550–1700* (Baltimore, 1984).

McMullan, J. L., Crime, law and order in early modern England, *British Journal of Criminology*, **27**, 1987, pp. 252–74.

Mack, P., The prophet and her audience: gender and knowledge in the world turned upside down, in *Reviving the English revolution*, eds G. Eley & W. Hunt (London, 1988), pp. 139–52.

Maitland, F. W., *Select pleas in manorial and other seignorial courts*, vol. 1, Selden Society, **II** (London, 1889).

Manchée, W. H., *The Westminster city fathers (the Burgess Court of Westminster) 1585–1901* (London, 1924).

Manning, B. (ed.), *Politics, religion and the English civil war* (Manchester, 1973).

Meldrum, T., Defamation at the church courts: women and community control in London 1700–1745, MSc thesis, London School of Economics and Political Science, 1990.

Miles, R., *The women's history of the world* (London, 1988).

Moogk, P. N., "Thieving buggers" and "stupid sluts": insults and popular culture in New France, *William and Mary Quarterly*, third series, **36**, 1979, pp. 524–47.

Morrill, J. S., *Cheshire 1630–1660: county government and society during the English revolution* (Oxford, 1974).

Morrill, J. S. et al. (eds), *Public duty, private conscience in seventeenth-century England. Essays presented to G. E. Aylmer* (Oxford, 1993).

Morris, A., *Women, crime and criminal justice* (Oxford, 1987).

Muchembled, R., *Les derniers bûchers* (Paris, 1981).

Muir, E., Introduction: observing trifles, in *Microhistory and the lost peoples of Europe*, eds E. Muir & G. Ruggiero (Baltimore, 1991), pp. vii–xxviii.

Muldrew, C., Interpreting the market: the ethics of credit and community relations in early modern England, *Journal of Social History*, **18**, 1993, pp. 163–83.

Murray, M., *The witch cult in western Europe* (Oxford, 1921).

Nelson, M., Why witches were women, in *Women: A feminist perspective*, ed. J. Freeman (Palo Alto, 1975), pp. 333–50.

North, R., *The lives of the right hon Francis North, Baron Guildford; the hon Sir Dudley North; and the hon and rev Dr John North* (3 vols, London, 1890).

Norton, M. B., Gender and defamation in seventeenth-century Maryland, *William and Mary Quarterly*, third series, **36**, 1979, pp. 3–39.

Notestein, W., *A history of witchcraft in England from 1558 to 1718* (Washington, 1911).

Nuttall, G., The emergence of nonconformity, in *The beginnings of nonconformity 1660–1665: a checklist*, Nuttall, G. (London, 1964), pp. 1–5.

O'Dowd, M., Women and war in Ireland in the 1640s, in *Women in early modern Ireland*, eds M. MacCurtain & M. O'Dowd (Edinburgh, 1991), pp. 91–111.

Oldham, J. C., On pleading the belly: a history of the jury of matrons, *Criminal Justice History*, **6**, 1985, pp. 1–64.

Oplinger, J., *The politics of demonology. The european witchcraze and the mass production of deviance* (London and Toronto, 1990).

Parish, E., *Hallucinations and illusions. A study of the fallacies of perception* (London, 1897).

Perry, M. E., *Gender and disorder in early modern Seville* (New Jersey, 1990).

Pitts, J. L., *Witchcraft and devil lore in the Channel Islands* (Guernsey, 1886).

Plucknett, T., *A concise history of common law*, fourth edn, (London, 1948).

Pollack, O., *The criminality of women* (Greenwood, Connecticut, 1950, reprinted 1978).

Prest, W. R., Law and women's rights in early modern England, *The Seventeenth Century*, **6** , 1991, pp. 169–87.

Prior, M. (ed.), *Women in English Society 1500–1800* (Oxford, 1985)

Prior, M., Women and the urban economy: Oxford 1500–1800, in *Women in English Society 1500–1800*, ed. M. Prior (Oxford, 1985), pp. 93–117.

Quaife, G. R., *Godly zeal and furious rage. The witch in early modern Europe* (London, 1987).

Quintrell, B. W., Government in perspective: Lancashire and the privy council, 1570–1640, *Transactions of the Historic Society of Lancashire and Cheshire*, **131**, 1982, pp. 35–62.

Rappaport, S., *Worlds within worlds: structures of life in sixteenth-century London* (Cambridge, 1989).

Reay, B. (ed.), *Popular culture in seventeenth-century England* (London, 1985).

Rees, W. D., The hallucinations of widowhood, *British Medical Journal*, **4**, 1971, pp. 37–41.

Reeve, A., The meaning and definition of 'property' in seventeenth-century England, *Past & Present*, **89**, 1980, pp. 139–42.

Roberts, M., Women and work in sixteenth-century English towns, in *Work in towns, 850–1850*, eds P. J. Corfield & D. Keene (Leicester, 1990), pp. 86–102.

Roper, L., *The Holy household: Women and morals in reformation Augsburg* (Oxford, 1989).

Roper, L., Witchcraft and fantasy in early modern Germany, *History Workshop Journal*, **32**, 1991, pp. 19–43.

Rose, H. J., *Primitive culture in Greece* (London, 1925).

Rosen, B., *Witchcraft* (London, 1969).

Rosenthal, J. T., Other victims: peeresses as war widows, 1450–1500, *History*, **72**, 1987, pp. 213–30.

Russell, C., *The causes of the Civil War: a comment* (Oxford, 1990).

Rushton, P., Women, witchcraft and slander in early modern England: cases from the church courts of Durham, 1560–1675, *Northern History*, **18**, 1982, pp. 116–32.

Sabean, D., *Power in the blood. Popular culture and village discourse in early modern Germany* (Cambridge, 1984).

Samaha, J. B., Hanging for felony: the rule of law in Elizabethan Colchester, *The Historical Journal*, **21**, 1978, pp. 763–782.

Sawyer, R. C., "Strangely handled in all her lyms": witchcraft and healing in Jacobean England', *Journal of Social History*, **22**, 1989, pp. 461–85.

Scarre, G., *Witchcraft and magic in sixteenth- and seventeenth-century Europe* (London, 1987).

Scott, J. W., *Gender and the politics of history* (New York, 1988).

Scott, J. W., Women's history, in Burke, *New perspectives*, pp. 42–66.

Scott, J., *Algernon Sidney and the English republic, 1623–1677* (Cambridge, 1988).

Scott, J. C., *Domination and the arts of resistance. Hidden transcripts* (Yale, 1990).

Searle, C. E., Custom, class conflict and agrarian capitalism: the Cumbrian customary economy in the eighteenth century, *Past & Present*, **110**, 1986, pp. 106–133.

Shanley, M. L., Marriage contract and social contract in seventeenth-century England, *The Western Political Quarterly*, **32**(1), 1979, pp. 79–91.

Sharpe, J. A., *Defamation and sexual slander in early modern England: the church courts at York*, Borthwick Papers, **58** (York, 1980).

Sharpe, J. A., "Such disagreement betwyx neighbours": litigation and human relations in early modern England, in *Disputes and settlements: law and human relations in the West*, ed. J. Bossy (Cambridge, 1983), pp. 167–87.

Sharpe, J. A., *Crime in seventeenth-century England. A county study* (Cambridge, 1983).

Sharpe, J. A., *Crime in early modern England* (London & New York, 1984).

Sharpe, J. A., The people and the law, in *Popular culture in seventeenth-century England*, ed. B. Reay (London, 1985), pp. 244–70.

Sharpe, J. A., *Early modern England: a social history 1550–1760* (London, 1987).

Sharpe, J. A., The history of crime in England, c. 1300–1914: an overview of recent publications, *British Journal of Criminology*, **28**, 1988, pp. 124–37.

Sharpe, J. A., *Judicial punishment in England* (London, 1990).

Sharpe, J. A., Witchcraft and women in seventeenth-century England: some northern evidence, *Continuity and Change*, **6**, 1991, pp. 179–99.

Sharpe, J. A., *Witchcraft in seventeenth-century Yorkshire: accusations and counter measures*, Borthwick Papers, **81** (York, 1992).

Sharpe, J. A., The devil in East Anglia: the Matthew Hopkins trials reconsidered, in, *Witchcraft in early modern Europe*, eds J. Barry *et al.* (forthcoming).

Sharpe, P., Poor children as apprentices in Colyton 1598–1830, *Continuity and Change*, **6**, 1991, pp. 253–70.

Shoemaker, R. B., *Prosecution and punishment: petty crime and the law in London and rural Middlesex, c.1660–1725* (Cambridge, 1991).

Sisson, C. J., *Lost plays of Shakespeare's age* (Cambridge, 1936).

Slack, P. A., *Poverty & policy in Tudor & Stuart England* (London, 1988).

Snell, K. D. M., *Annals of the labouring poor* (Cambridge, 1985).

Snell, K. D. M., Deferential bitterness: the social outlook of the rural proletariat in eighteenth- and nineteenth-century England and Wales, in *Social orders and social classes in Europe since 1500*, ed. M. L. Bush (London, 1992), pp. 158–84.

Spargo, J. W., *Juridical folklore in England illustrated by the cucking-stool* (Durham, NC, 1944).

Spufford, M., *Contrasting communities: English villages in the sixteenth and seventeenth centuries* (Cambridge, 1979).

Spufford, M., *The great reclothing of rural England: petty chapmen and their wares in the seventeenth century* (London, 1984).

Starkey, D., *The reign of Henry VIII; personalities and politics* (London, 1985).

Starkey, M. L., *The devil in Massachusetts: a modern enquiry into the Salem witch trials* (New York, 1950).

Staves, S., *Married women's separate property in England, 1660–1833* (Cambridge, MA, 1990).

Stenton, D. M., *The English woman in history* (London, 1957).

Stretton, T., Women and litigation in the Elizabethan Court of Requests, PhD thesis, University of Cambridge, 1993.

Stone, L., Interpersonal violence in English society 1300–1980, *Past & Present*, **101**, 1983, pp. 22–33.

Stone, L., *The family, sex and marriage in England 1500–1800* (London, 1977).

Stopes, C., *British freewomen: their historical privilege*, third edn (London, 1907).

Styles, J., Embezzlement, industry and the law in England, 1500–1800, in *Manufacture in town and country before the factory*, eds M. Berg *et al.* (Cambridge, 1983), pp. 173–206.

Summers, M., *The discovery of witches. A study of Master Matthew Hopkins* (London, 1928).

Swales, J. K. & McLachlan, H. V., Witchcraft and the status of women: a comment, *British Journal of Sociology*, **30**, 1979, pp. 349–58.

Tawney, R. H., *The agrarian problem in the sixteenth century* (London, 1912).

Teall, J. L., Witchcraft and Calvinism in Elizabethan England: divine power and human agency, *Journal of the History of Ideas*, **23**, 1962, pp. 21–36.

Thirsk, J., Foreword to *Women in English Society 1500–1800*, ed. M. Prior (Oxford,

1985), pp. 1–21.

Thomas, K., Women and the civil war sects, in *Crisis in Europe 1560–1660*, ed. T. Aston (London, 1965), pp. 317–40.

Thomas, K., *Religion and the decline of magic: studies in popular beliefs in sixteenth and seventeenth England* (London, 1971; 1988 edn).

Thomas, K., Age and authority in early modern England, *Proceedings of the British Academy*, **62**, 1976, pp. 205–48.

Thompson, E. P., Anthropology and the discipline of historical context, *Midland History*, **1**, 1972, pp. 41–55.

Thompson, E. P., Patrician society, plebeian culture, *Journal of Social History*, **7**, 1974, pp. 382–405.

Thompson, E. P., The grid of inheritance: a comment, in *Family and inheritance: rural society in Western Europe, 1200–1800*, eds J. Goody et al. (Cambridge, 1976), pp. 328–60.

Thompson, E. P., The crime of anonymity, in *Albion's fatal tree: crime and society in eighteenth-century England*, eds D. Hay et al. (London, 1977), pp. 255–308.

Thompson, E. P., *Customs in common* (London, 1991).

Thompson, J., "Her good name and credit": the reputation of women in seventeenth-century Devon, PhD thesis, University of Cincinnati, 1987.

Thompson, R., "Holy watchfulness" and communal conformism: the functions of defamation in early New England communities, *New England Quarterly*, **56**, 1983, pp. 504–22.

Tilly L. A. and Scott, J. W., *Women, work and family* (New York, 2nd edn, 1987).

Todd, B., The remarrying widow: a stereotype reconsidered, in *Women and work in pre-industrial England*, eds L. Charles, & L. Duffin (London, 1985), pp. 54–92.

Todd, B., Widowhood in a market town: Abingdon, 1540–1720, DPhil thesis, University of Oxford, 1983.

Trustram, M., *Women of the regiment: marriage and the Victorian army* (Cambridge, 1984).

Tyler, P., The church courts at York and witchcraft prosecutions 1567–1640, *Northern History*, **4**, 1969, pp. 84–109.

Underdown, D. E., The taming of the scold: the enforcement of patriarchal authority in early modern England, in *Order and disorder in early modern England*, eds A. J. Fletcher & J. Stevenson (Cambridge, 1985), pp. 116–36.

Underdown, D. E., *Revel, riot and rebellion*, (Oxford, 1985).

Underdown, D. E., *Fire from heaven: the life of an English town in the seventeenth century* (London, 1992).

Unsworth, C. R., Witchcraft beliefs and criminal procedure, in *Legal Record and Historical Reality*, ed. T. G. Watkin (London, 1989), pp. 71–98.

Vickery, A., Women and the world of goods: a Lancashire consumer and her possessions, 1751–81, in *Consumption and the world of goods*, eds J. Brewer & R. Porter (London, 1991), pp. 274–801.

Vickery, A., Golden age to separate spheres? A review of the categories and chronology of English women's history, *The Historical Journal*, **36**, 1993, pp. 383–414.

Wales, T., Poverty, poor relief and the life cycle: some evidence from seventeenth-century Norfolk, in *Land, Kinship and Life cycle*, ed. R. Smith (Cambridge, 1984), pp. 351–404.

Walter, J., Grain riots and popular attitudes to the law: Maldon and the crisis of 1629, in *An ungovernable people*, eds J. Brewer & J. Styles (London, 1983), pp. 47–84.

Walter, J., A "rising of the people"? The Oxfordshire rising of 1596, *Past & Present*, **107**, 1985, pp. 90–143.

Weatherill, L., Consumer behaviour, textiles and dress in the late seventeenth- and early eighteenth-centuries, *Textile History*, **22**, 1991, pp. 297–310.

Wertheimer, J., Some hypotheses about the genesis of visual hallucinations in dementia, in *Delusions and Hallucinations in Old Age*, eds C. Katona & R. Levy (London, 1992), pp. 201–208.

Whitelock, B., *Memorials of the English affairs*, vol.2 (Oxford, 1853).

Wiener, C. Z., Sex roles and crime in late Elizabethan Hertfordshire, *Journal of Social History*, **8**, 1974–5, pp. 38–60.

Willan, T. S., *Elizabethan Manchester*, Chetham Society, third series, **27** (Manchester, 1980).

Wood, A., Industrial development, social change, and popular politics in the mining area of north west Derbyshire, *c.*1600–1700, PhD thesis, University of Cambridge, 1993.

Woolf, D. R., Speech, text, and time: the sense of hearing and the sense of the past in Renaissance England, *Albion*, **18**, 1986, pp. 159–93.

Woolrych, A., *Soldiers and statesmen* (Oxford, 1987).

Worth, R. N., The siege of Plymouth: a chapter of Plymouth history re-written, *Annual Report and Transactions of the Plymouth Institution and Devon and Cornwall Natural History Society* **5**, 1876.

Wright, A., The ceremony of childbirth and its interpretation, and on women's experience of motherhood, *Women as mothers in pre-industrial England*, ed. V. Fildes (London, 1990), pp. 68–107.

Wright, S., Churmaids, huswyfes and hucksters: the employment of women in Tudor and Stuart Salisbury, in *Women and work in pre-industrial England*, eds L. Charles & L. Duffin (London, 1985), pp. 100–121.

Wrightson, K., & Levine, D., *Poverty and piety in an English village: Terling 1525–1700* (New York, 1979).

Wrightson, K., *English society, 1580–1680* (London, 1982).

Wrightson, K., Two concepts of order: justices, constables and jurymen in seventeenth-century England, in *An ungovernable people*, eds J. Brewer & J. Styles (London, 1983), pp. 21–46.

Wrightson, K., The social order of early modern England: three approaches, in *The world we have gained*, eds L. Bonfield *et al.* (Oxford, 1986), pp. 177–202.

Wrightson, K. The enclosure of social history, *Rural History*, **1**, 1990, pp. 73–81.

Wunderli, R., *London church courts and society before the Reformation* (Cambridge, MA, 1981).

Printed sources

Heinrich Bullinger, *The christen state of matrimonye*, tr. Miles Coverdale (Antwerp, 1541).

Edmund Bower, *Dr Lamb revived or witchcraft condemn'd in Anne Bodenham, a servant of his, who was arraigned and executed the Lent assizes last at Salisbury* (London, 1653).

Robert Clever, *A godlie form of household government: for the ordering of private families, according to the direction of Gods word* (London, 1598).

Sir Edward Coke, *The third part of the institutes of the laws of England* (London, 1660).

Sir John Comyns, *A digest of the laws of England*, 5 vols. (London, 1762–7).

Richard Crompton, *Star Chamber cases* (London, 1630).

M. Dalton, *The countrey justice: containing the practice of the justices of the peace out of their sessions* (London, 1635 and 1677 edns).

R. B. Fisher, *A practical treatise on copyhold tenure, with the methods of holding courts leet, court baron and other courts . . .* (London, 1794).

Ralph Gardiner, *England's grievance discovered, in relation to the coal-trade* (London, 1655).

John Gaule, *Select cases of conscience touching witches and witchcrafts* (London, 1646).

John Godolphin, *Reportotium canonicum* (London, 1678).

Henry Goodcole, *The wonderfull discoverie of Elizabeth Sawyer a witch, late of Edmonton, her conviction and condemnation and death* (London, 1621).

William Gouge, *Of domesticall duties: eight treatises* (London, 1622).

William Harrison, *The description of England*, ed. Frederick J. Furnivall, New Shakspere Society, series VI, (London, 1877–1881).

William Hawkins, *A treatise of the pleas of the crown*, 2 vols (London, 1716–21).

Matthew Hopkins, *The discovery of witches* (London, 1647).

John Kitchin, *Le court leet, et court baron* (London, 1580).

William Lambarde, *Eirenarcha: or the office of the justices of the peace in four books* (London, 1592).

John March, *Actions for slaunder, or, a methodicall collection under certain grounds of heads, of what words are actionable in the Law, and what not?* (London, 1647).

Henri Misson, *Memoires et observations faites par un voyageur en Angleterre* (La Haye, 1698).

Mary Moore, *Wonderfull news from the North: or, a true relation of the sad and grievous torments, inflicted upon the bodies of three children of Mr. George Muschamp, late of the county of Northumberland* (London, 1650).

Henry More, *An antidote against atheisme* (London, 1653).

Constantia Munda, *The worming of a mad dogge* (London, 1617).

Robert Plot, *The natural history of the Stafford-shire* (Oxford, 1686).

Reginald Scot, *The discoverie of witchcraft* (London, 1584).

William Sheppard, *A grand abridgment of the common and statute law of England*, 4 parts (London, 1675).

A. Sidney, *Discourses concerning government* (1698. Reprint, Indianapolis, Liberty Classics, 1990).

Lawrence Southerne, *Fearefull newes from Coventry, or, a true relation and lamentable story of one Thomas Holt . . . who through covetousnesse and immoderate love of money, sold himselfe to the devill* (London, 1642).

John Stearne, *A confirmation and discovery of witchcraft* (London, 1648).

Joseph Swetnam, *The arraignment of lewd, idle, froward, and unconstant women* (London, 1615).

Anna Trapnel, *Anna Trapnel's report and plea or a narrative of her journey from London to Cornwal, the occasion of it, the Lord's encouragements to it, and sign of presence with her in it* (London, 1654).

William Vaughan, *The spirit of detraction, coniured and convicted in seven circles* (London, 1611).

Charles Watkins, *Treatise on copyholds* (London, 1797).

The examination and confession of certain wytches at Chensford in the countie of Essex before the queens maiesties judges, the xxvi day of July anno 1566 (London, 1566).

A full and impartial account of the discovery of sorcery and witchcraft practis'd by Jane Wenham of Walkerne in Hertfordshire, upon the bodies of Anne Thorne, Anne Street, &c (London, 1712).

The lawes resolution of womens rights: or, the lawes provision for women. A methodicall collection of such statutes and customes, with the cases, opinions and points of learning in the law, as doe properly concern women (London, 1632).

The midwife's maid's lamentation in Newgate (London, 1693).

Modern reports, or select cases adjudged in the courts of King's Bench, Chancery, Common-pleas, and Exchequer, since the restauration of ... Charles II, 12 vols. (1682–1738).

Poor Robin's true character of a scold: or, the shrews looking-glass (London, 1678)

A prodigious and tragicall history of the tryall, confession and condemnation of six witches at Maidstone, in Kent, att the assizes held there in July, Fryday 30, this present year 1652 (London, 1652).

A true and exact relation of the severall informations, examinations and confessions of the late witches arraigned and executed in the county of Essex (London, 1645).

A true and impartiall account of the arraignment, tryal, examination, confession and condemnation of Col. James Turner . . . (London, 1663).

A true and just recorde of the information, examination and confession of all the witches taken at S. Oses in the countie of Essex, whereof some were executed and others treated according to the determination of the law (London, 1582).

A true relation of the most inhumane and bloody murther (London, 1609).

The tryal, condemnation and execution of three witches, viz Temperance Floyd, Mary Floyd and Susanna Edwards, who were arraigned at Exeter on the 18th of August 1682 (London, 1682).

The tryal of Richard Hathaway upon an information for being a cheat and imposter for endeavouring to take away the life of Sarah Morduck for being a witch (London, 1702).

Editions

Atkinson, J. C. (ed.), *Quarter sessions records*, VI (London, 1888).

Bateson, M. *et al.* (eds), *Leicester borough records*, 7 vols. (London, Cambridge and Leicester, 1899–1974).

Bateson, M. (ed.), *Borough customs*, 2 vols, Selden Society, 18, 21 (London, 1904–6).

von Bülow, G. & Powell, W. (eds), Diary of the journey of Philip Julius, duke of Stettin-Pomerania, through England in the year 1602, *Transactions of the Royal Historical Society*, new series, VI, 1892.

Chappell, W., & Ebsworth, J. W. (eds), *The Roxburghe Ballads*, 8 vols. (London and Hertford, 1871–95).

Cockburn, J. S. (ed.), *A calendar of assize records: Hertfordshire indictments James I*, (London, HMSO, 1975).

Cockburn, J. S. (ed.), *A calendar of assize records: Home circuit indictments Elizabeth I and James I* (London, HMSO, 1985).

Copnall, H. H. (ed.), *notes and extracts from ... the seventeenth century* (Nottingham, 1915).

Cunnington, B. H. (ed.), *Some annals of the borough of Devizes*, 3 parts in 2 vols. (Devizes, 1925–6).

Cunnington, B. H. (ed.), *Records of the county of Wiltshire* (Devizes, 1932).

Dale, T. C. (ed.), *The inhabitants of London in 1638*, 2 vols. (London, 1931).

Dewar, M. (ed.), *Sir Thomas Smith, De republica anglorum*, (Cambridge, 1982).

Earwaker, J. P. (ed.), *The court leet records of the manor of Manchester*, 12 vols. (Manchester, 1884–90).

L'Estrange Ewen, C., *Witch hunting and witch trials, the indictments for witchcraft from the records of 1373 assizes held for the home circuit AD 1559–1736* (London, 1929).

L'Estrange Ewen, C., *Witchcraft and demonianism: a concise account derived from sworn depositions and confessions obtained in the courts of England and Wales* (London, 1933).

Fenton, F. H. *et al.* (eds), *Manor of Tottenham series . . . court rolls*, 6 vols, in progress, (London, 1956).

Firth, C. H. and Rait, R. S. (eds), *Acts and ordinances of the Interregnum, 1642–1660*, I (London, 1911).

Gairdner, J. (ed.), *Three fifteenth-century chronicles, with historical memoranda by John Stowe*, Camden Society, new series, 28 (London, 1880).

Grange, W. (ed.), *Daemonologia: a discourse on witchcraft, as it was acted in the family of Mr Edward Fairfax, of Fuyston, in the county of York, in the year 1621: along with the only two eclogues of the same author known to be in existence* (Harrogate, 1882).

Griffiths, J. (ed.), *The two books of homilies appointed to be read in churches* (Oxford, 1859).

Haller, W. & Davies, G. (eds), *The leveller tracts 1647–1653* (Gloucester, MA, 1964).

Le Hardy, E. (ed.), *Calendar to the Middlesex sessions records*, 4 vols. (London, 1935–41).

Harte, W. J., Illustrations of municipal history from the act book of the Chamber of the city of Exeter, 1559–1588, *Reports and Transactions of the Devonshire Association for the Advancement of Science, Literature and Art*, **XLIV**, 1912.

Hearnshaw, F. J. C. & Hearnshaw, D. M. (eds), *Court leet records, vol 1 part 2, A.D. 1578–1602*, Southampton Record Society (Southampton, 1906), p.187.

Helmholz, R. H., *Select cases on defamation to 1600*, Selden Society (London, 1985).

Hewitson, A. (ed.), *Preston court leet records: extracts and notes* (Preston, 1905).

Heywood, T. (ed.), *The Moore Rental*, Chetham Society, Old Series, **XII** (1847).

Horrocks, J. W. (ed.), *The assembly books of Southampton*, 2 vols, Southampton Record Society, 19, 21 (Southampton, 1917–20).

Horsman, E. A. (ed.), *The pinder of Wakefield*, English Reprints Series, 12 (Liverpool, 1956).

Historic manuscripts commission, 13th Report. Manuscripts of his grace the duke of Portland, (London, 1891).

Historical Manuscripts Commision, 10th Report, Appendix, part IV. The manuscripts of the earl of Westmorland . . . and others (London, 1885).

Jenkinson, H., and Powell, D. L. (eds), *Surrey quarter sessions records*, **VII** (Surrey, 1935).

Larkin, J. F. (ed.), *Stuart royal proclamations*, **2** (Oxford, 1983).

Lister, J. (ed.), *West Riding sessions records*, 2 vols, Yorkshire Archaeological Society, Records Series, 3, 54, (Worksop and Leeds, 1888–1915).

Macfarlane, A., et al. (eds), *Records of an English village: Earls Colne, 1400–1750*, microfiche, (Cambridge, 1980–81).

Mayo, C. H. (ed.), *The municipal records of the borough of Shaftesbury* (Sherborne, 1889).

Melling, E. (ed.), *Kentish sources: VI, crime and punishment*, (Maidstone, 1969).

Palmer, W. M. (ed.), *Episcopal visitation returns for Cambridgeshire . . . 1638–1665* (Cambridge, 1930).

Ratcliff, S. C. and Johnson, H. C. (eds), *Warwick county records*, **IV** (Warwick, 1938).

Richardson, G. B. (ed.), *Extracts from the municipal accounts of Newcastle-upon-Tyne* (Newcastle, 1848).

Richardson, H. (ed.), *Court rolls of the manor of Acomb*, Yorkshire Archaeological Society: Record Series, 131, (York, 1969).

Rollins, H. E. (ed.), *A Pepysian garland: black-letter broadside ballads of the years 1595–1639* (Cambridge, MA, 1922).

Rollins, H. E. (ed.), *The Pepys ballads*, 8 vols. (Cambridge, MA, 1929–32).

Rye, W. (ed.), *Depositions taken before the mayor and aldermen of Norwich, 1549–1567,* Norfolk and Norwich Archaeological Society, (Norwich, 1905).

Sachse, W. L. (ed.), *Minutes of the Norwich Court of Mayoralty,* I, *1630–31,* II, *1632–35,* Norfolk Record Society, 15, 36, (London and Fakenham, 1942–67).

Sheils, W. J. (ed.), *Archbishop Grindal's visitation, 1575: comperta et detecta book,* Borthwick text and calendars: records of the northern province, 4 (York, 1977).

Stevenson, W. H., *et al.* (eds), *Records of the borough of Nottingham,* 9 vols, (London and Nottingham, 1882–1956).

Sutherland, J. ed., *L. Hutchinson, Memoirs of the life of colonel Hutchinson, with the fragment of an autobiography of Mrs. Hutchinson* (London, 1973).

Tait, J. (ed.), *Lancashire quarter sessions records: vol. I. quarter sessions rolls, 1590–1606,* Chetham Society, new series, 77 (Manchester, 1917).

Timmins, T. C. B. (ed.), *The Register of John Chandler, Dean of Salisbury, 1404–17,* Wiltshire Record Society, 39 (Devizes, 1984).

Wake, J., and Peyton, S. A. (eds), *Quarter sessions records of the county of Northampton,* Northants Records Society, 1 (Hereford, 1924).

Wellstood, F. C. (eds), *Records of the manor of Henley in Arden, Warwickshire* (Stratford-upon-Avon, 1919).

Williams, J. F. (ed.), *Diocese of Norwich: Bishop Redman's visitation, 1597. Presentments in the archdeaconries of Norwich, Norfolk and Suffolk,* Norfolk Record Society, 18 (Fakenham and London, 1946).

Willis, A. J. (ed.), *Winchester consistory court depositions, 1561–1602* (Hambleden, Lyminge and Folkestone, 1960).

Subject index